ONLINE RESEARCH AND RETRIEVAL WITH MICROCOMPUTERS

NAHUM GOLDMANN
SCIENTIFIC EDITOR: IAN EASSON, PH. D.

TAB Professional and Reference Books
Division of TAB BOOKS Inc.
P.O. Box 40, Blue Ridge Summit, PA 17214

[redacted]

To the memory of my mother, Brunia Zilberberg

FIRST EDITION

FIRST PRINTING

Printed in the United States of America

Library of Congress Cataloging in Publication Data

Goldmann, Nahum.
Online research and retrieval with microcomputers.

Includes index.
1. Online data processing. 2. Information retrieval. I. Title.
QA76.55.G65 1985 001.64'404 85-10047
ISBN 0-8306-1947-X

Contents

List of Online Services and Files Referred to in Figures

BRS online service

CHEMICAL ABSTRACTS SERVICE

DIALOG online service

ESA online service

Acknowledgments

The material in this book draws on work conducted in the last several years at the request and with the help of a number of scientists and other professionals involved in online information gathering. Particularly useful were countless discussions that we had with many of them when our *Subject Expert Searching Technique* was presented as a special course and during several seminars in various research institutions and private companies.

I am especially indebted to Dr. R. Whiting, Dr. S. Gupta, Dr. R. Maciejko, Dr. B.R. Shelton, D. Fox, P. Sampara, Dr. D. Halton, M.E. Easson, Dr. S. Beauchamp, Dr. R. McFadden, Dr. M. Tennassee, and many others who challenged me with their requests for information. Using our technique, we were jointly able to develop successful searching strategies, several examples of which are presented in this book.

My thanks are to Judy Biggin, who provided invaluable input when discussing the material that later became this book, to Dr. D.R. Richards, with whom I had a fruitful discussion on the subjects of associative problem solving and decision making, and to Dr. A.R. Kaye, for writing the foreword and for some valuable suggestions on the book's contents.

I was lucky to enjoy the cooperation of Ian Easson both in the development of the *Subject Expert Searching Technique* and in writing this book. His close involvement, firstly as a valuable opponent and later as an invaluable colleague and friend, has been a source of constant inspiration during the last several years of our joint work.

In preparing the material for this book, I am indebted to numerous individuals and corporations who supplied me with their advice, information materials, and searching time. Especially valuable was free searching time from such online services as DIALOG Information Services, Inc., MEAD Data Central, INFO GLOBE, CAS (Chemical Abstracts Service of the American Chemical Society), and I.P. SHARP Associates.

I am also thankful to those producers and vendors who gave me permission to publish records retrieved from their databases or online services.

Last, but not least, I am happy to acknowledge Natalya and Alice for their constant support, encouragement, and love.

Foreword

As we advance into the information economy, rapid access to information becomes increasingly important to all knowledge workers. At the same time, the rate of development of new knowledge in all fields of human endeavor is now such that it is difficult for the individual to keep track of all that is happening, even within a relatively narrow field, and quite impossible if horizons are broader. Paper-based methods of searching for information are becoming less productive than they used to be because of the sheer volume of material being produced. Yet, when we undertake a new endeavor, it continues to be of the utmost importance to know what has been done before because of the time and resources that knowledge may save us. So, increasingly, we turn to computer databases.

When we are searching for references in a mature field of knowledge, in which terminology is well defined and stable, we are usually quite successful. On the other hand, in new fields, especially those which cross the boundaries of several established disciplines, where terminology has not stabilized, a computer search frequently is less satisfactory than it might be. In such cases, one of the problems may be that the end-user, the subject specialist, has not involved himself sufficiently in the search.

Mr. Goldmann's book has an important message to subject specialists: A successful search may require your personal understanding of the subject under investigation because, in the end, only you can decide which references are truly responsive to your needs. Keywords are often poor indicators of real relevance. Searching for knowledge is too important to be entirely delegated to someone else.

This book explains how subject specialists can involve themselves more intimately in this crucially important part of their work. It will probably lead them to expect a good deal more from a computer search than has previously been the case but, on the other hand, it will help them and the research librarians who work with them to achieve those expectations.

A. Roger Kaye,
Mitel-Systemhouse Professor of Office Automation,
Carleton University, Ottawa, Canada.

Introduction

The book presents a newly developed searching technique intended for use in online information retrieval. Unlike other techniques that have been primarily developed for librarians, this technique is specifically developed for subject experts such as scientists, engineers, physicians, lawyers, businessmen, and other professionals.

The *Subject Expert Searching Technique* is organized as a set of simple, easy-to-follow rules. The strategy can be easily adapted to many publicly available information retrieval systems. Since the technique uses only a limited set of searching commands and principles, it is well-suited for use by the occasional searcher. The information gathering activity of a professional or a scientist can easily be organized around this basic searching procedure. This technique allows for the full realization of the potential of online information retrieval in the professional activity of the subject expert.

Chapter 1

The Place of Online Searching

In the last few years, computerized information systems have become a dominant factor in the establishment of world information flows—the nervous system of our civilization. They contain vast volumes of data that is increasing at an incredibly high rate. Furthermore, they are easily accessed from virtually any remote place, providing a technically sophisticated research resource.

ONLINE SEARCHING IS IN. THE TRADITIONAL LIBRARY IS OUT.

Online searching was born as the by-product of computerized typesetting for printed abstract publications. With time, however, it became a new instrument for information retrieval.

Online searching makes possible a great increase in the productivity of the information retrieval process. With the new medium, many complex operations on large masses of data can be performed easily. These operations were not feasible with hard-copy information sources.

The development of computerized searching, which can truly be considered an information revolution, to a great extent parallels the decay of the traditional specialized library serving the scientific and professional communities. For years the specialized library was considered a mandatory component of the scientific and professional establishment. Such a library attempted to be a major information center by collecting all the information available in its areas of specialization.

More recently, under economic pressure, acquisitions have frequently been restricted to only the leading publications in the field. More and more often, however, it has been recognized that even such a limited objective may be impossible to achieve.

It is increasingly difficult now for any library to keep up with the volume of materials published in its area of specialization, even if its subject area is well defined and relatively limited. It has become an almost impossible task if the library's area of specialization is relatively new, consists of several nonhomogeneous disciplines, or requires the collection of a substantial number of international and foreign language materials.

The reasons for such a decay are numerous. The great increase in the cost of books, periodic publications, publication storage, and personnel are factors that are most often cited.Also, specialization amongst professionals has become the standard practice. Such specialization, however, does not usually imply a single discipline, but rather a single subject of concern that is spread amongst several disciplines.

The multidisciplinary subject erodes the very idea of a compact library collection. For example, it is reasonable to expect that a good medical library should have literature on such diversified disciplines as biomedical engineering, ethics, and law, to name just a few subjects. However, such comprehensive collections of published materials are less and less readily available outside a few established scientific centers.

Another factor in the downfall of the traditional "comprehensive" library is the emergence of a multitude of scientific, technological, economic, and political centers in a number of new countries or new locations. It is no longer feasible to limit all world information exchange to a limited number of recognized focal points.

As often happens, the problem and the solution were born about the same time. Computerized information retrieval systems allow the elimination of many of the problems created by the destruction of the traditional library service. Rapid and convenient online connections allow the user to be more selective in his search for information.

Online searching also eliminates the expense of collecting and storing published materials that are of no immediate use. Such collecting is routinely done in the traditional library, even though up to 90 percent of library materials are never requested.

Essentially, the introduction of computerized information retrieval systems opens a new era in the organization of scientific and professional activities. Previously, in order to maintain a high level of work, scientists or professionals had to be located in recognized centers of scientific excellence. Proximity to large or specialized libraries was one of the major factors in selecting a location suitable for a leading research institution.

Online services eliminate the requirement for close proximity to the library as a precondition for professional excellence. A scientist working in a remote geographic area can now have the same access to state-of-the-art knowledge as his colleague who works at a world-class university.

WHY DON'T WE USE THEM? DO WE HAVE TO USE THEM?

Technically, the new computerized systems are quite sophisticated. However, from the end-user's point of view, they are still not very user-friendly.

One of the serious barriers to the use of information retrieval systems by the subject expert is that their structures, servicing, and educational networks are primarily tailored for use by librarians rather than by the end-user themselves. Searching techniques, educational courses, and manuals are not created for subject experts, whether they be scientists or professionals such as engineers, physicians, lawyers, or businessmen.

Most of the existing books on online searching are written for library staff and include many details that are of no use to the subject expert. They do not provide any coherent overall picture of modern information retrieval systems from the point of view of the end-user who has to perform information gathering as a part of his professional activities. Neither do they contain searching techniques suitable for this category of user.

As frequently noted in the specialized literature, online services are not sufficiently used by the subject experts themselves. Rather, they are searched by intermediaries who are generally not subject experts. As one of these surveys found, only 10 percent of all online searchers are the end-users of the retrieved information.

This is especially regrettable since, as will be demonstrated in this book, the retrieval of information by an intermediary (delegated searcher) is in principle impossible unless the search is controlled by the subject expert himself.

I hope that my analysis of the objective deficiencies of searches performed by intermediaries will not be taken as a criticism of librarians as a whole. My admiration for this noble profession can only be matched by my love for some of its finest representatives. Of course, there are poor librarians and there are good ones; the same may be said for members of any other profession—medical doctors, engineers, and lawyers alike.

In this book, however, I am not so much concerned with the quality, as with the relevance of the librarians' professional effort. After all, there were many highly qualified individuals amongst the scribes who used their quills. Despite this, the profession was wiped out with the invention of the printing press.

It is perhaps ironic that the typewriter, considered an automatic tool in the 19th century, is treated as a manual tool today. Not less ironic is the fact that the typewriter, the very invention that destroyed the occupation of calligrapher, is rapidly being eliminated now by this new small devil, the personal computer.

Likewise, it is unlikely that the library profession can survive in its present form, following the mass introduction of online searching and the parallel destruction of the traditional specialized library.

THE INFORMATION ECONOMY AND THE SUBJECT EXPERT

In the current economic environment, information has become a very important commodity. Proper information can save time and money, sometimes even lives. Possession of information gives significant advantages to its users.

Modern Western society is based to a great extent on the production, processing, and distribution of information. *The Information Economy,* a 1984 report commissioned by the Ontario Government, estimates that in Canada, information related activities constitute about half of the Gross Domestic Product. Similar estimates for the United States put the information related share of the GNP at 60 percent.

The structural shift towards information processing in modern technological society coincides with a fundamental change in the distribution of knowledge. Only 10 years ago the United States was the dominant source of technological innovation, producing 75 percent of the world's advanced technology. Today, according to the June 1984 issue of *EDN*, a well-informed Boston published journal specializing in electronic technology for engineers, the U.S. share has been reduced to 50 percent. This journal forecasts that the U.S. share in advanced manufacturing may shrink even further, reaching as little as 30 percent within the next 10 years.

With a reduced technological, economic, and scientific lead, the U.S. role as a dominant world source of scientific, technical, and social information will also likely diminish. This, in turn, may have fundamental implications for the information gathering activities of any subject expert, whether North American, European, or Japanese.

While, in the past, an expert might limit his information query to several well known "core" publications devoted to a particular subject, such an action is not easy to justify now. Today useful information originates outside the selected set of North American and Western European centers.

Japan is a good example of a new world-class center of technological innovation. However, Japanese information of interest to the outside world is not limited to technological areas alone. No less interest is directed towards the characteristics of the Japanese society and to the philosophy behind its industrial relations that made possible such rapid technological advances.

It is no longer proper for the expert to limit his information search to the scientific and technological sources that are exclusively devoted to the area of his specialization. More and more often knowledge transcends the narrowly defined boundaries of traditional disciplines. To be at the leading edge of development, an expert often has to have up-to-date information on many diversified subjects outside the nominal area of his specialization.

With the computer taking over many routine and auxiliary tasks, information gathering necessarily becomes the core of a professional's activities. A fundamental increase in its effectiveness and efficiency is often of primary concern. Whether an expert is up-to-date on important new developments in his field and has a clear overall vision of new trends in adjacent areas often determines the professional level of his work.

Online information retrieval systems allow the subject expert a rational organization of his overall information gathering activity. As a result, their consistent use could significantly raise his professional level.

The fact of the matter is that most organizations engaged in scientific, professional, or business activities have to change the way they conduct their information gathering activity. They cannot afford to keep their own libraries any longer. But do they still need them in the first place? A much more effective and less expensive solution is to integrate the use of online information retrieval systems into the everyday work of the subject experts.

Unfortunately, the fact that a significant share of the world's scientific and technical information flow is already computerized and may be easily accessed and processed at the request of the user, is not widely appreciated.

One of the most significant barriers between the subject expert and available information is that the scientists and professionals are unaware of the potential of online information systems.

THE PERSONAL COMPUTER AT THE SERVICE OF THE SUBJECT EXPERT

Professional activities have always been very difficult to mechanize. A microcomputer with its flexibility in applications is seen by many as a new revolutionary tool that would allow this mechanization. At present, the microcomputer is primarily used by the subject expert either for organizing his office activity (e.g., word processing or financial management) or to conduct various calculations, expressing the results in a numeric or a graphic form.

Online Data-Base, a market analysis report released in September 1984 by the California-based market research firm Creative Strategies International (CSI), sees personal computers as having the most dramatic impact on the information industry. According to this report, microcomputers are currently attracting a new wave of end-users. Thus, 60-90 percent of all new online service subscribers use personal computers as searching terminals, and not less than 10 percent of new micros sold become searching terminals.

Even though the proportion of professionals who use microcomputers for online information retrieval today is still very small, more and more searchers understand that it is advantageous to organize a search with the help of the microcomputer. Its use allows the searcher to make the connection procedure easier and to simplify the handling of materials gathered online after the search is finished.

If online searching has to become one of the end-user's primary activities, it is only reasonable to expect him to adapt to this powerful tool. Such an adaptation may require him to change not only his working habits but also the very way he thinks about problems.

The very rapid emergence of the IBM PC as the industry standard makes it necessary for us to describe, however briefly, an IBM PC configuration suitable for online searching.

The IBM PC was selected partially because the author himself makes use of this machine for online searching, amongst other applications. The main reason, however, was the numerous requests from users of our searching technique, many of whom invariably asked whether it is possible to organize effective searching with the help of their own IBM PC.

THE SUBJECT EXPERT SEARCHING TECHNIQUE—AN EFFECTIVE SOLUTION

This book examines the use of online information retrieval systems by subject experts themselves. It presents a specially developed Subject Expert Searching Technique, which is simple but reliable. This technique allows an expert to conduct online searching as an integral part of his professional tasks.

We do not expect any serious and detailed knowledge of computers and organization of online services from the reader of this book, nor is such a knowledge really necessary in order to create a successful searching strategy according to our technique.

With our searching technique, a professional or a scientist could organize the information gathering process as a state-of-the-art activity and thus fully realize the existing potential of contemporary computerized information retrieval systems. This technique is best suited for use as a part of a process in which the subject expert is involved.

The Subject Expert Searching Technique requires the active participation of a subject expert in the essential points of searching activity. Using this technique, the expert is firmly in charge of the information gathering process.

When searching has to be ordered through an intermediary, the principal elements of the Subject Expert Searching Technique can still be employed by the end-user. This can allow the subject expert to lead the information gathering process, to assure its quality, and to control the results of his search.

Our searching technique is actually one of the first information retrieval methods especially aimed towards searching a set of several online files rather than a particular secondary source or only one file. Together, these files are to a great extent representative of the whole Western flow of scientific, technical, and social information.

The Subject Expert Searching Technique is based on the presumption that it is more useful to understand the general principles of organization of online services and files than to memorize all the fine details of the commands used in a particular file or in a particular online service.

This broader understanding is important since the whole field is new and still in transition. Changes in content, format, query languages, and even in the existence of a particular online service or a file occur every day. Certain new features may become obsolete in a few years. Our technique allows the formulation of a search strategy in more general terms. Such a strategy may then be easily adapted to any information retrieval system.

Our searching technique uses only a limited set of searching commands and principles that can be easily understood by the subject expert. This is in contrast to the sophisticated operators and mnemonics introduced in some currently used techniques.

Since the technique does not require a detailed knowledge of the esoteric peculiarities of a particular file, it is well-suited for use by the occasional searcher, which we would expect the typical subject expert to be. Being fully up-to-date on an online service is not as important as being knowledgeable in the subject of the retrieval.

A TECHNIQUE IN STEP WITH THE EXPERT'S WORK

The Subject Expert Searching Technique is organized as a set of simple, easy-to-follow rules.

Information gathering activities of the professional may be easily organized around the basic searching procedure. Our technique also allows support staff to run nonessential but time consuming parts of a search. This may be important since the subject expert's time is limited and expensive.

If the subject expert's information gathering activity is at least comparable in quality with that of his other professional activities, the results of his

search almost always justify his personal involvement in the information retrieval process. In many cases, properly organized online information retrieval has a profound impact on the expert's professional accomplishments.

In general, the technique allows the subject expert to assure good cost-effectiveness of the information gathering process. There are alternative techniques that may be better suited for the extraction of data from a particular file. However, they are not suited for searching the whole flow of scientific and technical information, or for achieving the short and long-term objectives of an expert.

Our searching technique, of course, is not a universal solution for all kinds of problems that a searcher may encounter in his pursuit of information. This book is not a list of recipes that one can indiscriminately apply without thinking. It requires a high level of intellectual activity to formulate a good search, as with any other creative act.

Our experience, as well as that of other specialists using this technique, shows that most subject experts can expect the technique to be quite useful in at least 9 out of 10 searches that they have to perform. As in many other activities, a formal method is not a substitute for the generous application of one's professional knowledge and common sense.

THIS BOOK . . . AND OTHER SOURCES

One of the main reasons for writing this book was the realization that many who do not possess any knowledge of computers are afraid to switch on a computer terminal and start searching. Our task is to make the online information retrieval process as simple as the familiar manual library search, but at the same time to introduce the user to the powerful features characteristic of online services.

This book is intended to be a practical tool for the subject expert, introducing him to the general idea of online information gathering, giving examples of many useful databases that he can easily access, and guiding him in his attempts to formulate a simple but efficient search.

Our book does not attempt to provide a comprehensive analysis of online systems, databases, or computers. Neither was it created as a reference manual for various online files. Bringing together in one book all the information of interest to any user would be impossible. Therefore, this book had to be limited to the questions relevant to all subject experts.

Thus, we have attempted to avoid citations to the numerous publications on online information retrieval systems. Unfortunately, most of these publications are of no use to the majority of professionals. Even though this book includes references to major online information retrieval systems, you are expected to explore the existing online systems on your own.

A book by F.W. Lancaster *(Information Retrieval Systems: Characteristics, Testing and Evaluation*. J. Wiley & Sons, Inc, New York, 1979), is amongst a handful of publications that you could be advised to read in order to increase your general knowledge of online systems. Although primarily written for librarians and information scientists, this book provides a good introduction to various human factor problems involved in the online searching effort.

It could also be useful to follow several leading information science publications, particularly such magazines as *Online, Online Review,* and *Journal of the American Society for Information Science.*

The most fruitful strategy, however, for any online searcher who would like to upgrade his or her knowledge about online information retrieval systems is to search for this information online.

One of the additional sources that can be used by an occasional professional user as a practical tool in online information retrieval is *Goldmann's Glossary of Online Services and Databases.* This periodic newsletter is organized as a reference booklet, and is easy to use and to consult. In it are listed many important new developments in online services and databases. Some examples of useful information presented in the *Glossary* are also given in this book. More detail information on this newsletter may be requested by writing to P.O. Box 5145, Station F, Ottawa, Ont. K2C 3H3 Canada.

As many subject experts who have used our searching technique have already found, the quality of work and the overall productivity can be greatly increased with its use. Any method that allows a group of researchers to increase their intellectual productivity by as much as 25-50 percent undoubtedly has far reaching implications.

Only the formal education process may be compared with online information gathering in its ability to increase intellectual productivity. However, formal education at this moment is far more expensive and time-consuming than is online searching. This is not to imply, of course, that online searching can be considered a total substitute for formal education. I, however, would like to challenge anyone to provide an example where it is possible to achieve such a spectacular increase in intellectual productivity over such a relatively short period of time.

Our book and the *Glossary* will contribute to an awareness in the professional and scientific communities of the materials currently available online. Furthermore, our Subject Expert Searching Technique should allow professionals and scientists to organize information gathering in a fashion that better suits their needs.

YOU HAVE TO GET PERMISSION . . .

Almost all of the records that illustrate this book are unedited: no words were changed. Originally, they were retrieved online by me or by some of my colleagues in the course of our work. However, in order to assure that these records still exist online, I reretrieved each anew for this book. In those rare cases when original records were altered for one reason or another, it was done with the knowledge of their database producers, usually with a corresponding notice in the figure captions.

Several figures and most of the records used in the book are reproduced here courtesy of and with the permission of their authors or corresponding databases and online services. I have to admit that gaining such permissions for several dozen records retrieved online was at least as painful and slow as writing the book itself.

Only half of the permission forms that I mailed to database publishers came back to me within eight weeks. It took considerable effort, patience, and intelligence gathering activities to assure that the rest would ever be signed and mailed back. Despite my numerous letters and phone calls, some completed forms were received only more than a year later. This, I am sure, happened not due to any negative reaction on the producers' part. Rather, it is typical of the industry's inability to sort out the permission problem.

In the course of this mammoth task I did help several organizations to establish which executives were in a position to provide such permission. Surprisingly, amongst the slowest was a database producer that promotes itself as the largest in the field and that actively publicizes its copyright sign.

In that particular case, it took me more than a year, six letters, more than 20 long distance calls, and the befriending of a half a dozen executives, executive secretaries, and executive assistants to trace those two individuals who were responsible for copyright protection.

In at least one other case I was able to reconcile two different departments (Database Services and Permissions) in the same company, each of which claimed that permission could be obtained only from the other department. Both departments, located in the very same building, were communicating to each other only by sending letters to me (despite the fact that I happen to live in a different country). This process took several months to complete.

The only point on which both departments agreed was that I do not need permission to publish anything retrieved online from their database. Needless to say, a requirement to obtain such permission is prominently displayed in this database's promotional materials.

In a couple of cases I was totally unsuccessful in getting the required permission. One of these cases involved a leading U.S. scientific association as a producer. I was told by its executive staff members that the Association's bylaws do not have a provision for giving permission for publishing material retrieved from its database. I was, however, assured that the problem will be presented to the Association's Board of Governors at its next plenary session and will hopefully be resolved, maybe as early as 1986.

At least I was lucky on one account, since I did not have to get permission from the many databases shown in this book that are produced by U.S. government agencies. Surprisingly, the U.S. government is the largest producer of databases accessible through commercial online services. Most of the data generated by the government agencies in the United States are considered to be in the public domain. As such, they may be freely reproduced in the United States without special permission.

On the other hand, it would be much tougher if I were publishing this book outside of the United States. In this case, I would have been indeed required to obtain special permission from the U.S. government, whose materials are;

> . . . protected against copying or other reproduction outside of the United States under the provisions of Article II of the Universal Copyright Convention.

I simply hate to think how many phone calls to Mrs. Reagan it would take in order to convince the president to give such permission if I were publishing this book elsewhere.

I did have to obtain the database producer's consent, though, not only because this is a usual condition requested by any book publisher, but also because the contents of many databases are copyrighted by their producers. It is not unusual to find that according to conditions of use for many databases, no item retrieved from them can be published without written permission from their producers.

The trouble is that very often it is difficult to find who really is the database producer, never mind to secure its permission. The online database industry is so volatile that the ownership, address, and the very existence of the producer may be difficult to trace, even for the online services themselves. It may be even more difficult for those unfortunate clients who have to receive such permission.

Strictly speaking, many more users of online services are required by database producers to receive permission than is usually acknowledged. A disclaimer, such as that from the Drug Information Fulltext database (File 229 on DIALOG online service):

> No part of the database may be duplicated in hard-copy or machine-readable form without written authorization from the American Society of Hospital Pharmacists.

may potentially have far reaching legal implications for the average database user.

Evidently, this disclaimer makes it illegal even to make a photocopy of a record's printout. The fact that some database producers, explicitly recognizing this problem, specify that (IPA database, File 53 on DIALOG online service):

> . . . limited reproduction of printed, hard-copy output of up to twenty-five (25) copies is permitted for distribution within the subscriber organization only.

does not always solve it. Disclaimers like that from the Trademarkscan database (File 226 on DIALOG online service):

> Data may not be duplicated in hardcopy or machine-readable form without the prior written authorization from Thomson & Thomson, except that limited reproduction of printed output is permitted for distribution within the user's internal operation. Under no circumstances may copies produced under this provision be offered for sale.

prevent the online searcher from reselling the results of his search without written permission from the database producers. This further limits the possibility of online searching by intermediaries. Moreover, it makes difficult the business of those subject experts who would like to routinely integrate the results of their searches directly into their products.

Such integration is possible if, for example, bibliographic, numeric, or graphic data retrieved from a database are inserted directly into a final report. Thereafter, the report could be sold to a client who is unlikely to be a subscriber of the original database; this action makes the whole operation illegal. Without such integration, however, the wide penetration of online searching into the end-user community is questionable.

One of the main reasons for the use of electronic databases by the end-user is convenience in data manipulation. Normally, the user strives for consistency in all his operations. It is highly desirable from his point of view to receive information in electronic form, which would allow him to store and reprocess it later. The fact that many databases forbid such actions is a very serious stumbling block in the end-user's integration of online searching into his everyday work.

More important from some end-user's point of view may be the potential "power of refusal" that database producers can exercise over him in his quest for information. It is well known in the online industry that one of the leading producers was sued for its refusal to include a certain publication in its database. This action supposedly "undermined this publication's chances for wide circulation amongst the potential user community."

Interestingly enough, I happened to encounter a good example of the "power of refusal" during the production of this book as well. One of the leading producers, with several dozen databases on the market, categorically denied my request for presenting in this book a description of a certain publication (P.G. Adaikan, "Effects of Electrical Stimulation and Drugs on the Smooth Muscle of the Human Penis," *Proceedings of the 7th International Congress of Pharmacology,* Pergamon Press, Oxford, U.K., 1978) retrieved from its database.

The reason for not granting me the permission was, in the words of the producer, the "somewhat offensive" and "controversial" character of my example. Since I strongly feel that this little incident should not deny the readers of this book the opportunity of seeing an example from this leading database, I resubmitted my request with a less controversial entry. This one was promptly accepted.

Some readers of this book may notice that the wording of credit lines on various figures may differ substantially. This is because in some cases database producers specified a particular wording of the credit lines as a condition of use for the records retrieved from their databases.

I describe my dealings with database producers in detail here not only because I am pleased to share with the reader the fun of gathering this book's contents. I am doing it because the book is not so much about databases, as it is *about the end-user of online services.* The problem of how to handle a search is secondary here to the more important problem, namely that of *how the subject expert has to organize his information gathering activities as a part of his principal professional activities.*

The fact of the matter is that nontechnical aspects of online information retrieval are often many years behind the technical ones, and that often they preclude effective use of online services by the end-user. The user may find in organizing online information retrieval that political and legal barriers may be more difficult to penetrate than technical ones. The nontechnical problems must be solved if computerized information services are to become a truly universal media and their use integrated into the everyday activities of the subject expert.

Chapter 2

Information and the Subject Expert

Online searching is a kind of information gathering process. Therefore, the concept of *information* is of paramount importance in the establishment of any searching technique.

INFORMATION, KNOWLEDGE, AND DATA

There is a lot of confusion in defining information. Often *information* is confused with *data.*

In this book we accept the following definitions:

INFORMATION = NEW KNOWLEDGE

(Even though this definition of information is simple, its importance cannot be overestimated.)

KNOWLEDGE—understanding gained through past experience or association.

DATA—all quantities or characters that can be stored, transmitted, or retrieved and to which meaning might be assigned.

Examples of Data

kcvowp9uqI;lEir oeLoqylew ul'llm;xc c2sluqnw
010001111000
141592653589793 . . .

Examples of Knowledge

Ottawa is the capital of Canada
$2 \times 2 = 4$
September 15, 1985
ABCDEFGHIJKLMNOPQRSTUVWXYZ
$\pi = 3.141592653589793 \ldots$

Examples of Information

". . . our Christmas Party will take place on December 24, 1985. You may bring your wife(s) and/or girlfriend(s)."

". . . a number in the left bottom corner of this label represents in the binary code decimal (BCD) system the latest month when a drug may be used. Thus, in our example, 010001111000 stands for 4-78, i.e. April 1978"

Thus, *data, knowledge,* or *information* are not always synonymous.

The concept of *data* used in our book is wider than the concepts of knowledge or information. In everyday language and even in the specialized literature, these concepts are frequently confused. Knowledge is data, but not all data constitute knowledge or information.

A model for our concepts is shown in Fig. 2-1. You can see in this model that all existing knowledge can be expressed by means of data. Intellectual activity usually starts with existing knowledge but, in time, creates a body of new knowledge, namely information. Usually, but not always, information can be expressed in terms of existing data. With the passage of time, most information becomes incorporated in existing knowledge.

In some cases, a particular concept may be so novel that it requires the invention of a new data language to express it. The introduction of the 0 (zero) symbol by the ancient Indian civilization is a well-known example of such a fundamental intellectual development. This new kind of data was absolutely necessary for expression of the new philosophical idea of the absence of quantity.

Thus, in certain cases, what is considered to be new knowledge may to some extent be outside of the realm of the existing data. Subsequently, the very idea of data may be further modified and enlarged by new information.

Intellectual activity is the "driving force" in our model. Whether in relation to the individual or to society as a whole, intellectual activity makes reality of the human progress from data to knowledge to information. Unless a cataclysmic extermination of an existing civilization happens, intellectual activity constantly increases existing knowledge, and sometimes even the body of data symbols, by the creation of new information.

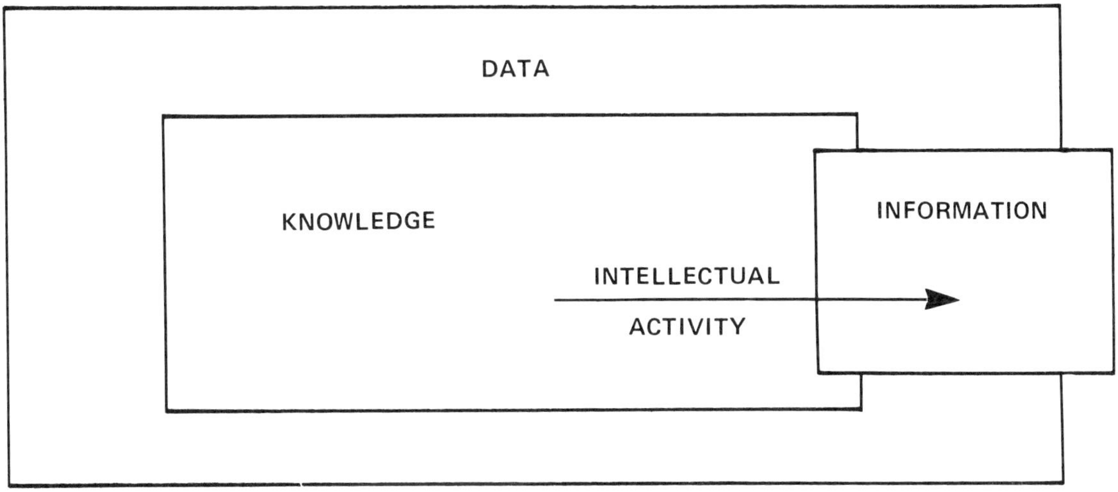

Fig. 2-1. A model for the concepts of *data, knowledge*, and *information*.

CHARACTERISTICS OF INFORMATION

Let us analyze the key definition:

INFORMATION = NEW KNOWLEDGE

The principal characteristics of data, knowledge, and information are as follows:

- The concept of data is different from the concepts of knowledge or information.
- Data is a collection of symbols or characters.
- Knowledge is a collection of facts.
- Knowledge presumes a degree of intelligence that we normally associate with the human being.
- Information is the same as new ideas.
- Information is something acquired that a user did not have before.
- Information transfer can take place only if the user comprehends the message.
- Information changes or widens a user's state of knowledge on a subject.
- Information is normally used to achieve a specific purpose.
- Information reduces uncertainty.
- Information is essential in decision-making.
- Data retrieved becomes "information" only when it is assembled and processed by the ultimate user who associates it with a certain context.
- Information is meaningful only in a certain context.

To sum up, the term *information* is associated with both:

An existing body of knowledge, and intellectual activity.

These two criteria are essential for defining the information gathering process as illustrated in Fig. 2-2.

> The information gathering process is possible only if somebody who has an extensive prior knowledge of the material, i.e., a *subject expert* (professional, specialist, scientist, information seeker, end-user, ultimate user, requester, searcher, nondelegated user, etc.) is actively involved in information retrieval.
>
> The opposite is generally true; that is without the active participation of a subject expert in information retrieval, the creation of information is impossible.

Our Subject Expert Searching Technique is based on the active participation of a subject expert in online information retrieval.

INFORMATION AND THE SUBJECT EXPERT

Let us again go back to our key definition:

INFORMATION = NEW KNOWLEDGE

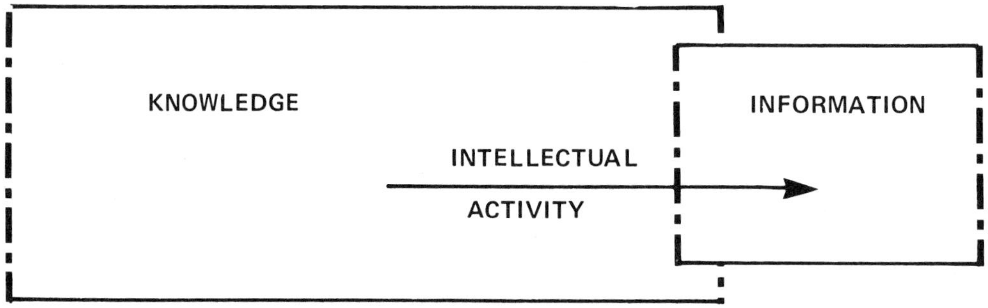

Fig. 2-2. A model of the information gathering process.

What kinds of human activity may be associated with this definition?

1. Educational
2. Scientific
3. Professional
   - medical
   - engineering
   - legal
   - business

What do all these activities have in common with our definition?

1. EDUCATIONAL ACTIVITY (study) is acquiring knowledge that is new for an individual but not for society.
2. SCIENTIFIC ACTIVITY (research) is acquiring knowledge that is new for both individual and society.
3. PROFESSIONAL ACTIVITY (development) is the use of existing knowledge in a new situation. At least some of the existing knowledge may be outside the expert's past experience and thus may be new for him. Therefore, the professional both consumes and creates information in the course of his work.

Here are some examples of professional activity:

- A doctor sees a patient, and, based on previous knowledge and the patient's symptoms, makes a diagnosis;
- An engineer surveys a river, and, based on previous knowledge and the results of the survey, constructs a bridge.

> Thus, there is an interdependence between information (as we defined it) and the different types of subject expert activity. Information constitutes an integral component in all of these kinds of activities.

The Subject Expert Searching Technique is especially suited to the professional or scientist as a part of his everyday activity.

> Successful intellectual activity is often *associative*. Many important scientific discoveries and professional achievements resulted from the use of associative logic.

For example, in many cases, a solution to a difficult technological problem was derived by the successful use of a known technology from a totally unrelated area.

> Continuous learning and the permanent development of scientific and professional knowledge is an important part of the subject expert's activity.

The main task of the Subject Expert Searching Technique is to realize and effectively use the associative, educational, and scientific potentials of the information gathering process.

Some examples of professional activities of a subject expert that include information gathering as their integral component are:

- Research and development
- Medical diagnostic and preventive practice
- Engineering consulting
- Business decision making
- Legal research
- Other

The above activities are "primary" in relation to the "supportive" information gathering processes. *A subject expert is a professional or a scientist who is actively involved in his area of knowledge and for whom information gathering constitutes an important supportive function of his primary professional activity.*

> Thus, information gathering is not a truly independent process; rather, it normally constitutes a part of some other more general activity. As such,

the organization of information gathering depends to some degree on how the primary professional activity is organized. Such information gathering may have certain peculiarities and limitations characteristic of the primary professional activity.

The opposite is also true. The results of a professional activity often depend on the quality of information gathering. In reality, there is an interdependence between the primary professional activity and the supportive information gathering process.

An example of the interdependence of primary professional activity and its supportive information gathering process is shown in Fig. 2-3. It is important to understand that this particular model represents only one kind of professional activity, namely, scientific activity, which is familiar to the majority of professionals.

Scientific activity includes many elements of information gathering that are common to other professional activities as well. At the same time, many other primary professional activities have their own peculiarities that make their supportive information gathering different from that shown on the scheme. The peculiarities of information gathering in some nonscientific activities will be shown later in this chapter.

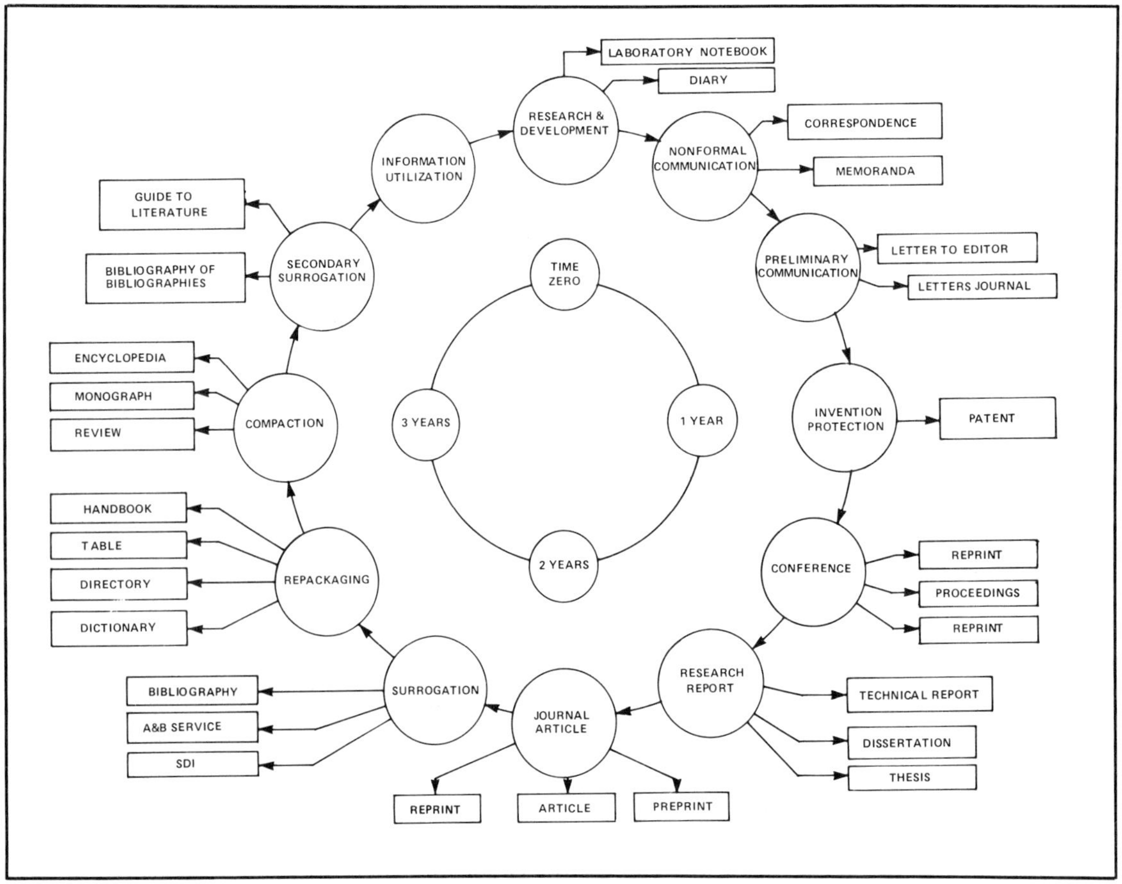

Fig. 2-3. The evolution of scientific information. (From *Encyclopedia of Library and Information Science,* vol. 26, Marcel Dekker, Inc., N.Y., 1979. Courtesy of Marcel Dekker, Inc.)

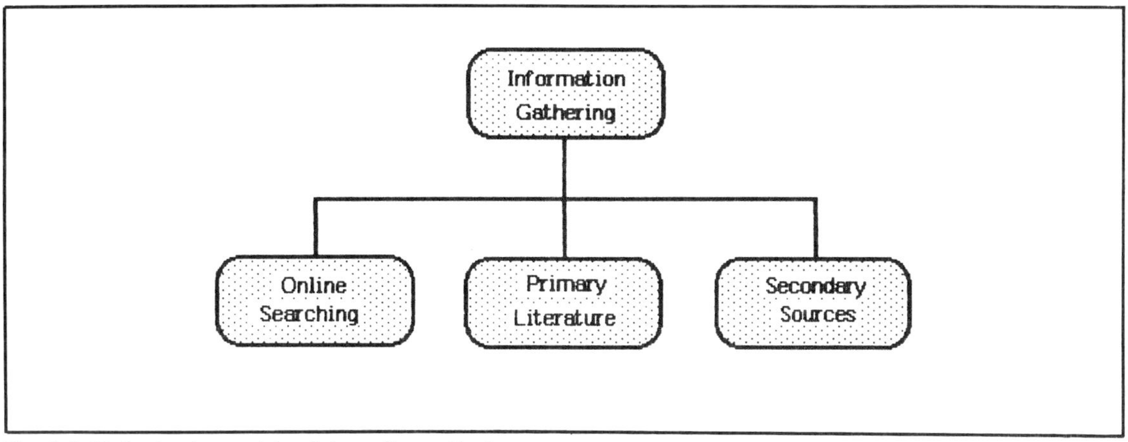

Fig. 2-4. Methods of organizing information gathering.

INFORMATION SOURCES

As is shown in Fig. 2-4, information gathering can be organized in various ways.

Use of primary publications or secondary abstracting sources is a more traditional kind of information gathering than online searching. However, the *information content* of online systems is frequently similar to that of the printed sources.

As Fig. 2-3 shows, information sources are primarily created at different stages of a complex research and development process.

What is common to all of the stages shown on this diagram?

> The answer to this question is: the general idea. Even though there may be certain modifications, improvements, and additions at the later stages, the main scientific objective remains about the same during all of the information dissemination process.

What is different in these activities?

> There is a difference in bibliographic formats, since the difference in tasks requires different product packaging.

Let us briefly examine the reason for the existence of traditional bibliographic sources.

Primary Literature

Laboratory notebooks and diaries are necessary to record results and to form the basis for more formal primary publications.

Nonformal communications are intended to solicit output from the scientific community, normally from a limited number of specialists with similar views or from the same scientific school. At this stage, up to a dozen specialists may be involved in discussing the results.

Letters to editors, conference presentations, and journal articles allow the scientist to formally establish precedence in having obtained certain scientific results. They also allow him to disseminate information more widely, primarily among specialists currently actively involved in the scientific area discussed. Normally, a primary source may be circulated among a few hundred or even a few thousand specialists. Such publications also open up possibilities for further information dissemination through secondary sources.

Patents are even more formal documents and are used to protect the invention when proprietary interests may be involved. In addition, published descriptions of patents also become a part of the primary scientific literature.

Research reports are normally required by the sponsoring agency as a proof of conducting and concluding scientific effort. Specific kinds of research reports, such as *dissertations* or *theses,* are primarily intended to acknowledge a certain scientific status of its author. Dissertations and technical reports traditionally are not considered to be "formally "published documents. However, in practice, with the introduction of new information dissemination methods and modern duplicating equipment (for example, photocopying machines or microfiche readers), the difference between these documents and "more established" sorts of publications has begun to rapidly vanish.

Item, problem	Information
Theoretical efficacy of the method	controlled trial
Applicability of the method in practice	operational study
Control of the vaccine, etc.	special studies
Risk of the disease in the society in question	epidemiological study
Population at risk	census data
Requirements of the procedure in terms of:	
(*a*) training in the procedures (*b*) vaccinations performed per unit of time (*c*) other technical requirements	from demonstration areas and expert opinion
Effect of the activity on the services	expert opinion (mainly from other information subsystems)
Attitude of the personnel and population	from expert opinion; can also be estimated from opinion surveys and participation rates
Side-effects and accidents related to procedure	individual reports to be stored and studied
Participation	data bank (as *ad hoc* study) that provides answers to questions such as which persons should be specially invited
Refusals	sample study of characteristics of refusals, rate of vaccinated persons by locality, cohort, etc.
Cases of disease	from notification and follow-up reports stored in a data bank
Other relevant items such as resources requested, cost, etc.	

Fig. 2-5. Information required for vaccination purposes. (From A.S. Härö, "Information Systems for Health Services at the National Level," In *Information Systems for Health Services. Public Härö in Europe No. 13,* WHO, Copenhagen, 1980, p. 13. Courtesy of World Health Organization.)

table 3–10

growth trend of product demand in customer industries (sample printout: corrugated shipping containers—sic 2653)

CUSTOMER INDUSTRY		VALUE OF PURCHASES IN MILLIONS OF SQUARE FEET						
SIC	DESCRIPTION	ACTUAL			PROJECTED		ANNUAL GROWTH RATES	
		1967	1972	1975	1980	1985	67-72	72-75
2032	CANNED SPECIALTIES	1124.6	1600.8	1700.4	2011.7	2380.0	7.24	3.40
2033	CANNED FRUITS, VEGETABLES & JAMS	2563.3	3504.7	3722.7	4404.3	5210.7	6.42	3.43
2034	DEHYDRATED FOOD PREPARATIONS	349.7	499.7	530.2	627.3	742.2	7.43	3.42
2035	PICKLES, SAUCES & SALAD DRESSINGS	688.2	961.6	1021.4	1208.4	1429.6	6.96	3.44
2037	FROZEN FRUITS & VEGETABLES	875.0	1288.9	1369.1	1620.0	1916.6	8.12	3.41
2038	FROZEN SPECIALTIES	925.4	1407.5	1495.0	1768.7	2092.5	8.81	3.42

Fig. 2-6. Samples of records from EIS files on business statistics. (From J.M. Gould *Input/Output Databases. Uses in Business and Government*, Garland STPM Press, 1979, p. 46. Courtesy of Garland Publishing.)

Secondary Sources

Secondary sources (such as *bibliographies* or *SDI—selective dissemination of information*) are intended to further disseminate scientific information among all the scientific community. They are better suited to be used to access primary literature at a later date. Certain kinds of secondary documents may examine in more depth a new idea and its possible applications (*monographs*); put a specific idea in proper perspective in relation to the more general scientific thought (*reviews*); or explain an idea in terms more suitable for educational or reference purposes (*handbooks, encyclopedias, dictionaries*).

An increasingly important kind of scientific literature which is omitted in Fig. 2-3 is *standards, regulations,* and *codes of practice.* Their importance is growing with the new trend towards incorporation of scientific results into social and economic life.

Figure 2-3 reflects the dependence of different bibliographic formats on *time.* Time is an important factor, which is essential to the development of information packages that are more refined and ready for consumption. However, a second important factor, which may be no less critical than time, is *resources.* Without proper resources, the normal developmental cycle may be aborted.

In reality, the progression of scientific information is, of course, not a closed process and constitutes a spiral rather than a circle. Utilization of information may lead to the generation of new ideas that will be further studied and developed, so that the evolution of scientific knowledge continues.

Professional activities other than scientific activities may require different kinds of information gathering processes.

An example of a health information system required for vaccination purposes is presented in Fig. 2-5. The table, which represents only a simple model of a much more complex program, has been developed by the Finnish National Board of Health.

Figure 2-6 shows an example of data that are used in *business decision making.* This example is taken from a book describing the Economic Information Systems (EIS) files, available online through the DIALOG online service. The author of the book, J.M. Gould, organized these files based on the principles of input/output economics developed by the Nobel Laureate Wassily Leontief.

Based on his previous knowledge and on the data available, a business analyst builds an economic model that may be used to forecast certain trends. An output of this forecast is used in business decision making.

Another example of statistical sources of information is shown in Fig. 2-7. Known statistics on the employment of scientists and engineers in the United States in 1900-1960 allowed Gould to make an assumption about exponential growth in the more recent history of the world. This was used to forecast the growth into the next century. The extrapolation of the curve into the past suggested that the model assumptions were reasonable. For the

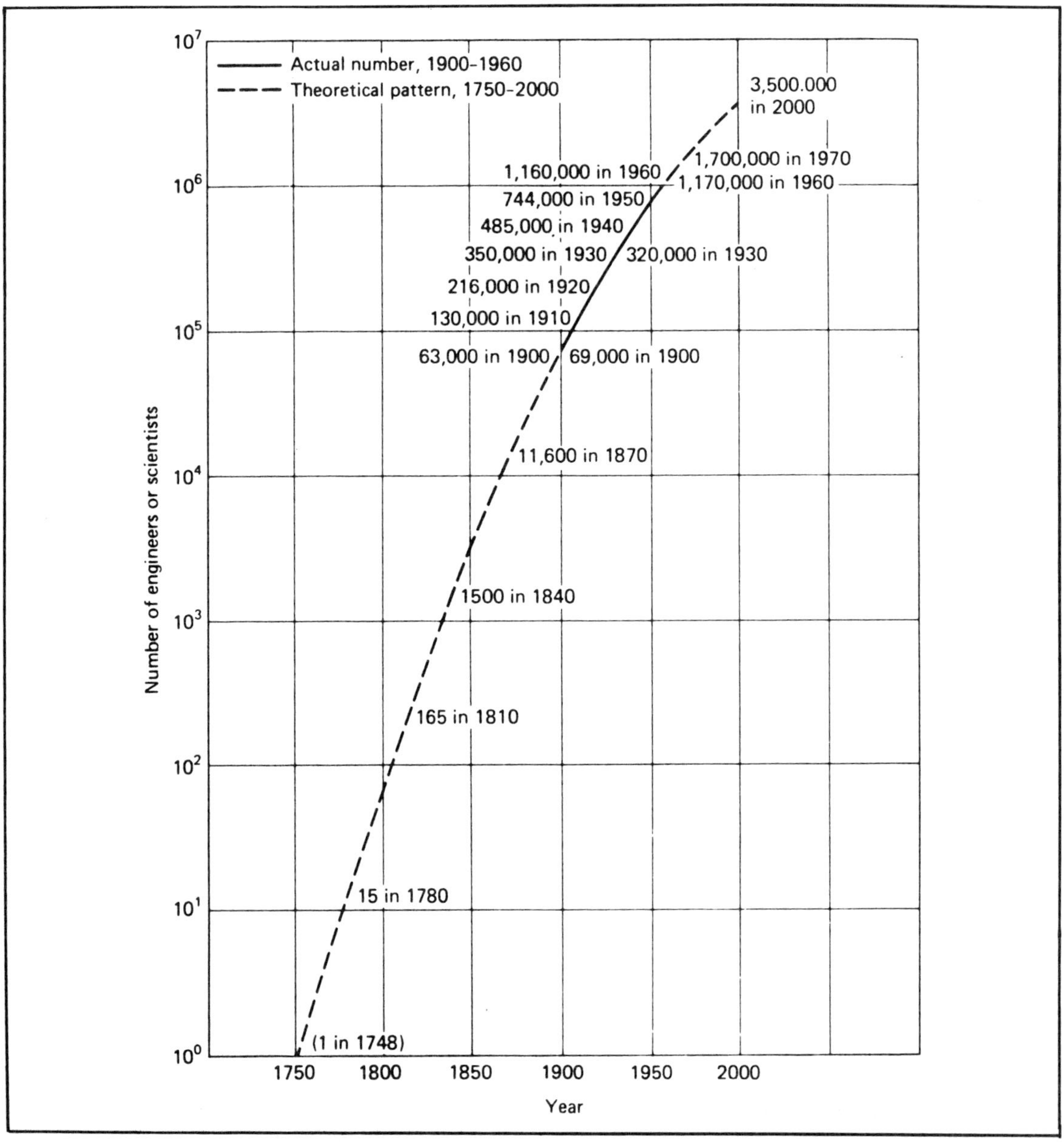

Fig. 2-7. Growth in the number of scientists and engineers in the USA. 1750-2000. (From J.M. Gould, *Input/Output Databases. Uses in Business and Government,* Garland STPM Press, 1979, p. 69. Courtesy of Garland Publishing.)

last twenty years, the forecasts of this model proved to be more or less accurate.

Traditional Information Sources

There are no accurate statistics on the primary scientific and technical literature and secondary publications published in the world. The estimates below are based on different sources.

- Figure 2-8 shows the estimates of proportions of publications according to their language of origin.
- Figure 2-9 shows the estimates of proportions of publications divided according to the area in which they were published.
- Estimates of the annual number of published books in science and technology in the world:

Total - 80,000 to 100,000 per year

New titles - 40,000 to 50,000 per year

- Estimates of number of periodicals in science and technology in the world:

Total - 50,000 per year

PUBLICATIONS AND THE USER

How intensively is an average scientific publication utilized by the users?

The following statistics give an inside look at the average article utilization (from H.Wooster, "The Future of Scientific Publishing . . .," *Journal of the Washington Academy of Sciences,* vol.60, no.2, June 1970, pp.41-45. Courtesy of the Washington Academy of Sciences):

- The most common frequency of scientific journal publication is quarterly.
- Average circulation is 4,400 copies.

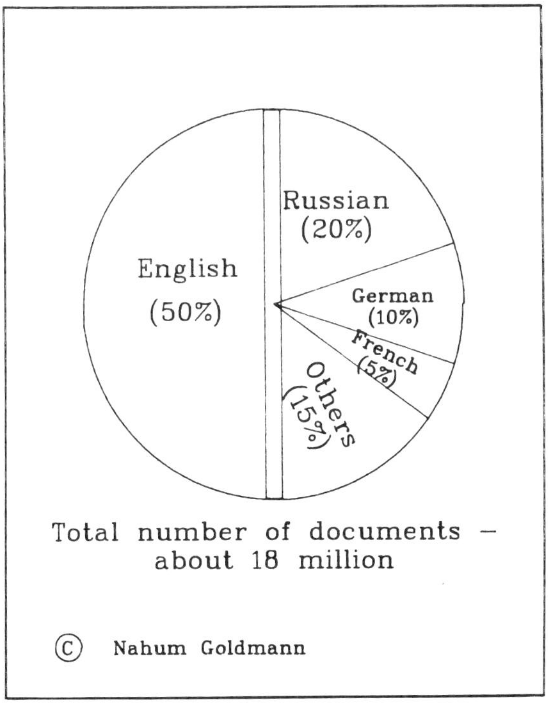

Fig. 2-8. Estimates of annual distribution by the language of origin of the world scientific and technical flow.

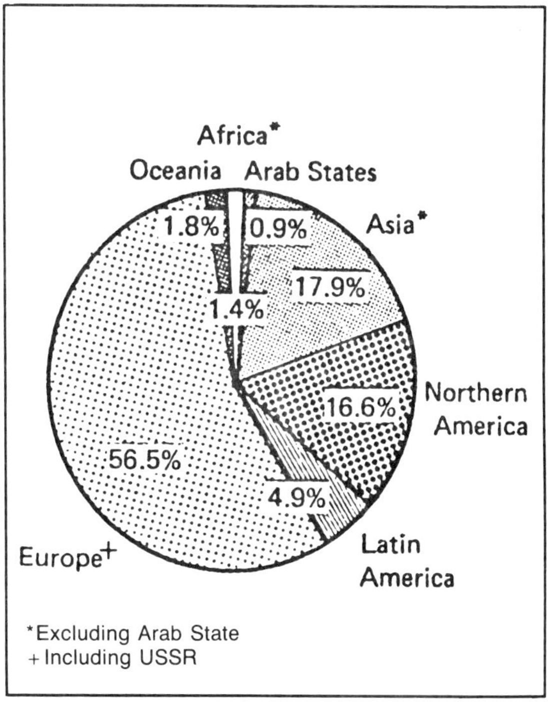

Fig. 2-9. Distribution of book production by continents and major areas: estimated percentage, 1979. (From *1980 UNESCO Statistical Yearbook*. ©Unesco 1980. Courtesy of Unesco.)

- The average annual publication is a 1,000 pages/per journal.
- One paper will reach about 100 actual readers.
- About 50 percent of the papers in core journals are read in detail by no more than 1 percent of readers; no paper is read by more than 7 percent of readers.
- About 90 percent of the authors receive reprint requests.
- The average number of reprint requests per published article is 11-15 copies.

H. Wooster came up further with the following three numbers that apply to the use of periodic scientific and technical publications—10, 100, and 1,000.

- 10 - the maximum number of journals any average scientist can be expected to keep up with.
- 100 - will meet 90 percent of the needs of any reasonably specialized information center.
- 1,000 - probably the number of first class scientific journals in the world today.

Knowledge of the user's preference and ability in utilizing information is important for the organization of information gathering activity of the subject expert. A properly organized information system may greatly increase the effectiveness and professional level of the subject expert.

CONCLUSIONS

Let us briefly summarize the major points of this chapter.

The following key definition was accepted:

INFORMATION = NEW KNOWLEDGE

Our conclusions are that:

- The information gathering process is possible only if somebody who has an extensive prior knowledge of the material, that is a subject expert, is actively involved in information retrieval.
- Without the active participation of a subject expert in information retrieval, creation of information is generally impossible.
- Knowledge of the user's preference and ability in utilizing information is important to the organization of the information gathering process of the subject expert. A properly organized information system may greatly increase the effectiveness and professional level of the subject expert.
- Information gathering is not a truly independent process. In reality, there is an interdependence between a primary professional activity and its supportive information gathering process. This interdependence was illustrated by the examples of the scientific process, a health information system, and a business decision making process.

Our *Subject Expert Searching Technique* may be characterized by the following:

- It is based on the active participation of a subject expert in online information retrieval.
- It is especially suited to the subject expert as a part of his everyday activity.
- It is intended to realize and effectively use the associative, educational, and scientific potentials of the information gathering process.

Chapter 3

An Overview Of Online Systems

The following is a brief description of the present state of online services.

FILE, PRODUCER, AND ONLINE SERVICE

Since online searching is a relatively new field, its terminology has not yet been well developed and standardized. Confusion is especially high in relation to three key-terms, *file*, *producer*, and *online service.*

Throughout this book we describe a *file* as a collection of textual, numeric, or graphic data that are stored in a rapid-access computer. With its data content, a file is similar to a traditional publication.

An online file is useful because it may be accessed almost immediately from any geographic location. It also provides the capabilities of sorting data and of retrieving data in a specified order of preference. Such operations can be conducted rapidly.

In different publications, instead of the term *file*, other terms such as *database* or *data base, data bank, vendor, producer,* or *supplier*, are used. These terms are not always interchangeable. In many cases this collection of data that we name as a file is only a segment of a much larger collection of data. The whole collection is called a *database*.

The division of a database into files is similar to the division of a large encyclopedia into separate volumes. Just as with the volumes of encyclopedia, the files that constitute a database share a great similarity in data structure.

In this book, we make a distinction between the terms database and file only when it is crucial to the understanding of the material. Otherwise, we tend to use the term file.

We describe a *producer* as an organization that creates a file's con-

tent. A producer may act as its own vendor, as well as market its files through other vendors.

Synonyms that are sometimes used instead of the term *producer* include *database, data bank, vendor, supplier, information center, secondary publisher, secondary services*, and *indexing and abstracting services.*

In this book the term *online service* is used to identify a collection of files that are maintained by the same vendor and have common connection and similar retrieval procedures.

Synonyms that are frequently used to describe online services include *databases, information or retrieval systems; information, retrieval,* or *search services; vendor services;* and *service suppliers.*

Generally, there is no one-to-one relationship between these three terms.

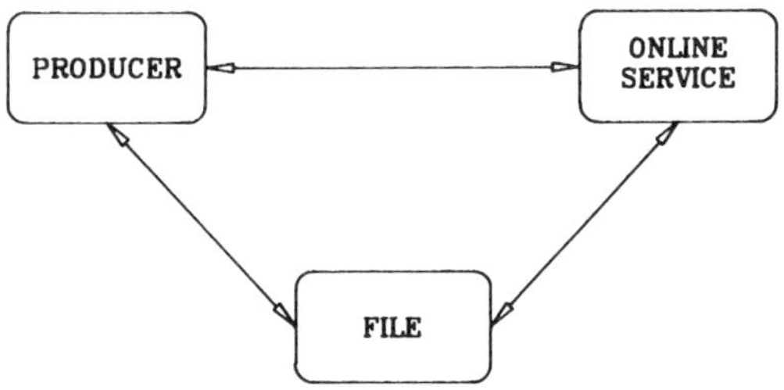

WHAT IS AVAILABLE ONLINE

The number of publicly available files and online records has rapidly increased during the last few years. Thus, the annual update rate on online systems for bibliographic records alone has reached ten million records per year (see Fig. 3-1). Of course, the overall number of records, including various nonbibliographic materials, is much higher.

The Spring 1984 *Directory of Online Databases*, issued by Cuadra Associated Inc., describes 2225 publicly available files. For the last several years, the number of files covered in this directory has steadily increased with an annual rate of nearly 50 percent. The number of online services has also steadily increased.

One way of illustrating this process of growth is to review the number of publicly available files on the DIALOG online service, which increased more or less steadily in 1979-84 with an average annual growth rate of 19 percent (see Fig. 3-2).

However, the average online connect rate for the DIALOG online service in the same period, taking inflation into account, has actually been slightly decreasing, although one may argue, not as fast as is desirable for the mass use of this service by the end-user. This is in spite of the facts that during this time a set of relatively expensive patent files was added to DIALOG; and that online systems started to charge for printing online records, in ad-

	Total	Unique (without duplicates)
Cumulative number of online records	70 million	40 million
Annual update rate	10 million	6 million

Fig. 3-1. Number of bibliographic records available online in 1982. (According to J.L. Holl and M.J. Brown, *Online Bibliographic Databases: A Directory and Sourcebook, Third Edition*, ASLIB, London, 1983, p. 1).

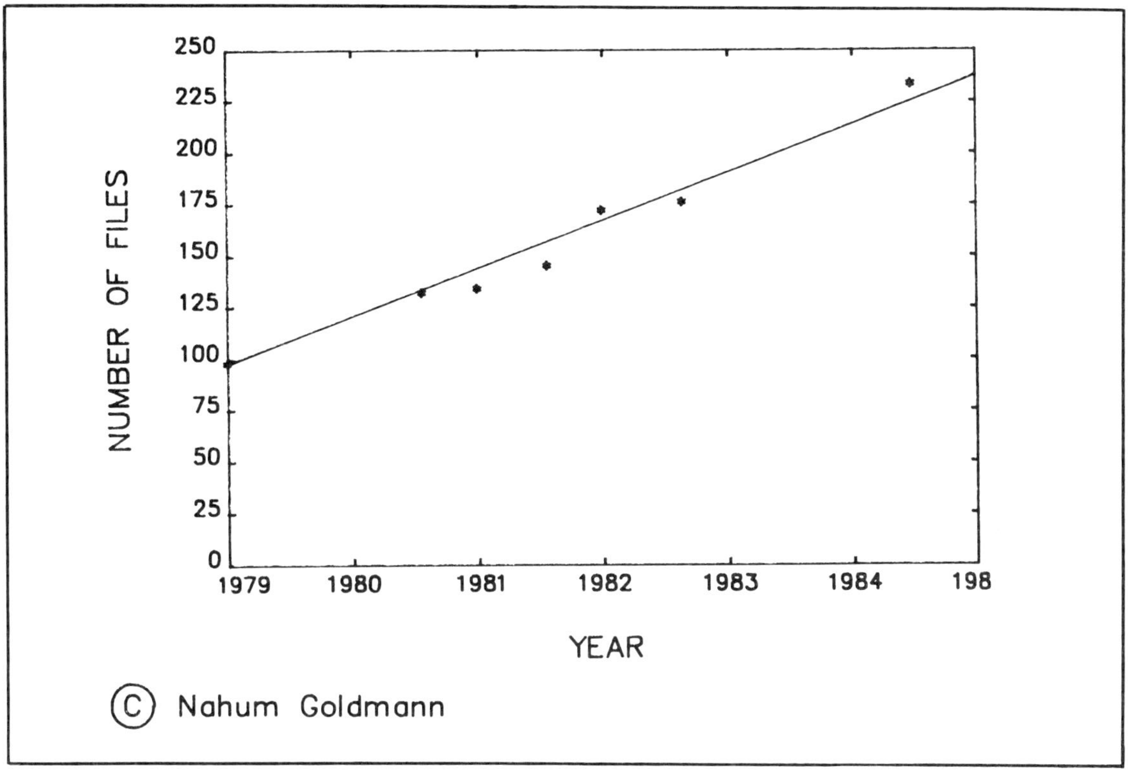

Fig. 3-2. Numbers of publicly available files on the DIALOG online service, 1979-84.

dition to the previous charges for online connect times (see Fig. 3-3).

Figures 3-4 through 3-6 provide some statistics on distribution of online materials by subject area, place of origin of file suppliers, and time since publication.

Figure 3-7 presents a table of the cumulative results of searches performed on three files that constitute the large computerized database EMBASE (Excerpta Medica; Files 172, 73, and 72), which together cover worldwide publications in medical journals since 1976. The choice of EMBASE amongst more than two hundred files currently available online through DIALOG was due to its well developed and highly consistent classification for both geographic and subject descriptors.

Searches in EMBASE were performed on subfile 35 "Occupational Health," which among all three file segments accounted for more than 45,000 records. Results of these searches are expressed in Fig. 3-7 as percentages of the total number of records in subfile 35.

Additional free-text searches on the same subject were performed on 15 DIALOG files representing such diversified branches of knowledge as medicine, biology, engineering, environmental, and pollution studies. The precision of these searches was generally lower than for EMBASE. However, their results were consistent with numbers presented in Fig. 3-7, regardless of the specified subject area of each file. This fact is not surprising when you take into account that occupational health is one of the few multidisciplinary fields concerned with almost all areas of scientific and professional knowledge.

The analysis of data shown in Fig. 3-7 is clearly representative of the limitations that are characteristic of North American hard-copy secondary publications and online services. For exam-

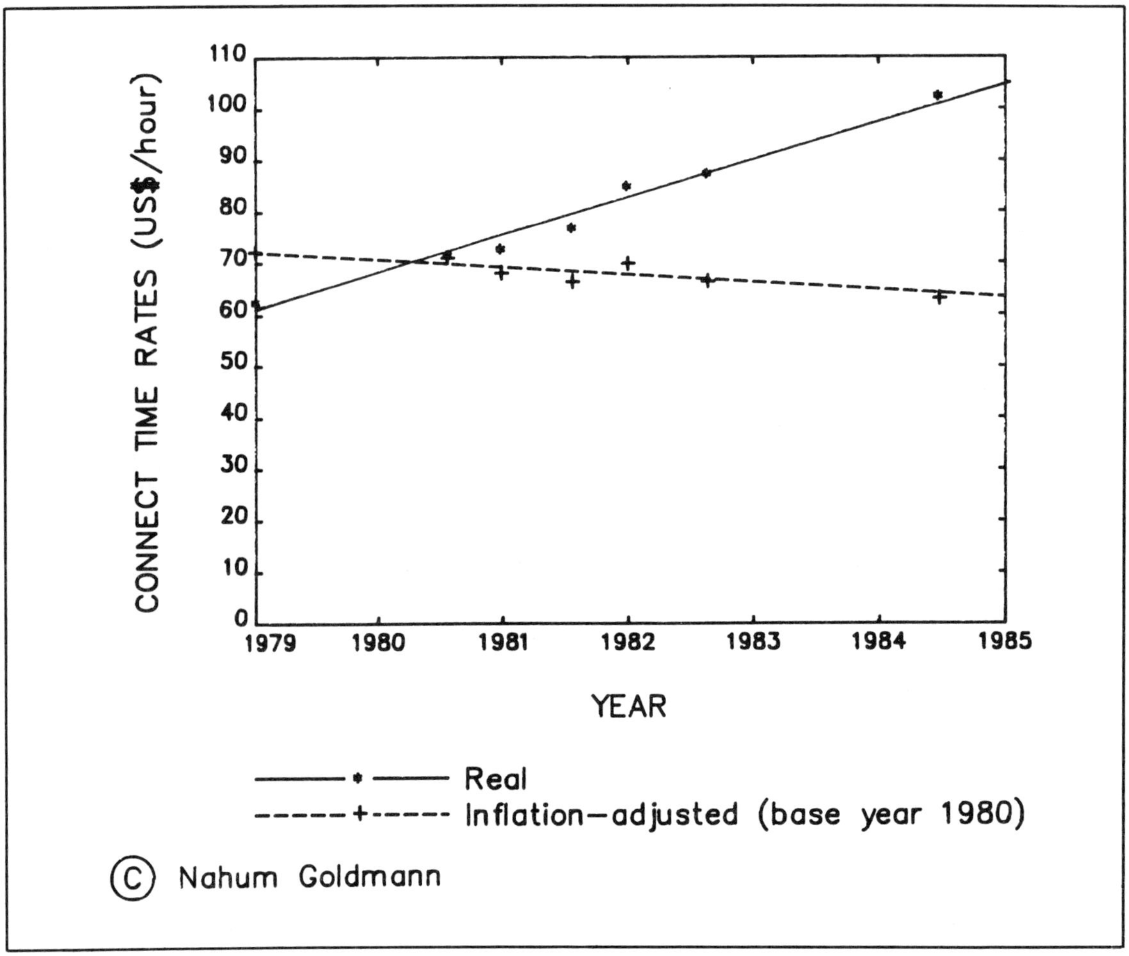

Fig. 3-3. Average online connect time rates for publicly available files on the DIALOG online service, 1979-84.

The rates are expressed in real terms and also in inflation-adjusted U.S. dollars with a base year of 1980. The data shown are the result of averaging of the sum of an online hourly rate and of an online type rate per 100 full records, where applicable. For more expensive files whose price for typing one record is higher than $3.00, we added to the hourly rate the price of typing only 10 full records instead of 100.

ple, numerous Soviet and East European publications, which are so important in this area, have been practically left outside of Western information sources. A similar situation exists in many other areas of scientific and professional knowledge.

THE QUALITY OF ONLINE DATA

> Comparing different figures, you may note that a greater percentage of the world collection of scientific and technical knowledge is put online every year. A significant portion of this knowledge has already been stored in computers.

Since online access provides a much better opportunity for information retrieval than traditional bibliographic methods, you may expect that eventually most of the world's information flow will be computerized. Economic considerations are contributing greatly to the process of computerization.

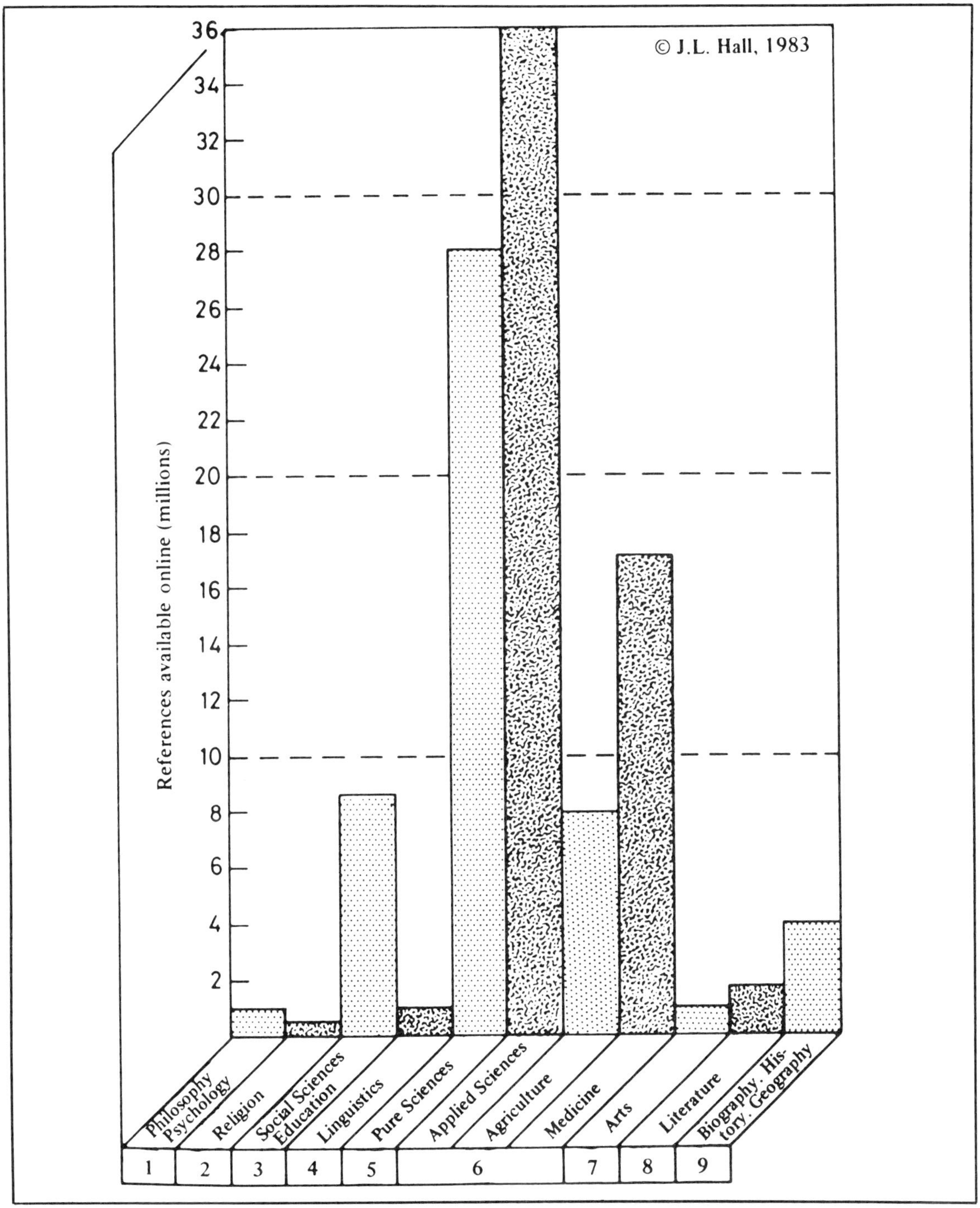

Fig. 3-4. The main fields of knowledge with an indication of the number of bibliographic references (in millions) available for online search. (From J.L. Holl and M.J. Brown, *Online Bibliographic Databases: A Directory and Sourcebook, Third Edition*, ASLIB, London, 1983, p. 25. Courtesy of James Logan Hall.)

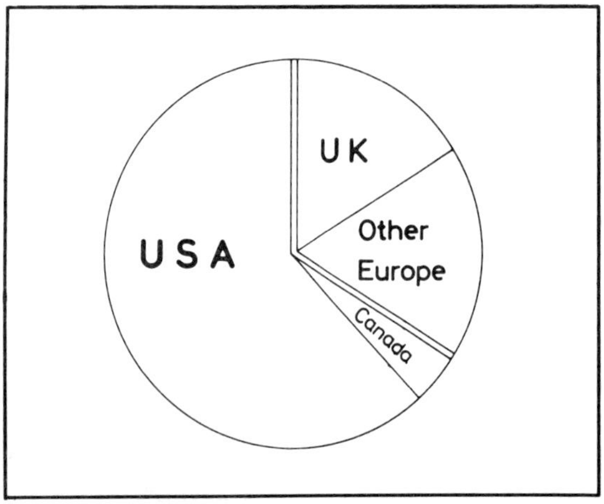

Fig. 3-5. Place of origin of online bibliographic file suppliers. (From J.L. Holl and M.J. Brown, *Online Bibliographic Databases: An Intermediate Directory, Second Edition*, ASLIB, London, 1981. p. xxiii. Courtesy of James Logan Hall.)

This is because the price of traditional publishing and distributing is increasing much faster than the price of online information retrieval. The latter may even decrease in the future.

Especially important for many practical applications may be the following limitations of publicly available online services:

- File suppliers first and foremost represent Western industrial developed countries.
- English-language materials dominate in the Western information flow. American-originated publications make up an especially large share of this flow.
- At present, publicly available online services cover approximately one-third of 18 million scientific and technical documents published annually in the world. However, this coverage is unevenly distributed among different geographic regions and publication languages. Documents published in nonEnglish languages are underrepresented in the Western secondary sources and correspondingly in the online services. This is especially so with the information generated by the Soviet Union and Eastern Europe, Japan, and the Third World countries, but to some extent also true of the Western European countries

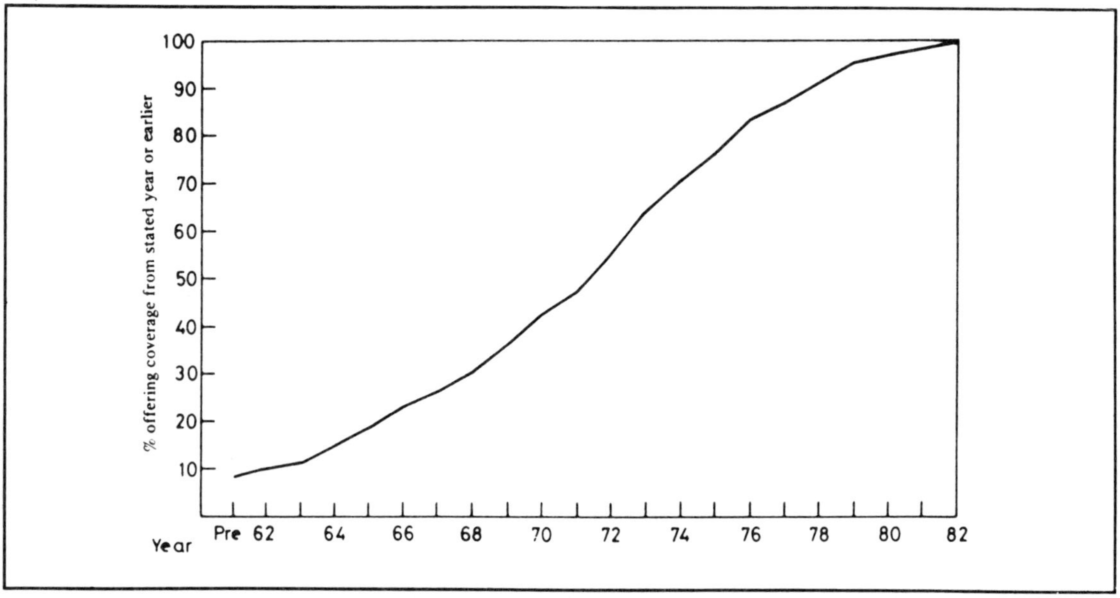

Fig. 3-6. Time-span on bibliographic files available online. (From J.L. Holl and M.J. Brown, *Online Bibliographic Databases: A Directory and Sourcebook, Third Edition*, ASLIB, London, 1983, p. 29. Courtesy of James Logan Hall.)

Sixty-one percent of the files provide coverage of at least the last 10 years.

© by Nahun Goldmann

Country	Percentage of the total number of records (45,209) in subfile 35 "Occupational Health"
United States	31.6%
Canada	3.1
United Kingdom	8.2
W Germany	8.7
France	6.2
Sweden	2.7
Netherland	1.4
Italy	4.4
Australia	1.1
Japan	5.0
USSR	4.0
East Germany	3.5
Poland	3.0
Bulgaria	1.1
China (PR)	0.02
India	1.3
Argentina	0.06
Brazil	0.15
Total	85.5%

Fig. 3-7. Geographic distribution of online references in the occupational health field. DIALOG online service. Files 72, 73, and 172:EMBASE (Excerpta Medica).

with "exotic" languages.

- Very rough evaluations show that online services cover about 60 percent of the annual U.S. scientific and technical bibliographic flow. About 40-50 percent of the annual volume of the West European scientific and engineering publications are represented online, especially those documents published in English. Our estimate for the current USSR and East European publications reflected in North American online services put this figure at only 10-20 percent and for the Third World countries at a mere 5-10 percent. This should not be too surprising as online geographic distribution parallels the trend in leading Western hard-copy abstract journals, which has been evident for decades.
- Online services are often created as by-products of printed indexes and bibliographies. Therefore, they cover mainly the scientific and technical information that has been published since the time when computer conversion started. Information published prior to this is represented online only

fragmentally. As Fig. 3-6 shows, only half of all online services cover documents that were published in 1970. Also, older online records are usually less informative than newer records. For example, in many of the older records the abstracts are not included.

- More than 80 percent of all requests for scientific and technical information submitted by the end-user normally concern documents published during the last two of three years. This probably results more from difficulties in accessing older hard-copy abstract publications than from any other reason. In the online form, a description of an old document is in principle as accessible as the newer one. This fact may lead to the possibility of significant increases in the lifespan of scientific and technical literature.
- The online conversion may be instrumental in increasing the accessibility of noncore publications, providing, of course, these publications have found their way into computerized information retrieval systems in the first place. Correspondingly, the publications that do not find their way online may in the future have a slim chance of being accessed.

> **The quality of information retrieved from the computer is limited by the quality of data put into the computer in the first place. At present, the existing online services still do not fully represent scientific and technical knowledge.**

Online data may be sufficient for solving many problems; however, in some cases the necessary data may be lacking in online services.

> **At the present stage of online services development, an online search, however complex, cannot provide all the published documents on any chosen subject.**

> **The degree of coverage of information which a subject expert may be seeking online depends on the nature of the problem being explored.**

The existence online of seemingly relevant knowledge does not automatically mean that it is exhaustive or useful. It may be biased for ideological, political, or other reasons, or because it represents a particular school of thought.

CONCLUSIONS

The chapter is primarily devoted to the existing online systems. I defined three important terms for online searching: file, online service, and producer.

I also noted that the number of publicly available files and online records has rapidly increased during the last few years. A significant portion of the world's collection of scientific and technical knowledge has already been stored in computers. Economic considerations are contributing greatly to the process of computerization. This is because the price of traditional publishing and distributing is increasing rapidly, much faster than the price of online information retrieval, which may even decrease in the future.

However, publicly available online information sources are biased towards English-language materials, especially U.S.-produced documents, and are limited in time, mainly covering publications since 1965. At present, the existing online services still do not fully represent world scientific and technical knowledge. One may hope, however, that eventually most of the world's information flow will be computerized.

At the present stage of online service development, an online search, however complex, cannot provide all the published documents on any chosen subject. At the same time, the existence online of seemingly relevant knowledge does not automatically mean that it is exhaustive or useful. It may be biased for ideological, political, or other reasons or because it represents a particular school of thought.

The degree of coverage of information that a subject expert may be seeking online depends on the nature of the problem explored.

Chapter 4
The Contents of Online Services

A viable online service usually consists of several dozen, and sometimes several hundred, files that include information on various subjects. A typical file has a well-defined subject such as biology, medicine, mathematics, physics, sociology, or the law. However, since modern science is quite multifaceted, a file often represents various aspects of the subject and may be a good source of information on many related topics. This is especially so with new subjects that are on the boundary of various disciplines.

Thus, if you are looking for information on a subject that formally belongs to mathematical physics, it is only logical to perform a search in both physics and mathematics files available online, such as American Institute of Physics' File SPIN or American Mathematical Society's Mathfile. Moreover, you may find useful information on this subject in certain engineering, computer, and general science files, for example Compendex, International Software Database, Scisearch, NTIS, Dissertation Abstracts Online, or Conference Papers Index.

Printed references in traditionally published secondary (bibliographic) journals are usually found with the help of the table of contents, or various indexes, such as the subject index. The indexes in these publications are normally organized according to their principal subject. It is, therefore, very difficult to find in a bibliographic journal a reference that is of interest to the end-user, but is not considered to be of principal importance by the journal publisher. For example, apparently peripheral subjects in scientific papers, such as experimental methodology, instrumentation used, or computational methods, are virtually inaccessible in many secondary publications, even though the authors may originally mention them in the abstract.

The situation is quite different with computerized information retrieval systems. Typically, all the words in online records are equally accessible, including words in titles and abstracts that are normally created by the authors themselves. It is, therefore, quite possible to retrieve a record that includes information considered to be of marginal importance by the indexer. This possibility greatly enhances the universal character and multidisciplinary use of online files.

TYPES OF FILES

Even though bibliographic files are fairly common now, there are many online files that are not bibliographic. Nonbibliographic files are sometimes referred to as *data banks* or *data files*. Their formats vary since they differ in scope and in the type of data that they contain.

Figure 4-1 shows how online files can be classified. The following are the three general categories of online files:

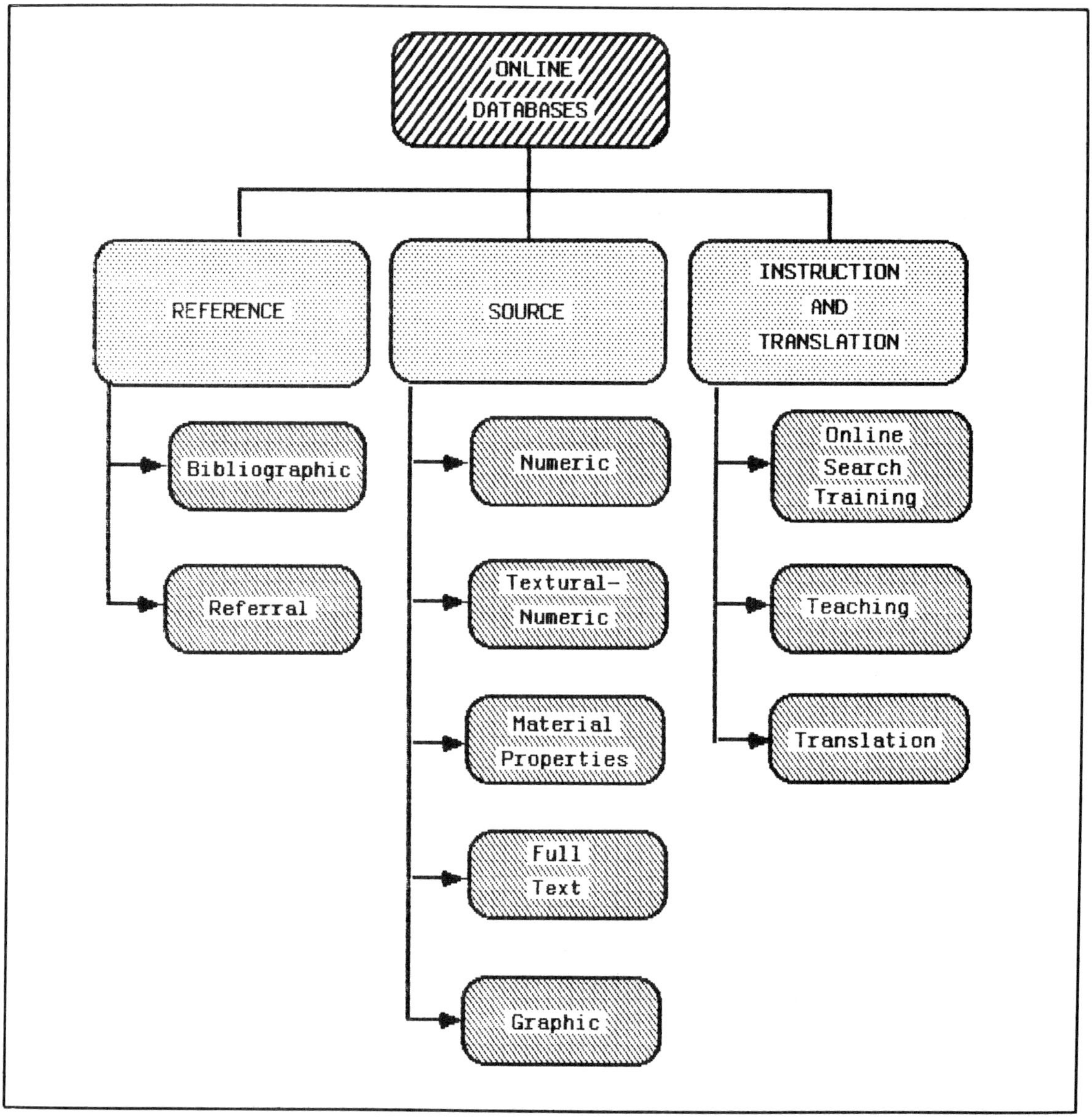

Fig. 4-1. Classification scheme of online files.

Reference files. Refer users to another source (for example, a document, an organization, or an individual) for additional details or for the complete text.

Source files. Contain complete data or the full text of the original source information.

Aid files. Intended to be used as tools for computer-aided education, skill training, translation, or design. Skill training involves more manual or routine tasks than does education. Amongst various skill training files, this book is primarily concerned with the narrower category of online-search training files.

REFERENCE FILES

Bibliographic files contain citations to the printed literature, including journal articles, books, conference proceedings, reports, dissertations, patents, standards, or newspaper items. Figures 4-2 through 4-9 show sample records from bibliographic files.

Referral files contain references to nonpublished information. They generally refer users to organizations, individuals, audiovisual materials, grants, business opportunities, and other nonprint media for further information. Also, they may contain thesauri or classification schemes for bibliographic files. Figures 4-10 through 4-15 show sample records from referral files.

SOURCE FILES

Numeric files contain original survey data and/or statistically manipulated representations of data. They are generally in the form of a time series that represents measurements (for example, tons or dollars) over time for a given variable (for example, production or shipment statistics for a given product or industry). Figure 4-16 shows a sample record from a numeric file.

Textual-numeric files contain records combining text and numeric data. Fig-

```
3/5/9
EJ292445  SP513540
  A+ Schools: Portraits of Schools that Work.
  Instructor, v93 n5 p20-21,24 Jan    1984
  Available from: UMI
  Language: English
  Document Type: PROJECT DESCRIPTION (141)
  Teachers,  students,  and parents at Tecumseh Harrison Elementary School
(Vincennes, Indiana)  are pulling together to make the school the best that
it  can be.  Innovative approaches include learning centers (on publishing,
for example), individualized instruction, and videotaped lessons. (PP)
  Descriptors:  *Educational Quality;  *Educational Strategies;  Elementary
Education; *Elementary Schools; Individualized Instruction;  *Instructional
Innovation;  *Learning Centers (Classroom);  Teaching  Methods;   Videotape
Recordings
  Identifiers: *Tecumseh Harrison Elementary School IN
```

Fig. 4-2. A unit record containing a citation to a journal article. DIALOG online service. File 1:ERIC (Education Resources Information Center).

```
-1-
AN   - 82-001552
TI   - How to buy : an insider's guide to making money on the stock market /
       Justin Mamis.
AU   - Mamis, Justin
SO   - New York : Farrar Straus Giroux, c1982.
NU   - ISBN 0374173346
NO   - ix, 245 p. : ill. ; 22 cm.
LA   - eng
AV   - Holding Library: LC
CALL- LC: HG4921.M325 1982
DC   - 332.6322
IT   - Stocks--United States--Handbooks, manuals, etc.
```

Fig. 4-3. A unit record containing a citation to a book. ORBIT online service. File LC/LINE. (Courtesy of System Development Corporation.)

The file represents U.S. Library of Congress catalogues and covers 1968 to August 1982 holdings.

ure 4-17 shows a sample record from a numeric file.

Like full text files, the textual-numeric reviews represent mainly the opinion of their authors and often are not without bias.

Properties files contain dictionary or handbook-type data, typically chemical, physical, or biomedical properties. Figure 4-18 shows a sample record from a properties file.

Full text (natural language) files contain records of the complete text of an item; for example, a newspaper article,

```
79075152    v7n9
  Kant's concept of geography and the importance of his deliberations of
the scientific basis for the contemporary study of the geography of
religion
  Buettner, M.
  Ruhr-Univ., Bochum, W. Ger.
  Association of American Geographers Annual Meeting 792 2106
Philadelphia, Pennsylvania  22-25 Apr 79
  Association of American Geographers
  Abstracts (Eng) in "AAG Program-Abstracts" booklet, Apr 79, for
information: Dr. J. W. Nystrom, Exec. Dir., AAG, 1710 16th St., N.W.,
Washington, D.C. 20009
  Descriptors: GEOGRAPHY
  Section Heading: GEOSCIENCE
  Section Class Codes: 5500
```

Fig. 4-4. A unit record containing a citation to a conference proceeding. DIALOG online service. File 77:Conference Papers Index. (Courtesy of Cambridge Scientific Abstracts.)

```
TYPE 5/4/1
DOE/SF/00115-T3  NTIS  84033573
  Battlefield Radiation Study
  Lee, H.; Millican, R.
  Stanford  Research  Inst.,  Menlo  Park, CA.*Department of Energy,
Washington, DC  (013999000 5911000)
  30  Jun  73,   27p,   Contract:  AM03-76SF00115,   NTIS Prices: PC
A03/MF A01
  A  system  for  radiological  assessment of battlefield conditions
during  a  technical  nuclear conflict is discussed. Recommendations
for an improved system are presented
  Fld: 18H, 15F, 15G, 6R, 77G, 74H, 74G, 68F, 68G, 57V
  Controlled  terms:  *Nuclear  weapons  /  *Radiation  monitoring /
*Local  fallout  /  *Risk  assessment  / Radiation hazards / Nuclear
explosions / Recommendations / Military personnel
  Uncontrolled terms: ERDA/450202 / NTISDE
```

Fig. 4-5. A unit record containing a citation to a report. ESA online service. File 06:NTIS (National Technical Information Service).

a specification, or a court decision. Figures 4-19 through 4-21 show sample records from full text files.

Graphic files contain records in graphic form; for example, chemical structure diagrams. Records may also include textual or numeric information. Figure 4-22 shows a sample record from a graphic file.

AID FILES

Online search training (online training and practice) files intended to be used by inexperienced searchers of complex or expensive files for low-cost training purposes. Normally these include small, simplified portions of main files. They may also include additional self-training instructions, self-evaluating procedures, and exercises. However, some commands that are used in the original files may not be valid in the training files. Figure 4-23 shows a sample record from an online search training file.

Computer Aided Learning (CAL) files are intended to be used for educational purposes, such as for the online learning of languages, mathematics, or physics.

Computer Aided Design (CAD) files are intended to be used for design purposes, with the help of various graphic and analytical tools.

Translation files perform machine translation from one language to another.

FILES WITH VARIOUS FORMS OF PRESENTATION

The classification of different files given above is, to a great extent, conventional. It is hoped that in the future computerized files will be capable of storing data in various forms.

A good example of data output simultaneously presented in several forms would be a printed version of an encyclopedia, with its variety of full text, numeric, graphic, bibliographic, and referral data.

```
1/5/4
836299  ORDER NO: AAD84-04863
  A HISTORY OF SOME RECENT APPLICATONS OF SURVEY SAMPLING FOR HUMAN
POPULATIONS  213 PAGES.
  BRITTON, GARY L.  (D.A.  1983  UNIVERSITY OF NORTHERN COLORADO).
  PAGE 3452 IN VOLUME 44/11-B OF DISSERTATION ABSTRACTS INTERNATIONAL.
  STATISTICS
  As the use of survey sampling for public opinion polls has increased in
recent years there has been a greater need for public understanding about
the procedures used in such pools.  To help meet this need, this
dissertation is written for those instructors and users of survey sampling
who are not experts in the field.  The development of both theory and
application of selected major aspects of survey sampling are included. Each
of the survey sampling procedures discussed is illustrated by detailed
reference to specific studies which have been conducted using that
procedure and reported elsewhere.
      Evidence justifying the use of systematic sampling is cited.
Theorems, first proved by W. C. Madow and L. H. Madow in 1944, expressing
the variance of the sample mean in terms of various internal correlations
are stated and proved. These theorems determine under which conditions
systematic sampling gives a better estimate than simple random sampling.
      Random digit dialing, which was first used in 1962, has enabled
telephones to be used for both sample selection and data gathering.  This
use is contrasted with telephone directories merely as sampling frames for
systematic sampling. Modifications of random digit dialing which have
appeared in the literature since 1964 are explained. Results of studies
which conclude that the telephone is an effective tool in survey research
are included.
      The inaccuracies of the 1936 Literary Digest presidential election
poll have long been attributed to its use of telephone directories in the
sampling frame.  This charge is analyzed using the results of Literary
Digest pools from 1916 to 1936.  It is shown that the sample was only
partially at fault in this erroneous prediction.  The failure to detect a
shift in voter preference as the election neared was also a major factor in
1936, as it was in 1948 and 1980.  The sampling used in pools for these
elections is examined.
      Randomized response, as proposed by S. Warner in 1965 for sensitive
issue surveys, is explained.  The need for such a method is shown by citing
evidence of respondent dishonesty in political polls. Modified and extended
randomized response models, as proposed since 1965, are discussed.
  DESCRIPTOR CODES: 0463
  INSTITUTION CODE: 0161
```

Fig. 4-6. A unit record containing a citation to a PhD dissertation. DIALOG online service. File 35:Comprehensive Dissertation Index. (Courtesy of University Microfilms International.)

Even today, certain online files, especially source files, may include several different kinds of presentation. Thus, it is difficult to classify a particular file as, for example, being strictly numeric or strictly graphic.

An example of an existing file in which data may be presented to the user in several forms is shown in Fig. 4-24. First the user retrieved common stock prices for two corporations that list their shares on the New York Stock Exchange. The

```
PN US 4445469.
PD MAY 01, 1984.
TI Engine heater.
IV Suhayda-Louis.
IA Montgomery IL 60538.
AP 365375 APR 05, 1982.
OR 123/142-5R0.
XR 123/179-H00.  432/221.
IC F02N 17/02.  EDITION 3.
RU 1380687, JUN 1921.  1460668, JUL 1923.  1862114, JUN 1932.  2078116,
   APR 1937.  2295177, SEP 1942.  2404394, JUL 1946.  2410353, OCT 1946.
   2414214, JAN 1947.  2418097, MAR 1947.  2464165, MAR 1949.  2851027,
   SEP 1958.  2916030, DEC 1959.  3131864, MAY 1964.  3233077, FEB 1966.
   3400700, SEP 1968.  3451663, JUN 1969.  3454266, JUL 1969.  3809527,
   MAY 1974.  3870855, MAR 1975.  4010725, MAR 1977.  4280452, JUL 1981.
AB An engine heater for airplanes or automobiles burning propane gas to
   heat the engine.  The heater employs electrical power to control the
   combustion of the propane gas and to propel the heated combustion
   products toward the engine.  The unit may utilize a building's usual
   line current of 115 volts a.c. it may also rectify this a.c. voltage
   to provide d.c. power capable of charging the battery on the vehicle.
   In the absence of the 115 V. a.c. the heater may simply connect to
   its own battery or the battery of the airplane or the automobile in
   order to warm the vehicle's engine and battery to facilitate the
   commencement of the vehicle's operation.  The heater unit includes
   connections to the appropriate source of power for the heater's
   operation.  When connecting the 115 volts a.c. source, it transforms
   the voltage to the appropriate magnitude to operate the heater.  The
   unit may also include a gas pilot light, an ignition coil for the
   pilot light, and two electrically controlled valves.  The first valve
   permits the passage of propane to the pilot light while the second
   valve allows the passage of the propane to assure the proper
   functioning of the unit.  Without a source of electricity to assure
   the proper functioning of the unit, both valves close and prevent the
   escape of propane.

              END OF DOCUMENT
```

Fig. 4-7. A unit record containing a citation to a patent. BRS online service. File PATS. (Courtesy of Bibliographic Retrieval Services.)

```
                    TYPE 5/4/1
103679  STANDARDS & SPECS.  82414716
  SAFETY STD. FOR STATIONARY AND FIXED ELECTRIC TOOLS
UL (UNDERWRITERS LABORATORIES, INC.)
Spec: 987  Date: 1978  In: ENGLISH
ADOPTED - DOD, APPROVED - ANSI
Classification Codes: 5310 (NUTS AND WASHERS)
NSA CARD NO: 89
Controlled terms: NUTS AND WASHERS
```

Fig. 4-8. A unit record containing a citation to a standard. ESA online service. File 44:National Standards and Specs. (Courtesy of National Standards Association, Inc.)

```
-2-
AN  - 8303-00004164
TI  - BECHTEL FAMILY SELLS CONTROL OF DILLON, READ & COMPANY
SO  - LOS ANGELES TIMES (LA), 83/03/09, SEC IV, PG 1, COL 1
CC  - 26097; 10699; 12037
IT  - INVESTMENT COMPANIES; BANKS & BANKING; CORPORATE ACQUISITIONS & MERGERS
ST  - BECHTEL GROUP INC.; BECHTEL FAMILY
```

Fig. 4-9. A unit record containing a citation to a newspaper article. ORBIT online service. File NDEX (Newspaper Index). (Courtesy of Bell & Howell.)

retrieved "raw" data are organized in a table with a user-assigned title.

Next, the user requested the system to calculate the percentage changes in the prices of these shares, based on the raw data from Table 1. The results of these calculations are presented in tabular form (Table 2) and also in graphic form (Display 1).

Most of the examples of online information retrieval that will be dealt with in this book relate to bibliographic databases and are simpler than the ones shown in Fig. 4-24. Nevertheless, this figure is representative of contemporary numeric databases, with their wealth of data that are accessible online and that allow the subject expert to perform numerical calculations and statistical analyses.

```
1/5/1009
0886974
WILCOX BURNER SERVICE
FUNNY RIVER RD
SOLDOTNA, AK 99669
TELEPHONE: 907-262-5226
COUNTY: KENAI-COOK INLET

SIC:
1711B .(HEATING & VENTILATION CONTRACTORS)
ADVERTISING CLASS: DISPLAY AD
CITY POPULATION: 1 .(1,000-2,499)

THIS IS A(N) FIRM
```

Fig. 4-10. A unit record containing a reference to an organization. DIALOG online service. File 507:Electronic Yellow Pages-Construction. (Courtesy of Market Data Retrieval, Inc.)

The record includes company name, address, and type of work performed. Also included is city population and advertising format.

PUBLICLY AVAILABLE ONLINE SERVICES

Table 4-1 lists some major publicly available online services. Because the availability of different databases and online services is continuously changing, reference data on them may become obsolete in about a year. In analyzing Table 4-1, you should keep in mind that there is a fair degree of duplication of databases amongst different online services and that many nonU.S. online services mainly supply databases produced in the United States. Also, some large databases may be divided by an online service into several files.

Up-to-date information on online services and databases may be monitored through numerous directories and periodic publications, including the following:

Directory of Online Databases
Cuadra Associates, Inc
Santa Monica, CA

Encyclopedia of Information Systems and Services
Gale Research Company
Detroit, MI

Computer Readable Databases. A Directory and Data Sourcebook
American Society for Information Science
Washington, DC

```
3/5/2
1003841
  TAYLOR GARY L
  GEORGE WASHINGTON UNIVERSITY  WASHINGTON DC  BACHELORS
  Major: ELECTRICAL ENGR-TECH; COMMUNICATIONS ENGR-TECH
  UNIV OF MARYLAND  COLLEGE PARK MD
  Major: ELECTRICAL ENGR-TECH; COMMUNICATIONS ENGR-TECH
  Overall Work Experience: 11 OR MORE YEARS EXPERIENCE
  Level of Education: COLLEGE
  Citizenship Status: UNITED STATES   Civil Service Register: NO
  Permanent  Address:  123 RICHARDS BLVD NO,   GIBSONIA PA 15044  412-123-4567
  Security Clearance: YES   Type: TOP SECRET
  A & B TELEPHONE CO. OF WA   FEB 1982 TO MAR 1983
  123 W BASELINE ST  VANCOUVER WA 22222
  Position/Title: DIVISION STAFF MANAGER
  Description of Duties:  MANAGED WA NETWORK OPNS SUPPORT ORG  INCL  BUDGET
SERVICE & MINICOMPUTER CNTRS
  Highest Salary: $69,100
  B T & T CO.   APR 1979 TO NOV 1981
  123 LAKE AVE  WEST HILL NJ 07090
  Position/Title: DIVISION MANAGER
  Description  of Duties:  SELECTED CONSULTANTS FOR PROCUREMENT STUDIES FOR
ANTITRUST DEFENSE
  Highest Salary: $65,800
  AMERICAN TELEPHONE INTL.   JUL 1977 TO MAR 1979
  TEHRAN, IRAN
  Position/Title: DIRECTOR OF OFFICE SERVICES
  Description of Duties: DIRECTED ALL COMPANY SUPPORT FUNCTIONS 1000 EMPLYS
PRIOR TO REVOLUTION
  Highest Salary: $60,000
  Occupational Preference:  TELECOMMUNICATIONS/11 OR MORE YEARS  EXPERIENCE
Function: CONSULTING; GENERAL STAFF-ADMINISTRATION
  Occupational  Preference:   COMMUNICATIONS,   GENERAL/11  OR  MORE  YEARS
EXPERIENCE  Function: CONSULTING; GENERAL STAFF-ADMINISTRATION
  Geographical Preference: SOUTHEAST;  INTERNATIONAL  City/Area Preference:
ST. PETERSBURG FL
  Date Available: OCT 1983
  Willing to Travel: 100%  Willing to Relocate: YES
  Salary Expectation: $80,000
  Special   Skills:   STRONG   INTERPERSONAL  SKILLS,   SEASONED  TELECOMM
ADMINISTRATOR, FOREIGN & DOMESTIC.
  Full Resume Available: YES
  Experience  Summary:  SEASONED  TELECOMMUNICATIONS  ADMINISTRATOR-STRONG
INTERPERSONAL  SKILLS-RECORD OF PRODUCING COST EFFECTIVE RESULTS IN FOREIGN
&  DOMESTIC CULTURES,  MANAGED ALL SUPPORT FUNCTIONS FOR 1000 EMPLOYEES  IN
IRAN.  COORDINATED  AN  ACCELERATED  BUILDUP  &   SUBSEQUENT  REDUCTION  IN
PERSONNEL AT TIME OF  REVOLUTION.  DOMESTICALLY  MANAGED  PLANT  OPNS  AND
FULFILLED  COMPLEX ASSGMTS INVOLVING INTERFACE WITH REPS OF GOVT.,  UNIONS,
INDUSTRY, AND MEDICAL PROFESSIONS.
```

Fig. 4-11. A part of a unit record containing a reference to an individual—a resume, submitted to the special agency. DIALOG online services. File 162:Career Placement Registry/Experienced Personnel. (Courtesy of Career Placement Registry, Inc. The names and addresses in this record have been changed with permission from the Publisher.)

```
2/5/1
0885944        MP
  Tuesday, May 19th, 1981
  PRODUCER: UNION CARBIDE CORP   (UCC)
    270 PARK AVE, NEW YORK, NY 10017
  DISTRIBUTOR: UNION CARBIDE CORP   (UCC)
    270 PARK AVE, NEW YORK, NY 10017
  PROD CREDIT: GLYN GROUP   (GLYNG)
    MILWAUKEE, WI
  YEAR: 77   ;  16MM FILM OPTICAL SOUND;  12 MIN
  LIBRARY OF CONGRESS: 78-700319  ; STOCK CODE: C
  Describes five tragic accidents that may occur if safety regulations
relating to chemical transportation are not observed.
  SUBJECT HEADINGS: Safety - Industrial;  Transportation - General
  SUBJECT CODES: L755400 ;  Y840005
```

Fig. 4-12. A unit record containing a reference to audiovisual material (16 mm sound film). DIALOG online service. File 46:NICEM (presently, AV-Online)—1979 Edition. (Courtesy of U.S. National Information Center for Educational Media. ©Access Innovations, Inc.)

Databook Directory of On-Line Services
Datapro Research Corporation,
Delran, NJ

In addition to the limited number of leading online services, dozens of smaller online services have started to proliferate during the last several years. Many of these services were created by various companies, government organizations, associations, or universities, first as private files for their own internal use, and only later as files available for public use.

The unrestricted proliferation of online services

```
4/5/1
0598771
 DESIGN AND DEVELOP SOFTWARE TO BE INTEGRATED INTO A SYSTEM designed to
perform time and frequency domain acoustic signal processing. Effort also
involves hardware interface, programming, system installation, and system
software maintenance. Offerors must demonstrate understanding of the signal
processing done in both the ASWOC update FTAS and the P-3C. Offerors must
be able to program DEC Vax Minicomputer, A Ramtek 9400-series display
computer, and multiple array processors. Offerors must possess a
confidential clearance in order to receive a copy of the RFP. Requests for
copies of RFP N60921-84-R-0142 must be submitted in writing to P K
Schmidtke, White Oak, Silver Spring, Code S23, 202/394-3780. See note 42.
(131)
 Sponsor: Naval Surface Weapons Center Silver Spring, MD 20910
 Subfile: PSE .(U.S. GOVERNMENT PROCUREMENTS, SERVICES)
 Section Heading: H  Expert and Consultant Services
 Legend: 1
 CBD Date: MAY 14, 1984
```

Fig. 4-13. A unit record containing a reference to the U.S. Government contracts for which the tenders are sought. DIALOG online service. File 195:Commerce Business Daily.

```
SS 1 /C?
USER:
tree heart

PROG:
Cardiovascular System  A7
    Heart  A7.541
        Endocardium  A7.541.207
        Fetal Heart  A7.541.278 (+)
        Heart Atrium  A7.541.358
        Heart Conduction System  A7.541.409 (+)
        Heart Septum  A7.541.459
        Heart Valves  A7.541.510 (+)
        Heart Ventricle  A7.541.560
        Myocardium  A7.541.704
        Pericardium  A7.541.795


SS 1 /C?
USER:
tree cardiovascular system

PROG:
Cardiovascular System  A7
    Blood Vessels  A7.231 (+)
    Heart  A7.541 (+)


SS 1 /C?
USER:
tree A7.541.278

PROG:
Heart  A7.541
    Fetal Heart  A7.541.278
        Ductus Arteriosus  A7.541.278.395
        Truncus Arteriosus  A7.541.278.930
```

Fig. 4-14. Three unit records containing parts of the U.S. National Library of Medicine (NLM) hierarchical thesaurus. MEDLARS online service. File MeSH Vocabulary.

The first record represents a hierarchial tree for the term "Heart". The second and third records represent higher and lower level terminology for the same term. (MeSH—Medical Subject Headings).

and databases may have some undesirable consequences. One of them is the unnecessary duplication of the same material in numerous small databases. Another is the low quality of searching software and insufficient support for the searcher.

However, in the highly competitive field of computerized information retrieval, there is a noticeable trend of concentrating the best databases amongst the online services that can provide a reasonable level of service and support. The databases that cannot compete for the user's attention are likely to be dropped from the leading online

```
Ref  Items   Index-term
E4       1  *CN=GALLIUM ARSENIDE
               (GAAS)
E5       1   CN=GALLIUM ARSENIDE
               PHOSPHIDE (GA2ASP)
E6       1   CN=GALLIUM BORIDE
               (GAB12)
E7       1   CN=GALLIUM BROMIDE
               (GABR3)
                                          -more-


2/5/1
  CAS REGISTRY NUMBER: 13450-88-9
  FORMULA: Br3Ga
  CA INDEX NAME: Gallium bromide (GaBr3) (8CI 9CI)
  SYNONYMS: Gallium bromide; Gallium tribromide

2/5/2
  CAS REGISTRY NUMBER: 12230-30-7
  FORMULA: B12Ga
  CA INDEX NAME: Gallium boride (GaB12) (8CI)
  SYNONYMS: Gallium boride

2/5/3
  CAS REGISTRY NUMBER: 12044-20-1
  FORMULA: AsGa2P
  CA INDEX NAME: Gallium arsenide phosphide (Ga2AsP) (9CI)
  SYNONYMS: Gallium arsenide phosphide

2/5/4
  CAS REGISTRY NUMBER: 1303-00-0
  FORMULA: AsGa
  CA INDEX NAME: Gallium arsenide (GaAs) (8CI 9CI)
```

Fig. 4-15. Four unit records from the classification scheme (inventory) of chemical substances. DIALOG online service. File 52:TSCA Inventory (TSCA—Toxic Substances Control Act).

The online classification schemes are primarily organized as auxiliary files to the bibliographic ones (here to the CAS-Chemical Abstracts service files). The records may be listed as a dictionary, that is, in alphabetical order by displaying only the necessary index terms. In full printed form, the same records would appear in some other order (here by decreasing CAS registry number).

services. Unless heavily subsidized by the government, they are on the way to oblivion. It is likely that an even more intense concentration of databases will take place in the future.

Thus, amongst 179 bibliographic databases which J.L. Holl and M.J. Brown list in their latest directory, the four largest online services, DIALOG, ORBIT, BRS, and ESA, give access to 81 percent of those databases (J.L. Holl and M.J. Brown *Online Bibliographic Databases: A Directory and Sourcebook, Third Edition,* ASLIB, London, 1983, p.28). A similar trend toward concentration is also characteristic of nonbibliographic databases.

For a book like this one, it does not make any

2/6/5
0194439
SAU3600003381056 STATE AND AREA EMPLOYMENT, HOURS, AND EARNINGS SUBFILE
AVERAGE HOURLY EARNINGS OF PRODUCTION WORKERS
ENGINEERING AND SCIENTIFIC INSTRUMENTS
DIV. OF INDUSTRY: MANUFACTURING, DURABLE GOODS
NEW YORK NY
UNADJUSTED DATA

CURRENT DOLLARS

YEARS	Q1	Q2	Q3	Q4
1984	11.21	NA	NA	NA
1983	10.21	10.42	10.92	11.06
1982	9.58	9.62	10.14	10.62
1981	8.74	9.05	9.34	9.50
1980	7.92	8.04	8.35	8.67

SOURCE: U.S. BUREAU OF LABOR STATISTICS DIALOG FILE 178
DATES AVAILABLE:(JAN. 1978-FEB. 1984)

Fig. 4-16. A unit record containing numeric data. DIALOG online service. File 178:BLS Employment, Hours, and Earnings.

4/5/1
100548
TABLE 5. PRODUCTION AND EXPORTS OF WHEAT FLOUR: JANUARY 1985 (CIR M-20A)
March 6, 1985
Section: 15 (Manufacturing Data)
(Quantity in 1,000 cwt.; value in $1,000)

Month	Wheat flour production		Exports of domestic merchandise(1)			Percent exports manufacturers' production	
	Quantity	Value	Quantity	Value at port	Estimated producers' value(2)	Quantity	Value
1984							
December...	23,656	(NA)	413	4,056	3,572	1.7	(NA)
November...	25,080	(NA)	776	2,951	2,599	3.1	(NA)
October....	26,289	(NA)	1,428	14,998	13,207	5.4	(NA)
September..	24,338	(NA)	732	7,506	6,610	3.0	(NA)
August.....	26,025	(NA)	565	6,643	5,850	2.2	(NA)
July.......	22,847	(NA)	1,813	21,458	18,896	7.9	(NA)
June.......	24,306	(NA)	2,992	41,974	36,962	12.3	(NA)
May........	26,630	(NA)	3,573	37,795	33,282	13.4	(NA)
April......	24,076	(NA)	3,204	32,545	28,659	13.3	(NA)
March......	25,931	(NA)	3,260	34,503	30,383	12.6	(NA)

Fig. 4-17. A unit record containing textual information and numeric data. DIALOG online service. File 580:Cendata. (*Continued* on page 42.)

```
February...   25,482   (NA)     1,464   12,354     10,879      5.7   (NA)
January....   24,766   (NA)     1,532   13,877     12,220      6.2   (NA)

   Note:  Comparison of SIC code (domestic output) and Schedule B export
numbers is as follows:

                    Domestic output          Export
                   20411--wheat flour    131.4010, 131.4030

   (NA) Not available.
   (1) Source:  Bureau of the Census report EM 546, U.S. Exports.
   (2) These values were derived by use of adjustment factors to exclude
freight, insurance, and other charges incurred in moving goods to the port
of export.  This adjustment is made to convert the values to an
approximation of the producers' value of exported goods.  Current
adjustment factors (0.8806 for industry group 204) are based on data for
1981 which are published in M81(AS)-5, Origin of Exports of Manufactured
Products, appendix B.

SOURCE:  Current Industrial Reports Series M20A(84)-1, Flour Milling
Products, for January 1985.  See summary for contact person and
subscription information.
```

Fig. 4-17. A unit record containing textual information and numeric data. DIALOG online service. File 580:Cendata. (Continued from page 41.)

sense to give more detailed information on various online services that you may need to access. After all, this information will become obsolete even before the book is published. More extended information can usually be obtained through numerous printed and electronic sources that the subject expert can consult.

Most of the major online services issue their own publications, such as manuals, file descriptions, and periodic newsletters, that describe their services. They also maintain a hot line (action desk, customer services) that provides assistance if a user

```
TDBN- 4376
NM  - GALLIUM ARSENIDE
RN  - 1303-00-0
MF  - AS-GA
ST  - 821101COMPLETE WITH PEER REVIEW COMMENTS INCORPORATED RLGTH:4964
MW  - 144.64
SY  - GALLIUM ARSENIDE [GAAS]
SY  - GALLIUM MONOARSENIDE
SY  - GALLIUM MONOARSENIDE (GAAS)
USE - [MERCK INDEX 9TH ED 561] IN SEMICONDUCTOR APPLICATIONS
      (TRANSISTORS, SOLAR CELLS, LASERS)
USE - [HAWLEY. CONDENSED CHEM DICTNRY 9TH ED 405] SEMICONDUCTOR IN
      LIGHT-EMITTING DIODES FOR TELEPHONE DIALS; MAGNETORESISTANCE
      DEVICES; THERMISTORS
USE - [HAWLEY. CONDENSED CHEM DICTNRY 9TH ED 405] MICROWAVE GENERATION
```

Fig. 4-18. A unit record from a dictionary describing properties of a certain substance. MEDLARS online service. File TDB (Toxicology Data Bank).

```
ARTICLE 1  -  1,075 MORE TO BE SCANNED  -  PAGE  1 OF  3
::::::::::::::::::::::::::::::::::::::::::::::::::::::::::::::::::::::::::::
850460135    FRI    FEB.15,1985      PAGE: B15
BYLINE: KAREN HOWLETT
CLASS:*ROB*Technology
DATELINE:                                                      WORDS: 512
::::::::::::::::::::::::::::::::::::::::::::::::::::::::::::::::::::::::::::
               ***Northern*Telecom*unveils new PBX line **
                            By  KAREN HOWLETT
In its pitched battle to hang on to the lead in the competitive $3.6-
billion U.S. market for private branch exchanges,*Northern*Telecom*Ltd.
has launched its newest generation of equipment.
   Known as Meridian, the new system links business telephones and
personal computers.
   The Mississauga, Ont., telecommunications giant is pitting its strength
against that of American Telephone and Telegraph Co. of New York. (Another
competitor, Mitel Corp. of Kanata, Ont., has already bowed to the
competition. As a percentage of total product sales, its U.S. exports have
fallen to 48 per cent of fiscal 1984 sales of $343-million, from 52 per
cent in 1983.)
   The rivalry is so intense that*Northern*Telecom*flew several of its
vice-presidents to Laguna Beach, Calif., where its new products were

ARTICLE 1  -  1,075 MORE TO BE SCANNED  -  PAGE  2 OF  3
unveiled and demonstrated for about 600 data processing managers from the
Fortune 500 companies. The announcement was made simultaneously to a small
gathering in Toronto, but the products were not demonstrated there. A
spokesman said the company could not get equipment hooked up in time for
the hurriedly called press conference.
   Private branch exchanges, which transmit data and voices over ordinary
telephone wires through a central switch, are considered a crucial tool in
linking automated office equipment.
  *Northern*Telecom*expects its future growth to come from the office
automation products area. Traditionally, almost 40 per cent of its sales
have come from large digital telephone switches - the company's most
important product - which are sold to telephone companies. But sales for
large switches are expected to be flat over the next few years.
   "Northern made a name for itself in medi
said Francis McInerney, executi
Information Inc.
slowly mo
```

Fig. 4-19. A part of a unit record containing the complete text of a newspaper article (*Globe and Mail*, Toronto, February 15, 1985, p. B15). INFO GLOBE online service. File Globe and Mail Online. (Courtesy of *The Globe and Mail*. ©The Globe and Mail.)

```
            RANK        1 OF       39,      PAGE       1 OF      4

                         *Professional*Engineers*Act

                              R.S.O. 1980, c. 394

      s. 27

                                   OFFENCES

      Offences, persons
        27.(1) Every person, other than a member or a licensee, who,
        (a) takes and uses orally or otherwise the title*"Professional*
        Engineer" or "Registered*Professional*Engineer" or uses any
        addition to or abbreviation of either such titles, or any
        word, name or designation that will lead to the belief that he
        is a*professional*engineer, a member or a licensee or, except
        as permitted by section 2, uses the title or designation
        "engineer" in such a manner as will lead to the belief that
        he is a*professional*engineer, a member or a licensee;
        (b) advertises, holds himself out, or conducts himself in any
        way or by any means as a member or a licensee; or
        (c) engages in the practice of*professional*engineering,

            RANK        1 OF       39,      PAGE       2 OF      4
      is guilty of an offence.

      Idem
        (2) Every person who,
        (a) wilfully procures or attempts to procure registration
```

Fig. 4-20. Part of a unit record containing the complete revised text of the Statues of Ontario (1980 and all amendments as of July 1, 1984). QL online service. File SO (Statutes of Ontario). (Courtesy of QL Systems Ltd.)

```
                          LEVEL 1 - 8 OF 13 CASES

            ERNEST DRUCKER, Petitioner v. COMMISSIONER OF INTERNAL
                              REVENUE, Respondent
                              Docket No. 11463-79.
                                 79 T.C. 605
                              September 30, 1982.

   SYLLABUS:
      Petitioner was employed as a concert musician with the Metropolitan Opera.
  The Opera did not provide its concert  musicians  with an area to use for
  individual  practice  but expected them to practice on an individual basis off
  the premises.  Held: Under sec. 280A, I.R.C. 1954, a room in petitioner's
  residence where he spent a part of his workday practicing is not his principal
  place of business, and he is not entitled to a deduction for the cost of
  maintaining the room.

   COUNSEL:
      Richard B. Sherman and Arthur Pelikow, for the petitioner.

                                  79 T.C. 605
```

Fig. 4-21. Part of a unit record containing the full text of a U.S. court decision. MEAD DATA CENTRAL online services. File Lexis. (Courtesy of Mead Data Central. Lexis© is a service of Mead Data Central). (Continued on page 45.)

```
    Julius Jove, for the respondent.

  OPINIONBY:
    WHITAKER
  OPINION:
    WHITAKER, Judge: Respondent determined a deficiency of $321 in petitioner's
 Federal income tax for 1976 and $265 for 1977.  After concessions by the
 parties, the sole issue remaining for our decision is whether petitioner is
 entitled to a home office deduction under section 280A, I.R.C. 1954.

    FINDINGS OF FACT
    Some of the facts have been stipulated and are so found.  The stipulation of
 facts and exhibits attached thereto are incorporated herein by this reference.
    Ernest Drucker (petitioner) resided in New York, New York, at the time he
 filed his petition herein.  His Federal income tax returns for 1976 and 1977
 were filed with the Brookhaven Service Center at Holtsville, New York.
    During taxable years 1976 and 1977, petitioner was a concert violinist
 employed by the Metropolitan Opera Association, Inc., (hereinafter the Met) at
                                  79 T.C. 605
 Lincoln Center, New York, New York.  As of 1976, petitioner had been a concert
 violinist for 47 years and had been with the Met for 30 of those 47 years.
    Petitioner, as a member of the Metropolitan Opera Orchestra n1 was covered by
 the terms of union contracts between Local 802, American Federation of Musicians
 (of which petitioner was a member) and the Met.  During 1976 and 1977,
```

Fig. 4-21. Part of a unit record containing the full text of a U.S. court decision. MEAD DATA CENTRAL online services. File Lexis. (Courtesy of Mead Data Central. Lexis© is a service of Mead Data Central.) (Continued from page 44.)

```
RN   26442-66-0                                                 ANS 1
IN   Pregn-4-en-21-al, 15.alpha.-hydroxy-20-oxo-, 21-(dimethyl acetal),
     p-toluenesulfonate (8CI)
SY   Pregn-4-en-20-one, 15.alpha.-hydroxy-21,21-dimethoxy-,
     p-toluenesulfonate (8CI)
MF   C30 H42 O6 S
ST   4:15A.PREGN
```

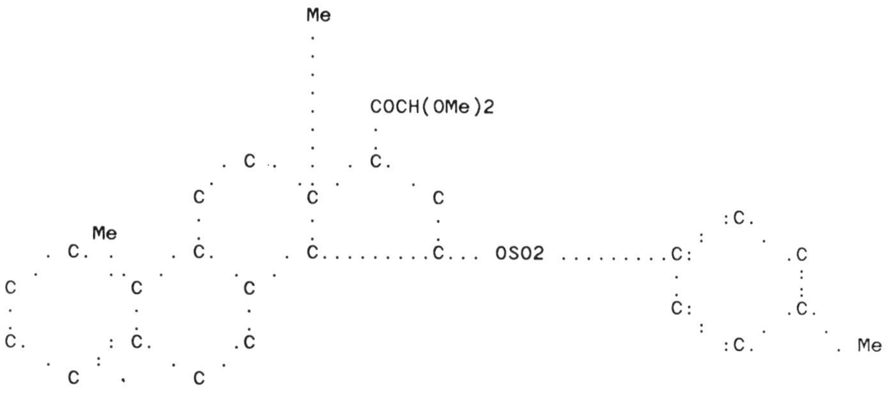


```
1 REFERENCES IN FILE CA (1967 TO DATE)
```

Fig. 4-22. A unit record containing a chemical structure in graphic format and the number of bibliographic citations that can be retrieved for this particular substance. CHEMICAL ABSTRACTS SERVICE online service. File REG. (Courtesy of Chemical Abstracts Service. ©American Chemical Society.)

The file covers more than 5.6 million substances. MF is a molecular formula and IN is an CAS index name of the substance.

```
PLEASE TYPE YOUR FIRST NAME AFTER 'USER:' IS PRINTED BELOW,
THEN PRESS THE 'CARRIAGE RETURN' OR 'SEND MESSAGE' KEY.  IF YOU
DO NOT WISH TO ENTER YOUR NAME, SIMPLY PRESS THE 'CARRIAGE
RETURN' OR 'SEND MESSAGE' KEY.

USER:
ann

PROG:
HELLO ANN!

IT IS IMPORTANT FOR YOU TO KNOW THAT THERE IS NO TIME LIMIT FOR
RESPONDING TO A *MEDLEARN* USER: CUE.  WE RECOMMEND THAT YOU
WORK THROUGH *MEDLEARN* WITH A MINIMUM OF INTERRUPTIONS AND AT
YOUR OWN PACE.

CHAPTER 1 OF *MEDLEARN* DISCUSSES THE USE OF A COMPUTER
TERMINAL.  HAVE YOU EVER USED A COMPUTER TERMINAL BEFORE?
(YES/NO)

USER:
no

PROG:
CODE=0100       USING THE COMPUTER TERMINAL

CODE=0110 MESSAGE TRANSMISSION AND ERROR CORRECTION

IN ORDER TO COMMUNICATE WITH MEDLINE FROM YOUR REMOTE COMPUTER
TERMINAL, THERE ARE TWO CONVENTIONS TO BE LEARNED.

     1.  HOW TO SEND MESSAGES TO THE COMPUTER.
     2.  HOW TO CORRECT TYPING ERRORS IN YOUR MESSAGES.

CODE=0111     TRANSMITTING MESSAGES TO THE COMPUTER
```

Fig. 4-23. A part of a session with an online search training file. MEDLARS online service. File Medlearn.

TABLE 1. CLOSING PRICES FOR IBM AND XEROX
AS REPORTED ON THE NEW YORK STOCK EXCHANGE

	6JUL84	13JUL84	20JUL84	27JUL84	3AUG84	10AUG84
IBM	105.75	105.25	106.50	109.00	120.00	121.13
XEROX	38.75	36.75	34.13	35.50	37.13	38.88

TABLE 2. WEEK-TO-WEEK PERCENTAGE CHANGES
IN THE CLOSING PRICES FOR IBM AND XEROX
AS REPORTED ON THE NEW YORK STOCK EXCHANGE
(CALCULATED)

	6JUL84	13JUL84	20JUL84	27JUL84	3AUG84	10AUG84
IBM		-0.47	1.19	2.35	10.09	0.94
XEROX		-5.16	-7.14	4.03	4.58	4.71

DISPLAY 1

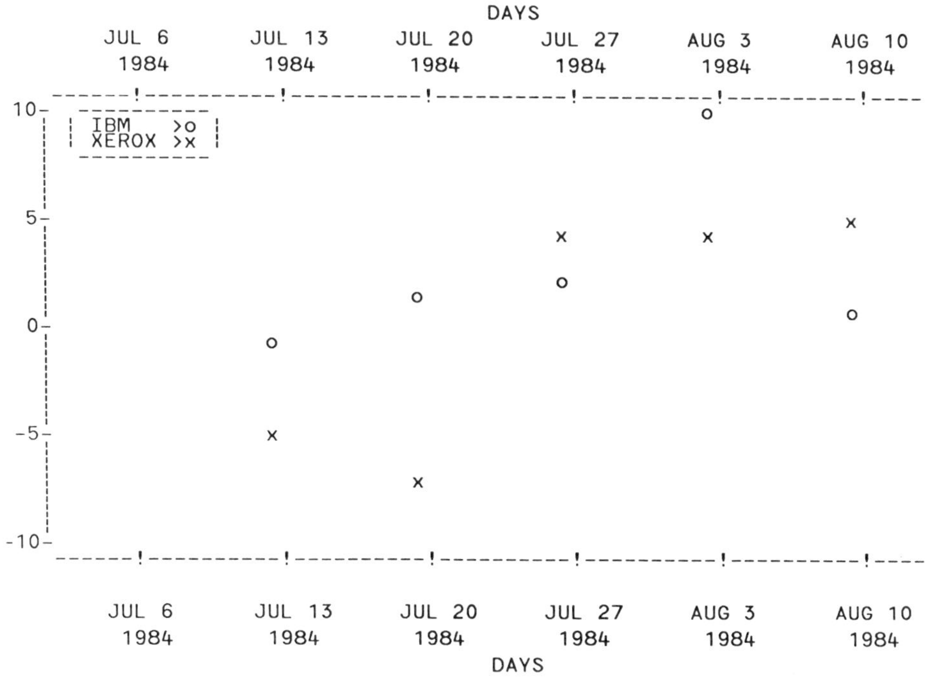

Fig. 4-24. Example of a database with various forms for presenting data. I.P. SHARP ASSOCIATES online service. File NASTOCK (North American Stock Market). (Courtesy of I.P. Sharp Associates Limited.)

Table 4-1. Major Publicly Available Online Services.

Online service	Service vendor	Location	No. of databases (approximate) (1984)	Online service	Service vendor	Location	No. of databases (approximate) (1984)
ACI	ACI Computer Services	Victoria, Australia	17	GENERAL ELECTRIC	General Electric Information Services Company	Rockville, MD	51
BRS	Bibliographic Retrieval Services	Latham, NY	81	INFO GLOBE	Info Globe	Toronto, Canada	6
CAN/OLE	Canadian Institute for Scientific and Technical Information	Ottawa, Canada	26	INKA	INKA Karlsruhe	Karlsruhe, W. Germany	48
CHASE ECONOMETRICS	Chase Econometrics/ Interactive Data	Bala Cynwyd, PA	131	INTERACTIVE MARKET	Interactive Market Systems, Inc.	New York, NY	44
COMPUSERVE	CompuServe, Inc	Columbus, OH	76	I.P.SHARP	I.P.Sharp Associates	Toronto, Canada	111
DATA RESOURCES	Data Resources, Inc	Washington, DC	93	MEAD	Mead Data Central	Dayton, OH	23
DATA-STAR	Information Industries, Ltd.	Bracknell, U.K.	42	MEDLARS	National Library of Medicine	Bethesda, MD	21
DIALOG	Dialog Information Services, Inc.	Palo Alto, CA	201	NEWSNET	NewsNet, Inc	Bryn Mawr, PA	158
DIMDI	Dimdi	Cologne, W. Germany	41	ORBIT	SDC Information Services	Santa Monica, CA	61
DOE	U.S. Department of Energy	Washington, DC	32	PERGAMON-INFOLINE	Pergamon InfoLine	London, U.K.	31
DOW JONES	Dow Jones & Company, Inc.	Princeton, NJ	23	QL	QL Systems Ltd	Ottawa, Canada	59
ESA/IRS	ESRIN	Frascati, Italy	59	QUESTEL	Telesystemes-Questel	Paris, France	62
				THE SOURCE	Source Telecomputing Company	McLean, VA	27

```
ENTER DATA BASE NAME:     news

*SIGN-ON   20.18.26                        08/06/84:
########################################

SYSTEM NEWS                                2          3-31-83
DATABASES ONLINE                           3          WEEKLY
DATABASES OFFLINE                          4          3-25-83
X FILES                                    5          WEEKLY
DATABASE CHARGES                           6          6-12-84
UPCOMING PRICE CHANGES                     7          7-13-84
TRAINING SCHEDULE                          8          7-30-84
DATABASE NAMES AND SEARCH LABELS           9          5-8-84
BRS COURSE DESCRIPTIONS                    10         6-8-84
PSYCHINFO TRAINING WORKSHOPS               11         7-17-84
ABSTRAX 400 AVAILABLE!                     12         5-8-84
AUTOMATIC SDI                              13         6-4-84
ABI-INFORM TRAINING CLASSES                15         7-20-84
CFTX ONLINE SURVEY                         18         11-23-83
WHAT'S IN PRINT AT BRS                     20         7-24-84
BRS OFFLINE CHARGES                        30         4-5-83
PREM AND PREP CHANGES                      33         1-30-84
*
PLEASE ENTER THE DOCUMENT NUMBER.  DO NOT ENTER DOC=N
ENTER DOCUMENT NUMBER RANGE :     3

DATABASES ONLINE

#

THE FOLLOWING FILES ARE AVAILABLE FOR ONLINE SEARCHING, LISTED BY
LABEL, INCLUDING DATES OF COVERAGE AND FULL FILE NAME.

#

DATABASE LABEL & COVERAGE   FULL NAME OF DATABASE

#

AAED(THRU JUN 1984)         ACADEMIC AMERICAN ENCYCLOPEDIA
A400(JUN)                   ABSTRAX 400
ABLE(JUL 1984)              ABLEDATA
BBIP(1979-JUL 1984)         BOOKS IN PRINT
BEBA(1978-JUL 1984)         BILINGUAL EDUCATION BIBLIO. ABSTRACTS
BIOB(1970-1977)             BIOSIS BACKFILE
BIOL(1978-AUG 1984)         BIOSIS
BOOK(THRU JUN 1984)         BOOKSINFO
CAIN(1970-MAY 1984)         AGRICOLA
CCML(THRU JUN 30,1984)      CRITICAL CARE MEDICAL LIBRARY
CFTX(1980-JUL 1984)         AMERICAN CHEM. SOC. PRIMARY JOURNALS
CHEB(1970-1976)             CA CONDENSATES (CA SEARCH BACKFILE)
```

Fig. 4-25. Example of useful online information. BRS online service. (Courtesy of Bibliographic Retrieval Services.) (Continued on page 50.)

Command *news* retrieves a menu that lists current online news. In this example, the searcher selected menu item *3*, which lists files that are accessible online.

```
CHEM(1977-JUL 1984)             CA SEARCH
COMP(1976-JUL 1984)             COMPENDEX
CRFW(1963-APR 1984)             CATALYST RESOURCES FOR WOMEN
CROS(POSTINGS-ONLINE FILES)     CROSS
CULP(THRU JULY 1982)            CALIF. UNION LIST OF PERIODICALS
DISC(1928-AUG 1984)             DATA PROCESS. & INFO. SCIENCE CONTENTS
DISS(1861-JUN 1984)             DISSERTATION ABSTRACTS
DRSC                            DRUGINFO
DRUG(1968-MAR 1984)             DRUGINFO-ALCOHOL USE & ABUSE (CONCAT.)
ECER(1966-MAR 1984)             EXCEPTIONAL CHILD EDUCATION RESOURCES
EMED(JAN 1980-JUN 1984)         EXCERPTA MEDICA
ERIC(1966-JUL 1984)             EDUCATIONAL RESOURCES INFO. CENTER
ETSF(APR 1984)                  EDUCATIONAL TESTING SERVICE FILE
FILE(JUL 84)                    FILE
FNTL(MAY 1982-DEC 1982)         FINTEL
FSIS(1978-APR 1984)             FROST & SULLIVAN MARKET RESEARCH
GPOM(NOV 1976-JUN 1984)         GPO MONTHLY CATALOG
HARF(1979-JUL 1984)             HARFAX INDUSTRY DATA SOURCES
HAVC(JAN 1983)                  HEALTH AUDIOVISUAL ONLINE CATALOG
HBRO(1976-APR 1984--            HARVARD BUSINESS REVIEW ONLINE. FULL TEXT.
                                                     1971+ BIBLIOGRAPHIC
HLTH(1975-AUG 1984)             HEALTH PLANNING AND ADMINISTRATION
INFO(1971-JUL 1984)             ABI-INFORM
INSB(1970-1976)                 INSPEC BACKFILE
INSP(1977-AUG 1984)             INSPEC
IPAB(1970-JUL 1984)             INT'L PHARMACEUTICAL ABSTRACTS
```

Fig. 4-25. Example of useful online information. BRS online service. (Courtesy of Bibliographic Retrieval Services.) (Continued from page 49.)

encounters difficulties during a search.

Certain instructions and updated information, such as an up-to-date list of available files, can usually be requested by a searcher during an interactive online session. An example of useful online information is shown in Fig. 4-25.

CONCLUSIONS

In this chapter a classification scheme for online files was introduced. The three general categories of online files are reference files, source files, and instruction and translation files. The chapter includes examples of online records for many types of online files. The knowledge of what types of information are available online is important for the subject expert in planning a search.

Chapter 5

Computers, Terminals, and Telecommunications

Our task in this book is to give only the information necessary for a subject expert to organize a search. Fortunately, successful search activity does not require any deep knowledge of data processing.

Let us briefly examine the different elements of a *computer communications network* as represented in Fig. 5-1.

TERMINALS

There are many types of *terminals* on the market today. Printing terminals type characters on paper. Video display terminals are less convenient for searching than printing terminals, unless they are connected to a printing device that keeps track of a search on paper.

Terminals may differ in:

- Speed of communication (usually 100, 300, or 1200 baud).
- Availability of memory. Intelligent terminals have some memory and may perform processing operations that make searching easier.
- Reliability. At present, some terminals may require a lot of maintenance.
- Portability.
- Simplicity of operation.
- Speed and quality of print.
- Ergonomic qualities and visual appearance.
- Cost.

The selection of a terminal is a very important step in the organization of your searching activity. Certain types of terminals may be better suited for specific tasks or correspond to the operator's preferences. The most effective way to organize searching activity is to use intelligent terminals, which actually are computers themselves. Organization of searching with the help of the IBM PC microcomputer is described in more detail in the following chapter.

TELECOMMUNICATION PROCEDURES

A terminal normally requires certain ad-

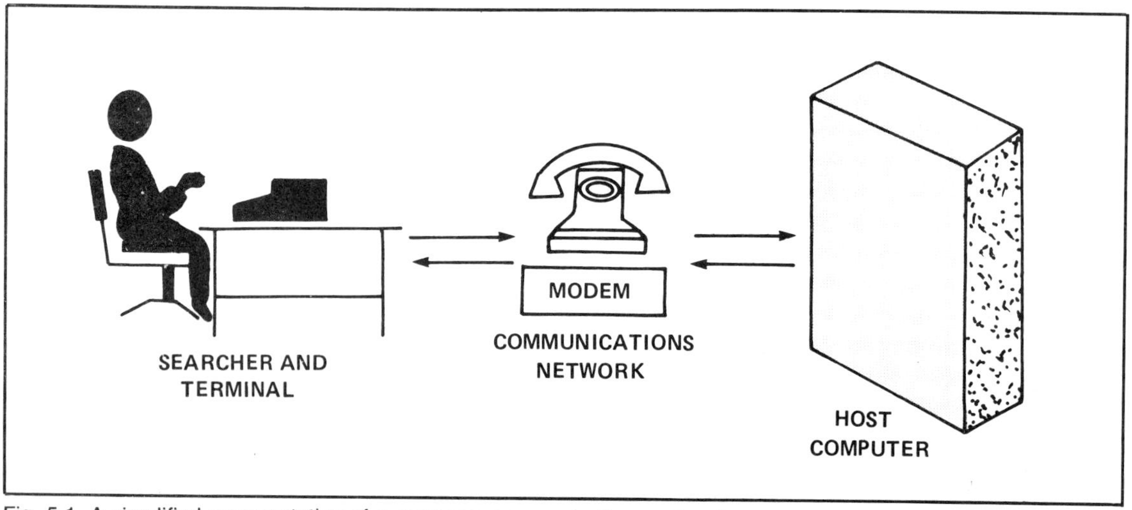

Fig. 5-1. A simplified representation of a computer communications network.

justments before an interactive session with a particular online service can start. The nature of these adjustments depends on the type of terminal and on the online service connection requirements.

There may be special switches to make such adjustments or special procedures to set up the terminal for proper operating conditions. Lack of proper terminal settings is a frequent cause of unsuccessful connection.

There are at least three communication characteristics that require connection adjustments in the terminal. They are:

- Communication speed (*100, 300,* or *1200* baud). Communication speed is chosen based on the terminal capabilities and online service connection requirements. There are often different telephone numbers for high speed (1200 baud) and low speed (100 and 300 baud) connections.
- Duplex (full duplex/half duplex.) *Full duplex* means that data are going into the communication network simultaneously from both directions. In the *half duplex* communication only one direction may be used at a time. A choice of duplex depends mainly on the online service requirements and is normally specified in the online service connection procedure.
- Parity (*odd/even/off*).A computer uses *parity* in order to automatically check whether a data message has been damaged during the communication process. The choice of parity depends on the online service requirements and is normally specified in the online service connection procedure.

MODEMS

Modem is an abbreviation for the words *Mo*dulator-*Dem*odulator. Modems are sometimes called *couplers.*

Modems convert machine-readable digital messages into special signals that can be transmitted over telephone lines. A modem is connected to a terminal and to a telephone.

Without such a conversion device, computer-to-terminal communication would require special connection lines that are expensive. A modem provides the possibility of using the existing telephone lines and makes possible a connection with a computer from any point where there is a telephone.

There are two types of modems—acoustic and direct-connect.

An *acoustic modem* is portable, inexpensive, and

very flexible since it can be used with any standard telephone. However, connections with acoustic modems are less reliable and are not recommended for use with communication speeds over 300 baud.

A *direct-connect* modem provides more reliable connections but is more expensive than an acoustic modem and not as flexible in terms of connections.

> A modem may also require a simple adjustment procedure before connection. Among other settings, establishment of proper speed and duplex may be necessary.

An example of setting up a terminal and a modem prior to connection is shown in Fig. 5-2.

COMMUNICATION NETWORKS

The *communications network* is one of the major factors assuring a high degree of accessibility of online information. These networks have special local telephone numbers in every large and medium size North American city, as well as in many large cities around the world.

The networks are specially designed to handle data transmitted to and from computers effectively. They markedly increase the capability and the efficiency of communication channels such as telephone lines and satellite systems. The low usage cost of communication networks makes the use of computers that are located far from the searcher an inexpensive activity. This cost is a fraction of normal long-distance rates and in many cases does not depend on distance.

The three major networks used in the United States are TELENET, TYMNET, and UNINET. These three networks may differ slightly in choice of online services, connection price, and reliability.

DATAPAC is the internal Canadian communications network. A Canadian user can be connected to U.S. online services through DATAPAC, which in turn accesses these online services through the U.S. networks. A U.S. user trying to access a Canadian online service uses the opposite procedure.

TELEGLOBE is a Canadian network which is linked to DATAPAC and serves users outside North America.

EURONET-DIANE is a new general-purpose European network which serves the members of the European community.

COMPUTERS

The most important part of the computer com-

```
ACCESSING INFO GLOBE THROUGH TYMNET

1.   Set the switches on your terminal and modem as follows:

     MODEM        Power          ON
                  Speed          300 or 1200
                  Duplex         Full

     TERMINAL     Power          ON
                  Speed          300 or 1200
                  Duplex         Full
                  Parity         Odd, Null or Mark
                  Online/Local   ONLINE
```

Fig. 5-2. Requirements for setting various switches on a terminal and a modem prior to the connection procedure. INFO GLOBE online service. (From *Info Globe User's Manual*, Toronto, January 1983. Courtesy of the Globe and Mail. ©Info Globe.)

munications network is the computer itself. Computers make possible the maintenance and updating of online services. They also perform all the logical operations necessary to match the user's requests with the content of the online service and keep track of the searches performed.

The computer that maintains an online service is often referred to as a *host* computer. This term distinguishes it from the microcomputers employed by many users as intelligent terminals at the other ends of the communications network.

To maintain online services, large and powerful time-sharing computers are usually used in real-time operations. *Time-sharing* refers to the capability of a very large number of users to carry on simultaneous interaction with an online service. The term *real-time* (also *online, interactive, conversational,* or *direct communication*) implies that the computer responds relatively quickly during online searching (within a matter of three to five seconds). A significant advantage of online searching is the ability of a searcher to participate in a two-way conversation with the computer, to alter a search strategy, or to discontinue the search if he is not satisfied with its preliminary results.

The sensitivity of an online service to variations in the number of simultaneously connected searchers, its speed, and the reliability of the connection are very important characteristics from the searcher's point of view. These characteristics, which often determine the success or the failure of a particular online service, are dependent on the quality of its software and hardware.

If an online vendor does not pay constant attention to upgrading his software and hardware, there is a strong tendency on the part of the users to switch to another online service with more up-to-date facilities, provided that the new service has comparable data online.

Even software that was initially well-designed requires constant upgrading in order to keep the online service in satisfactory shape. The changes are necessary due to the constant improvements in various query languages, which are very important in the highly competitive environment of online information retrieval systems.

The alternative to real-time data processing is *batch processing*, in which the programs to be executed are collected into groups to permit convenient, efficient, and inexpensive data processing.

For the information retrieval systems that are presented in this book, batch processing is often referred to as *offline searching.* The search is processed by a computer after the user has logged off, normally during night hours when the computer is less busy. The results are printed at the host computer site and are mailed to the user shortly thereafter.

> If a large amount of searching is being performed, offline searching may be less expensive. A serious disadvantage of offline searching is the searcher's inability to correct the search strategy during the retrieval session.

CONCLUSIONS

This chapter includes a description of the principal elements of the computer communications network. Briefly discussed here are the basic characteristics of the computers, modems, terminals, and various communication networks that are essential to the subject expert in the organization of his searching activity.

Chapter 6

The IBM PC and Information Gathering

Like many other recent publications, this book has been produced with the help of a microcomputer. In my case the microcomputer used was an IBM PC. In addition to word processing, my IBM PC was also used for many other purposes. One of the most important activities in the writing of this book was the retrieval of necessary data from various online sources, both for gathering new knowledge on the subject and for illustrating the book with relevant examples.

HOW THE IBM PC FOUND ITS WAY TO THESE PAGES

Actually, there is something almost magical in the fact that the IBM PC is more and more often used for various applications and in various capacities. This computer is not exceptionally powerful in comparison with some other microcomputers on the market. One may certainly find a system that is better suited to a particular application.

The answer to the remarkable success of the IBM PC lies primarily in various external factors. Thanks to the company's established reputation in the computer field and to its aggressive marketing strategy, the IBM PC has become de facto an *industry standard.*

> This industry standard allows various software packages to be compatible to some extent and permits the user to combine diversified applications together. As a result, hundreds of applications were developed for the IBM PC by various software houses. In addition, many older software packages written for minicomputers and even for mainframes are currently being transferred to this microcomputer.

For years and years, the first advice of computer pundits to naive laymen was not to concentrate on the hardware when buying a computer.

Instead, the buyer was supposed to make sure that software available for a computer considered for purchase could support all the intended applications.

Unfortunately, far too often this good advice has been disregarded. The inexperienced user was forced into a purchase by pushy salesmen, unclear advertising, or his lack of understanding of his own needs. Frequently, the honeymoon with a new software package was over after just a few attempts to use it. As a result, the owner was stuck with a useless machine, good only for playing trivial and boring games on the color screen.

In a sense, the existence of an industry standard makes life much easier for the inexperienced user—by far the majority of the computerized population. It allows him not to worry too much about the hardware and instead to concentrate on various applications available on the market. If at a later stage it is necessary to expand the system's capabilities in order to accommodate new applications, it is much easier to do so with the standard basic system.

Most of the successful application packages, almost by definition, can be run on the "standard" microcomputer. The availability of the many hundreds of software packages assures that the user may select the most efficient or the most friendly ones (which frequently are the same). Also, in case there is no application software that suits the user's particular needs, there is a good chance that one will be available in the not-too-distant future.

A computer that is the industry standard attracts a large number of users. Such a large user-community is the best assurance that many more programs will emerge on the market, including the ones that satisfy fairly exotic needs and perform esoteric functions. Large numbers of programs also guarantee fierce competition, and in the long run, low prices and high quality of surviving software packages.

Of course, long-term assumptions are very difficult to make in the volatile area of microcomputer technology. Changes in today's technology will inevitably make obsolete even the best industry standard in the future. However, the users of the IBM PC cherish the hope that whatever the future developments are, they will have to be compatible with the existing IBM PC hardware and software.

The online searcher is not, by all means, limited to the use of the IBM PC. Our own Subject Expert Searching Technique described later in this book is not linked to any particular computer and can be implemented with quite simple technological means. However, an IBM PC-based computerized system is quite powerful and versatile and may be convenient to use for online searching. Such a system would allow the user to organize his searching activity in the most efficient way. In addition to the information retrieval process, the subject expert can use his IBM PC microcomputer for many other applications that are essential in his professional activity.

Our own experience in the application of various hardware and software is, of course, not binding on any other user. We hope, however, that it may be quite beneficial to the readers of this book.

THE MULTITUDE OF APPLICATION PROGRAMS FOR THE IBM PC

The multitude of application programs designed for the IBM PC is one of the main assets for a professional who uses this microcomputer. Online information gathering is only one of many functions a user has to perform in his everyday activity.

This book is primarily devoted to the organization of information gathering for various kinds of professional or scientific activity. Consuming information is very important for any professional or scientist. However, you should not forget that it is the *production of information* that is really the main function of any subject expert.

Professionals and scientists are normally judged on the information contents of their output. Therefore, their interest in the outside information is primarily determined by its relevance to the results of their professional activity.

We developed a microcomputer workstation with the assumption that online information retrieval is only one of many important tasks that constitute the subject expert's overall activity. For example, one of the first functions that we decided to implement on our IBM PC was word processing, rather than computer communications. The overall task was to organize our professional output properly.

Thus, our first purchase of application software was a *word processor,* MULTIMATE. This powerful package is an imitation of the very effective and user-friendly software previously developed by Wang Laboratories for its word processing systems.

Being menu-driven, MULTIMATE is easy to learn for a novice, and not boring to an experienced user. A beginner can start with a limited number of commands that are quite adequate to create and edit a simple document. Gradually, a user can build proficiency, improving his knowledge of various options and his overall performance.

As with some other software packages, MULTIMATE allows for a simple conversion to and from *ASCII format.* This standard code is very important for many of our applications, particularly for online information retrieval. ASCII (American Standard Code for Information Interchange) is a kind of a universal computer alphabet, that allows various word processors, data communication programs, and associated equipment to communicate among themselves.

With the help of a *data communication program,* it is possible to perform certain operations that allow you to capture received information for subsequent manipulation.

In addition to downloading various data to the memory of your microcomputer, you can automate the technical side of such procedures as connection and searching. These procedures may be quite irritating and slow to perform manually without the use of an intelligent terminal.

Thus, good data communications software can save the user a lot of time and effort, reduce the overall retrieval and word processing time, and improve the reliability of the telecommunication process.

CROSSTALK-XVI, the data communication program that we selected, is used for two different purposes. First, it allows us to perform information retrieval from various online services. Second, we use this software to send and receive electronic mail. In both cases we use the IBM PC microcomputer as an intelligent terminal of the host computer system.

The flow of data is controlled in computers with the help of an *operating system.* DOS (Disk Operating System) allows various pieces of hardware and software to interact. DOS constitutes the basis of most of the popular software packages that exist today on the market, including both MULTIMATE and CROSSTALK-XVI. In addition, DOS allows the user to perform some important basic operations that other software packages do not support (such as disk-formatting or diskcopy).

In addition to word processing and data communication programs, each user may have other favorite application packages, ones that could support his own applications. For example, a scientist may use software packages that perform data acquisition during an experiment. An engineer could use a graphic application program for the computer-aided design (CAD) of a PCB-board. A physician could use his microcomputer to keep track of his patients, and a market researcher could build his charts based on the information that he gathered online. The versatility of a microcomputer workstation allows the subject expert to tailor it for any necessary application.

THE HARDWARE CONFIGURATION

Computer dealers advertise certain computer brands, such as IBM PC, PC-AT, Macintosh, or

Compaq. These brand names normally represent certain configurations of hardware and software. Like a child's construction toy, each of those microcomputers consists of several parts that can be assembled in numerous combinations, depending on the application requirements.

The heart of any computer is its *CPU,* or *central processing unit.* This unit performs all calculations under the guidance of the computer software. Also important is the *read-only memory,* or *ROM*—a device that, among other things, controls the CPU's interactions with the peripherals, such as its monitor, keyboard, or disk drive.

In the IBM PC, the CPU and ROM are contained in the so-called *system unit*—the part that is usually the most important and expensive among those components that constitute a microcomputer configuration.

Many manufacturers have introduced their own versions of the IBM PC. These "clones" undercut the relatively high price of the original version, yet they allow a user to execute the multitude of programs originally produced for this microcomputer. However, the user should be aware that none of the clones existing on the market have so far full compatibility with the original IBM PC. In practice, the definition of a *PC-compatible* computer varies from manufacturer to manufacturer.

Specialists list several levels of compatibility of PC clones with the original machine. At the lowest level operators working with different machines might use similar types of commands. At the highest level, all programs originally developed for the IBM PC can be run on the clone computer without any modification.

It is impossible, however, to achieve a true full compatibility with the IBM PC. This would require duplication of the IBM-developed software built into the microcomputer's ROM. Without such a violation of the copyright law, no manufacturer could claim that his computer is able to run all the programs developed for the IBM PC.

A potential user who is not concerned with the distant possibility of running an exotic software package that can be run only on the original IBM PC may seriously consider a clone as a substitute for the more expensive original system. Such PC-compatible clones as Compaq or Columbia may run up to 95 percent of the software developed for the IBM PC, thus satisfying the needs of the majority of microcomputer users.

On the other hand, the user whose requirements are not as well established might opt for the original IBM PC System Unit. Such a choice would guarantee that future applications could be performed without undesirable and expensive modifications to the software or to the computer itself.

My own microcomputer workstation has been built around the most basic IBM PC configuration, which includes 64K user memory, one 320K disk drive, and a keyboard. Actually, my initial preference was for an even simpler basic system, since I was planning to purchase a less expensive and better developed version of the keyboard elsewhere. Unfortunately, I was not able to obtain from IBM a totally stripped-down configuration.

For many applications it is necessary to have a much larger system memory than the 64K provided with the most basic configuration. Therefore, I upgraded the microcomputer memory to 256K. The most recent versions of the basic IBM PC come with 256K memory.

The upgrading was done by inserting several dozen chips, purchased separately, into the special slots on the *memory board,* a part of the original system. This relatively simple operation is characteristic of various manipulations that are necessary to put a microcomputer together. Typically, a person with an elementary knowledge of handling a screwdriver can successfully perform most of the required operations, thereby eliminating the initial dealer's charge for putting the machine together.

As was mentioned above, the original IBM PC is not an ideal computer. Layout and performance of its various components may certainly be improved, as has been done by many manufacturers of compatible systems. As long as it does not jeopardize the idea of compatibility itself, such improvements will only be welcomed by the user. In addition to advanced performance and quality of the overall system, these improvements may also result in considerable money savings.

Almost any peripheral for the IBM PC microcomputer can be successfully selected from the numerous brands available on the market. Whether or not to substitute a clone for almost any other part of the IBM PC configuration is an easy decision to make compared with the choice of the system unit itself.

The visual presentation of information is made possible through the use of a *monitor*—a screen similar to that of a television set. Depending on applications and ergonomic requirements, a user can select a simple and inexpensive one-color screen. Alternatively, he can choose among a high-resolution "Cadillac" of displays intended to represent drawings and multicolor graphics. Between these two choices lie many types of monitors capable of doing a more or less adequate job when connected to your microcomputer.

The choice of a monitor is important, as this device directly relates to your online performance and productivity. If the display has low resolution or flickers, the operator may become weary after only a short work period. More serious problems, such as long-lasting headaches or permanent effects on the eyes are known to occur when one disregards the required quality of visual information.

No less important, by the way, are the external conditions in the workplace. Such factors as proper office lighting or adequate furniture should not be underestimated in the development of the computerized workplace.

For my system, I selected an Amdek-310A amber monitor for its good performance characteristics and low cost. In addition, its ergonomic characteristics, particularly the sharpness of characters on its amber color screen, compares favorably with the ergonomic characteristics of the IBM's own green color screen.

A microcomputer controls its visual display with the help of a special *monitor card*—an internal board that is installed in the system unit. Usually such a card also controls the operations of the computer printer.

The original IBM PC monochrome monitor/printer card is adequate to support the use of alphanumeric characters. More advanced graphics/printer boards, such as the Hercules, also have the capability for high resolution graphics, which may be important in some applications.

The choice of a printer is very important. Being a mechanical device, a printer is relatively expensive, and prone to breakdown. Usually, a printer should be able to support such contradictory operations as fast print in a draft mode, letter quality print in a final mode, and even graphics printing. It should be reliable and simple in operations and maintenance. It also should provide variations in the print styles and sizes.

For my system, I selected an Epson FX-80 dot matrix printer. Being relatively inexpensive and simple in operation, it provides a variety of letter styles and sizes that is quite adequate for my applications. In addition, it can also support various graphic applications.

I used the Epson printer primary for draft print applications. In order to produce a final copy of the figures, I used the Corona LP-300 laser printer. This new and relatively inexpensive device allows the IBM PC user to produce high quality prints that are suitable for inclusion in a book.

Some graphic materials in this book were also produced with the help of my IBM PC system.

When not in memory, data are kept on permanent storage media, which in the case of IBM PC consists of 5-1/4" floppy disk. Many of the programs that run on this microcomputer require simultaneous use of two floppy disks—one for the program itself and another for data created during the session. It was therefore necessary to add another disk drive in addition to the one included in the basic configuration. For these purposes I selected a Tandon disk drive which is identical to the IBM PC drive but costs only a fraction of the original unit's price.

The modem is an indispensable part of a microcomputer workstation developed for effective online searching. I selected the Rixon PC-212A board, capable of supporting communication at 1200 baud. A modem internally installed in a system unit is more convenient to use than the traditionally employed separate box. An internal board configuration also allows for more space on the usually busy desk of the operator, is less prone to accidental damage, and last but not least, costs less.

The Rixon PC-212A modem, which does not require an action telephone for operation, permits many useful features to be implemented. Among them is the direct dialing of a telephone number from a keyboard, multiple redials of the last number dialed, automatic alternations of several telephone numbers if the first attempts to connect fail, and time-delays during dialing, which may be important when it is necessary to dial a sequence of several telephone numbers.

Most of the named characteristics of a modem may sound quite fancy for an inexperienced user. These characteristics, nevertheless, could be vitally important in allowing you to achieve an effective and reliable connection and may save you considerable amounts of time and effort during an information retrieval session. Whichever modem you select, make certain it is compatible with the communications program you plan to use.

A general view of the IBM PC-based microcomputer workstation that was used for online searching is shown in Fig. 6-1.

ASSEMBLING YOUR OWN MICROCOMPUTER SYSTEM

Altogether the bits and pieces of software and hardware mentioned previously constitute quite a powerful microcomputer workstation, capable of realizing many diversified applications. Its total cost in our case can be compared very favorably with the cost of the

Fig. 6-1. An IBM PC-based microcomputer system suitable for online searching with a Rixon PC-212A modem board being installed. (Courtesy CASE RIXON Communications, Inc.)

similar systems sold by IBM PC dealerships, whereas its potential to support various usages is higher.

Of course, an individual user with his unique set of requirements has to create his own system, more relevant to his own line of applications.

Careful shopping around, for example through computer ads in large city newspapers, as well as concerted efforts in putting various pieces of equipment and application software together may cut the cost of the final system in half. In addition, shopping around may significantly improve the system's performance and its capability of supporting various applications.

Advice from an independent subject expert who is familiar with the user's potential applications may be especially valuable in putting together a computer configuration. A computer dealer representing a certain line of products may be biased towards it. It is not uncommon that a dealer proposes as a first choice an expensive system whose features are not all needed at the first stage of its use.

Potential for expansion, which the IBM PC-standard provides, allows the user to add necessary hardware and software at a later stage, when the real need for a new application arises. Otherwise, the user may be forced to deal with software that was purchased ahead of time and that became obsolete before its turn to be used came.

One of the hard-earned lessons of any experienced microcomputer user is that he should be extremely selective in his choice of a new piece of hardware or software. It is always a dubious practice for a busy professional or scientist to possess several pieces of software that perform essentially the same functions. Besides the direct cost factor, every software package requires considerable time and effort to become acquainted with and to be put into effective use. Such a high "upfront cost" of a microcomputer application frequently turns off potential users altogether.

This sad sequence of events will not, however, happen to the user who builds his microcomputer workstation step-by-step, in accordance with his overall professional objectives. An experienced user would have in his library only a handful of familiar application software packages, each of which is compatible with his other software packages and supports a certain aspect of his work.

The acquisition of a new software package for such a skilled user is a relatively rare event. It would always follow intensive sessions of gathering intelligence on the new software's qualities and characteristics. Acquisition of a new software package requires intensive educational sessions even for the experienced user. In addition, the user always has to reevaluate whether it is necessary to stop using some of his older application packages or at least some of their features that may be more effectively performed with the new software. A subject expert with a busy schedule can accept such a major disruption only infrequently.

In the selection of a software package, subject experts should be guided primarily by the following four criteria:

- Efficiency and productivity: the software must be rated as a top application package by an independent evaluator.
- User-friendliness: two important subcriteria are that the software should be easy and quickly learned by a new user, yet be effective enough to support an experienced user in more sophisticated applications.
- Compatibility: the software should allow the user to move data easily to and from it, permitting it to be used in conjunction with other packages. This, however, does not imply a preference for the "integrated" program packages that promise to perform everything for everybody; their components are often quite inefficient compared with the best specialized programs on the market.
- Software support: the user must have a reasonable expectation that the software producer will support his product. Some important elements of the producer's support are notifications of periodic revisions and updates, a telephone or an electronic mail hot-line that would allow the user to solve his problems

quickly and efficiently, and a newsletter that keeps the user informed on new developments and offers hints on how to use certain features of the system.

In evaluating software efficiency, productivity, and the degree of user-friendliness, the advice of a more experienced user will often do. However, a much better way is to read evaluation reviews produced by microcomputer specialists. Such reviews frequently appear in the numerous journals devoted to personal computers.

A good general rule to follow is to select a piece of software that has been on the market for at least a year. It is more likely that such software has already been independently evaluated, and that the software producers have had a chance to fix the most obvious problems found in the program by the first wave of users. Even better is to choose a microcomputer program that imitates a well-established piece of software previously introduced for another computer system.

In gathering such information, it helps to remember that online searching is a very effective tool for retrieval of up-to-date knowledge found in the multitude of the published sources. There are by now several online databases that are devoted to microcomputer software, hardware, and applications. Even more up-to-date sources of online information are the various *bulletin boards,* some of which contain the full text of newsletters and uncensored comments from users.

The same approach that we recommend for software selection is also effective when you are looking for hardware. As a rule, the prospective buyer should already be reasonably informed when he calls a computer dealer for the first time. More than with any other purchase, even a small amount of homework may save the buyer a lot of money and embarrassment.

An alternative to the creation of the computer system from scratch is to use a workstation that is put together by others. This solution may be more acceptable to the subject expert unskilled in computer use. Such a user should, however, be prepared to pay the consequences, if he finds out later that what he has got is not suitable for his use.

A reasonable compromise is to use the services of a skilled computer expert together with the intensive self-educating session. Such a session may not produce a new computer expert, but it certainly would give the future user an appreciation of the problems involved, as well as the principal solutions and compromises.

Such self-education sessions are necessary at the start of a "computerization drive" for any subject expert, regardless of his level of computer literacy. After all, the decision to "computerize" may well be one of the most important professional decisions for a specialist to make. Whether he likes it or not, the implications of such decisions may predetermine many of the subject expert's actions for the rest of his career.

RUNNING A SEARCH WITH YOUR MICRO

Below we describe some typical manipulations that you have to perform in order to run a search with the help of the microcomputer workstation based on the IBM PC and Rixon board modem, that is, the system that was described previously. This procedure may vary somewhat among different types of microcomputer-based workstations, depending on their level of sophistication. However, automatic information retrieval with the help of such an intelligent terminal may differ quite significantly from an online search performed with the aid of a terminal that does not have the processing capabilities of a microcomputer.

At present, the difference between automatic and nonautomatic systems primarily concerns convenience and time savings. These benefits may be reaped during technical procedures such as connection, data capturing and reprocessing, and to some extent, accessing auxiliary information during the online session.

In the future, microcomputers will undoubtedly be powerful enough to perform more complex tasks, such as translation of a natural language search request into various query languages, optimization of a search strategy, or condensation of results into a more meaningful form. Although such tasks are outside of the reach of today's computers, certain software packages that are available on the market today implement some features of those more complex tasks.

In order to run a search session with IBM PC, the user would need to insert two floppy disks into the microcomputer drives. On the first disk there should be a communications program (in our case it is CROSSTALK-XVI). The second disk is used in order to record (download) the online session, including data obtained from the host computer.

After issuing the initial command:

xtalk

a Status Screen (menu) of the system will be displayed , as shown in Fig. 6-2.

The system messages displayed on the highlighted *command line* at the bottom of the display guide the user during the connection procedure. For example, in Fig. 6-2 the system requests the user to provide the number of the service that he would like to search online. The user can choose amongst several *command files* listed just above the command line.

Suppose that in our example the user selected the *DIALOG* online service by pressing number *1*. Some of the initial (default) settings listed on the display will immediately change (see Fig. 6-3) and the system will start to dial DIALOG through one of several communication networks.

If the telephone is busy or the network does not respond, the system will automatically dial again, using various alternative telephone numbers or communication networks until the connection is established.

At a suitable moment during this connection procedure, the system is programmed to make a brief pause and ask the operator whether he would like to capture the search onto a floppy disk inserted into drive B. In the case of a positive answer, all subsequent interaction between the operator and

```
                 ┌──── CROSSTALK - XVI Status Screen ────┐        Off line

NAme    CROSSTALK default settings                  LOaded   A:STD.XTK
NUmber                                              CApture  Off

┌───── Communications parameters ─────┐            ┌──── Filter settings ────┐
SPeed 1200   PArity None   DUplex   Full            DFbug    Off   LFauto   Off
DAta  8      STop   1      EMulate  None            TAbex    Off   BLankex  Off
POrt  1                    MOde     Call            INfilter On    OUtfiltr On

┌──────── Key settings ───────────┐                 ┌── SEnd control settings ──┐
ATten   Esc                COmmand ETX (^C)         CWait    None
SWitch  Home               BReak   End              LWait    None

┌──────────────── Available command files ────────────────┐

1) DIALOG    2) ORBIT    3) MEDLARS      4) BRS           5) ENVOY-100
6) QUESTEL   7) ESA      8) THE SOURCE   9) COMPUSERVE   10) DOW JONES

 Enter number for file to use ( 1 - 10 ): _
```

Fig. 6-2. The typical initial setting of the CROSSTALK-XVI Status Screen. (Courtesy of Microstuf, Inc.)

```
             ┌──── CROSSTALK - XVI Status Screen ────┐          Off line

NAme     DIALOG                                   LOaded    A:DIALOG.XTK
NUmber   92345678                                 CApture   Off

┌───────── Communications parameters ─────────┐  ┌────── Filter settings ──────┐
 SPeed 1200    PArity None    DUplex   Full       DEbug     Off    LFauto    Off
 DAta  8       STop   1       EMulate  None       TAbex     Off    BLankex   Off
 POrt  1                      MOde     Call       INfilter  On     OUtfiltr  On

┌──────────────── Key settings ───────────────┐  ┌─── SEnd control settings ───┐
 ATten  Esc                   COmmand  ETX (^C)   CWait     None
 SWitch Home                  BReak    End        LWait     None

┌────────────────────── Available command files ──────────────────────────────┐

 1) DIALOG     2) ORBIT    3) MEDLARS      4) BRS              5) ENVOY-100
 6) QUESTEL    7) ESA      8) THE SOURCE   9) COMPUSERVE      10) DOW JONES

DIALING: T92345678

┌──────────────────────────────────────────────────────────────────┐
│ Dialing -  92345678 - Waiting for connection... 27               │
└──────────────────────────────────────────────────────────────────┘
```

Fig. 6-3. Setting of the CROSSTALK-XVI Status Screen during telephone dialing of the DIALOG online service. (Courtesy of Microstuf, Inc.)

the computer will be recorded on the disk and the information obtained during the session can be reprocessed later.

In addition to automatic telephone dialing, CROSSTALK-XVI can also respond to certain messages from the host computer or communications network. For example, it can keep in its memory all the identification numbers and the passwords that are necessary for normal connection and provide them in response to the host computer's request. It also can be programmed to recognize error messages indicating a disconnection from the host computer. In such a case, an alarm would sound, and an automatic reconnection procedure would be initiated, all under program control.

The software can also speed up the searching time quite considerably in cases in which the online service allows the searcher to print only a small portion of text at a time, and requests his permission to continue every several minutes. A properly programmed microcomputer will automatically supply the host computer with a positive answer and thus can greatly reduce overall online time.

Another convenient feature of the CROSSTALK-XVI communication software is that instead of typing a whole command or even a string of commands during a searching session, the user can press only one key, which is preprogrammed to initiate the required action.

Also useful is the ability to develop the initial version of a search statement on the microcomputer, without connection to the host computer. Such an action obviously allows the user to save on the computer and communications costs. More importantly, it considerably reduces the level of stress that is normally associated with online searching, and it usually results in much more effective and productive online sessions.

After connecting to the host computer, the user

can send his prefabricated search strategy statement to the host computer with one command.

At the end of the searching session, I normally use a special command to convert the download data from the standard ASCII format, used for interchange between the computers, to MULTIMATE documents. Conversion to MULTIMATE greatly facilitates further data processing and editing activities. Converted documents are also easy to insert into final reports.

CONCLUSIONS

This chapter describes the IBM PC-based microcomputer workstation, which amongst many other applications can be used for online information retrieval. The IBM PC was selected to become the basis of the workstation due to the high popularity of this microcomputer; popularity that lead to the emergence of the IBM PC as a de facto industry standard.

This industry standard allows various data to be passed from one program to the other and permits the user to combine diversified applications. As a result, hundreds of applications were developed for the IBM PC by various software houses. In addition, many older software packages written for minicomputers and even for mainframes are currently being transferred to this microcomputer.

The online searcher is not, by all means, limited to the use of the IBM PC. Our own Subject Expert Searching Technique described later in this book is not linked to any particular computer and can be implemented with quite simple technological means. However, an IBM PC-based system is quite powerful and versatile and is convenient to use for online searching. Such a system allows the user to organize his searching activity in the most efficient way. In addition to the information retrieval process, the subject expert can use his IBM PC microcomputer for many other applications that are essential in his professional activity.

Online information retrieval can be performed effectively with the help of a data communication program. Such a program can greatly facilitate the connection process and allow the user to capture received information for subsequent manipulation.

Altogether, the bits and pieces of software and hardware described in this book constitute a powerful microcomputer workstation, capable of realizing many diversified applications. Its total cost is moderate, whereas its potential to support various usages is quite high.

This chapter describes some criteria that should guide you in your selection of software and hardware. Even though these criteria are quite basice, they can be beneficial when you start to assemble your own microcomputer system.

This chapter also includes examples of some typical manipulations that you must perform in order to run a search with the help of the described microcomputer workstation.

Chapter 7

Overview of the Online Retrieval Process

The following material describes various steps typically involved in the online searching process.

SEARCHING STEPS

A simple online search usually consists of the following principal steps (see Fig. 7-1):

1. Connecting (including the logon procedure)
2. Selecting a file
3. Performing a search
4. Printing out the results
5. Disconnecting (logoff procedure)

More complex searches may include some additional steps, such as displaying online parts of the indexes, saving a search, running a search through several additional files, and so on.

> Each online service has its own distinctive set of commands (query language) that describes these steps. Although these relatively simple commands vary in appearance from one online service to another, they often represent the same computer actions.

This similarity in the functioning of the basic searching steps and commands in different online services often makes it possible for a searcher to adapt his original search strategy to various online services. Such adaptation is easier to achieve if the original search strategy is expressed using the most basic commands. This, in fact, constitutes one of the most important aspects of our Subject Expert Searching Technique.

The process of "translating" a search from one online service to another is relatively easy to perform with the help of *Goldmann's Glossary of Online Services and Databases.* This periodic newsletter is a practical tool for an occasional searcher. A scientist or a professional is likely to spend only a small fraction of his time on online searching and thus almost always is an occasional searcher.

```
TELENET ◄──────────────────────────────────────── CONNECTING
205 16D

TERMINAL=

@c 213 170

213 170 CONNECTED

ENTER YOUR DIALOG PASSWORD
XXXXXXXX  LOGON File1 Wed 23may84 21:14:26 Port056

? b122 ◄────────────────────────────────────────── SELECTING
                                                    A FILE
           23may84 21:15:14 User12345
     $0.20 0.013 Hrs File1*
     $0.10 Tymnet
     $0.30 Estimated Total Cost

File122:Harvard Business Review - 1971-84,Mar/Apr
(Copr. Harvard 1984)
          Set Items Description
          --- ----- -----------
? s investment ◄────────────────────────────────── PERFORMING
                                                    A SEARCH
            1   628 INVESTMENT

? t1/5/1 ◄──────────────────────────────────────── PRINTING
                                                    THE RESULTS
1/5/1
120375          842160          **COMPLETE TEXT AVAILABLE**
   Internal Auditors Can Cut Outside CPA Costs
   Wallace, Wanda A. - Southern Methodist Univ. School of Business
   HARVARD BUSINESS REVIEW, Mar/Apr 1984, p. 16
   DOCUMENT TYPE: HBR Article
   FEATURE NAME: Ideas for Action
   CORPORATE FUNCTIONS: Finance and accounting.

   ABSTRACT:
   Companies are creating and augmenting internal auditing departments to
cut external auditor fees. Internal auditors can lower outside fees by
improving a company's accounting controls and by performing financial
examinations. They can also help outside auditors by providing
organizational support and review and testing assistance; help in
preparation and drafting of footnotes to financial statements; and provide
general help as needed.
   A study of 32 companies that compared the costs of inside and outside
audit services found, by regression analysis, that every dollar spent on
internal auditing can be expected, on average, to reduce the external audit
fee by roughly a nickel. The study suggests that the payback of
expenditures on internal auditing might be improved by allocating more
hours of internal audit assistance to the companies' outside CPAs.
```

Fig. 7-1. Principal steps involved in a simple online search. DIALOG online service. File 122:Harvard Business Review. (Courtesy of John Wiley & Sons, Inc. ©John Wiley & Sons, Inc.) (Continued on page 68.)

```
   GRAPHS AND EXHIBITS:
   The  relationship  of internal audit activities to external audit fees -
Costs.

   SUBJECT DESCRIPTORS: *Audits; *Internal controls; *Accounting.
   COMPANY/ORGANIZATION DESCRIPTORS:  Public Accounting Report;

? logoff ◄──────────────────────────────────────────────  DISCONNECTING
          23may84 21:16:31 User12345
    $1.65  0.022 Hrs File122 1 Descriptor
    $0.18  Tymnet
    $1.83  Estimated Total Cost

LOGOFF 21:16:32
DATAPAC: call cleared - remote request(45B)
```

Fig. 7-1. Principal steps involved in a simple online search. DIALOG online service. File 122:Harvard Business Review. (Courtesy of John Wiley & Sons, Inc. ©John Wiley & Sons, Inc.) (Continued from page 67.)

THE CONNECTION PROCEDURE

The *connection procedure* usually consists of the following stages (see Fig. 7-2):

- The selection of a communication network through which an online service is accessed
- The specification of the terminal characteristics
- The selection of an online service
- The identification of the user (using ID, password, etc.)
- The automatic connection to a default file
- The automatic initiation of various counters keeping track of the duration and cost of the online session
- A brief presentation by the computer of online service news
- The presentation of a *prompt* that requests the start of a search.

The length, duration, and reliability of a connection procedure greatly varies between different online services. Small and less popular online services sometimes have a tendency to make this procedure as long, costly, and miserable for the user as possible. On the other hand, the better online services give their users only new and highly useful information during the connection procedure.

> It is beneficial for a user to develop standard connection procedures and to use them for every interactive session. An example of such a procedure, which is taken from *Goldmann's Glossary of Online Services and Databases*, is shown in Fig. 7-3.

A standard connection procedure can save a lot of trouble for the user. This is especially important, as an interactive session requires a lot of concentration and can be highly stressful.

FILE SELECTION

The connection procedure described above includes automatic connection to a *default file*. Most of the online services select as a default file the one which is most popular and the least expensive.

Thus, DIALOG selects a popular and relatively inexpensive file called 1:ERIC as a default file. The main subject of this file is education. The file is fairly large and has a wealth of data on various subjects only peripherally related to education. Therefore, the file may be quite useful to almost every subject expert during the initial formulation stage of his search.

The choice of the most recent File Medline as a default file on MEDLARS is quite logical, as it is by far the most popular file on this online service.

In the ORBIT online service, a special file called Orbit, which contains no records, is used as a default file. This file allows the user to rapidly and inexpensively enter many commands and logical operators that can be saved and later used automatically in more expensive files with records.

Certain online services allow the user to change his default file either himself (for example ORBIT), or on written request (DIALOG). This feature can save quite a bit of money, especially for the frequent user who does not want to waste his money by being connected to an expensive file that is useless for him.

Each online service with more than one file has a special command that allows the searcher to se-

```
AFTER A TELEPHONE CONNECTION WITH THE COMMUNICATIONS NETWORK IS
MADE, THE CARRIAGE RETURN (cr) IS HIT TWICE BY THE SEARCHER.
THE SYSTEM RESPONDS WITH:


TELENET
602 11L

TERMINAL= (cr) <------------------------------------  SPECIFYING
                                                      TERMINAL
                                                      CHARACTERISTICS

@c 213 33 <-----------------------------------------  SELECTING AN
                                                      ONLINE SERVICE
213 33 CONNECTED
/login usercode <-----------------------------------  IDENTIFYING
                                                      THE USER
YOU ARE ON LINE LE8

HELLO FROM SDC/ORBIT IV.  (08/10/84  6:07 P.M.  PACIFIC TIME)  CLOCK
                                                               INITIATION
ENTER SECURITY CODE:
tree <----------------------------------------------  USER'S
                                                      PASSWORD
PROG:
****
ENERGYLINE NOW PROXIMITY-SEARCHABLE! SEE EX ENERGYLINE FOR DETAILS. <-- NEWS

****
ELECTRONIC MAIL SERVICE NOW AVAILABLE! SEE EX MAIL FOR DETAILS.
****
INSPEC NOW PROXIMITY-SEARCHABLE! SEE EX INSPEC FOR DETAILS.
****
THE FOLLOWING FILES WILL BE UNVAILABLE FROM 4:00-6:00PM (PST) AUGUST 8:
INFORM, METADEX AND WPIL.
****
YOU ARE NOW CONNECTED TO THE ORBIT DATABASE. <------  CONNECTION TO
FOR A TUTORIAL, ENTER A QUESTION MARK.  OTHERWISE, ENTER A COMMAND.   A
                                                      DEFAULT FILE

SS 1 /C?
USER: <---------------------------------------------  PROMPT FOR A
                                                      SEARCH STATEMENT
```

Fig. 7-2. An example of a connection procedure. ORBIT online service. (Courtesy of System Development Corporation.)

- 9 - Goldmann's Glossary

SUBJECT	DIALOG	ORBIT	MEDLARS
Connecting in the U.S. (con't)	Access through TELENET: The terminal must be set in FULL DUPLEX. Switch terminal and modem "on". Dial local TELENET number ___-___. If you have a "dumb" terminal, after receiving a high-pitched tone connect the telephone handset to a modem (or push a red "Hold" button on the telephone). If you have an intelligent terminal with an attached modem, such a link may be established automatically. CR CR After receipt of the message: "TERMINAL=" enter your TELENET terminal model identifier:_________ If you don't know your identifier, produce default value by entering CR If this causes problems, obtain your terminal identifier from DIALOG. After receipt of: "@"	Access through TELENET: The terminal must be set in FULL DUPLEX. Switch terminal and modem "on". Dial local TELENET number ___-___. If you have a "dumb" terminal, after receiving a high-pitched tone connect the telephone handset to a modem (or push a red "Hold" button on the telephone). If you have an intelligent terminal with an attached modem, such a link may be established automatically. CR CR After receipt of the message: "TERMINAL=" enter your TELENET terminal model identifier:_________ If you don't know your identifier, produce default value by entering CR If this causes problems, obtain your terminal identifier from ORBIT. After receipt of: "@"	Access through TELENET: The terminal must be set in FULL DUPLEX. Switch terminal and modem "on". Dial local TELENET number ___-___. If you have a "dumb" terminal, after receiving a high-pitched tone connect the telephone handset to a modem (or push a red "Hold" button on the telephone). If you have an intelligent terminal with an attached modem, such a link may be established automatically. CR CR After receipt of the message: "TERMINAL=" enter your TELENET terminal model identifier:_________ If you don't know your identifier, produce default value by entering CR If this causes problems, obtain your terminal identifier from MEDLARS. After receipt of: "@"

Fig. 7-3. An excert from the description of a standard setup procedure. *Goldmann's Glossary of Online Services and Databases, Sixth Edition*. 1985.

lect a new file, that is, to switch from one file to another (see Fig. 7-4). At the same time, this command usually erases the results of the previous search from computer memory.

In some online services, it is possible to switch to another file temporarily without losing the results of the previous search (see Fig. 7-5). However, it is usually not possible to perform joint logical operations on the records selected from two different files.

PRINTING THE RESULTS

Unit records found during a search can be printed during the current session (*online print*) or after the session, using the fast high-quality printers owned by the online service, and then mailed to the end-user through the ordinary or rush mail service (*offline print*).

The choice between online and offline printing depends on such factors as:

- End-user requirements, particularly time and money constraints
- The quality of the online service hardware and software, particularly its tolerance towards the simultaneous connection by a number of searchers

```
ENTER DATA BASE NAME:  ptsd ◄──────────────────   SELECTING
                                                    A FILE
*SIGN-ON    20.53.34        08/06/84:

BRS/PTSD/AUG 1984 (ISS 31)

BRS - SEARCH MODE   - ENTER QUERY
    1:     lubricat$ adj oil$1 ◄───────────────   PERFORMING
                                                    A SEARCH
    RESULT   1

    2:      ..print 1 bibl/doc=1 ◄─────────────   PRINTING
                                                    THE RESULTS
     1

AN 055419 PROMT, 8408, Entry Date: 84/07/26.
SO CPI-Purch, Issue: 84/04/00 pp 74,76.
YR 84..
TI SUPPLY NEWS: Special purpose refineries to be upgraded.

R0601 * END OF DOCUMENTS IN LIST

BRS - SEARCH MODE   - ENTER QUERY
    2:      ..c/emed ◄─────────────────────────   SWITCHING FROM
                                                    A FILE TO A FILE
*CONNECT TIME0:01:33 HH:MM:SS     0.026 DEC HRS     SESSION  46*

* COPYRIGHT ESP B V EXCERPTA MEDICA 1984 *

BRS/EMED/1980 - ISS 25-26 1984

BRS - SEARCH MODE   - ENTER QUERY
    1:     lubricat$ adj oil$1 ◄───────────────   PERFORMING
                                                    ANOTHER SEARCH
    RESULT 17

    2:      ..print 1 bibl/doc=1 ◄─────────────   PRINTING
                                                    THE RESULTS
     1

AN 84091875 8421.
TI Toxicological characteristics of refinery streams used to manufacture
   lubricating oils.
AU Kane-M-L, Ladov-E-N, Holdsworth-C-E, Weaver-N-K.
SO AM-J-IND-MED, 1984, 5/3 (183-200).

      END OF DOCUMENT
```

Fig. 7-4. An example of switching from one file (PTSD—Predicasts Prompt Weekly Update) to another (EMED—Excerpta Medica) during the same session. BRS online service. (File PTSD courtesy of Predicasts, Inc. Database© by Predicasts, Inc. File EMED courtesy of Elsevier Science Publishers. ©Elsevier Science Publishers BV/Excerpta Medica. All rights reserved.)

```
SS 1 /C?
USER:
file ca82 ◄──────────────────────────────────  SELECTING
                                               A FILE
PROG:
ELAPSED TIME ON ORBIT: 0.05 HRS.
YOU ARE NOW CONNECTED TO THE CAS82 DATABASE.
ACS COPYRIGHT 1984
COVERS 1982 THROUGH VOL 101 #2 (8414)
SEE ALSO CA77, CA72, AND CA67. LEFT-HAND TRUNCATION AVAILABLE.

SS 1 /C?
USER:
pipes and creep(w)damage ◄─────────────────────  PERFORMING
                                               A SEARCH
PROG:
SS 1 PSTG (5)

SS 2 /C?
USER:
prt fu ◄───────────────────────────────────  PRINTING
                                               THE RESULTS
PROG:

-1-
AN  - CA96-203578(24)
TI  - Assessment of the creep damage and residual life of steam pipes
AU  - Auerkari, Pertti; Kemppainen, Helena
OS  - Tech. Res. Cent. Finland, Metallilab., Espoo, Finland
SO  - Tutkimuksia - Valt. Tek. Tutkimuskeskus (TUTUDX), V 59, 26 pp., 1982
DT  - J (Journal)
LA  - Swed
CC  - SEC55-12
IT  - 39411-23-9, prop: (creep damage and residual life detn. of steam pipes
      of)
IT  - Pipes and Tubes: (chromium-molybdenum steel, creep damage and residual
      life detn. in steam)
IT  - Steam: (steel pipes for, creep damage and residual life detn. of)
ST  - pipe; accelerated; electron; microscopy


SS 2 /C?
USER:
tfile cassi ◄────────────────────────────────  SELECTING
                                               A FILE
    PROG:                                      TEMPORARILY
```

Fig. 7-5. An example of a search in one file with a temporary switch to another file. ORBIT online service. Files CAS82 (Chemical Abstracts Service) and CASSI (Chemical Abstracts Service Source Index). (Courtesy of Chemical Abstracts Service. ©American Chemical Society.) The searcher temporarily switches to another file (CASSI) in order to find out more on the origins of the record of interest to him, without losing the results of the previous search. (Continued through page 74.)

File CASSI provides bibliographic data, library holdings and information on publishers and document suppliers, primarily for journals, serials, monographs, and conference proceedings cited in the CAS database.

```
ELAPSED TIME ON CA82: 0.14 HRS.
YOU ARE NOW CONNECTED TO THE CAS SOURCE INDEX DATABASE.
ACS COPYRIGHT 1983
COVERS 1907 THRU 2ND QTR (8402).
***
TRANSFER MORE THAN 140 TERMS FROM SINGLE PRINT RECORD TO  SELECT LIST!
SEE EX PRINT SELECT NOWRAP FOR DETAILS.
*TMP* SS 2 /C?
USER:
tutkimuksia ◄────────────────────────────── PERFORMING
                                             A SEARCH
PROG:
SS 2 PSTG (2)

*TMP* SS 3 /C?
USER:
prt fu ◄─────────────────────────────────── PRINTING
                                             THE RESULTS
PROG:                                        OF A TEMPORARY
                                             SEARCH
-1-
JC  - TUTUDX
TI  - Tutkimuksia - Valtion Teknillinen Tutkimuskeskus [Research Reports -
      Technical Research Centre of Finland], (Tutkimuksia - Valt. Tek.
      Tutkimuskeskus) (TUTUDX)
      TUTKIMUKSIA / VALTION TEKNILLINEN TUTKIMUSKESKUS. -- ESPOO, FINLAND.
SO  - Valtion Teknillinen Tutkimuskeskus (Valt Tek Tutkimuskeskus),
      Vuorimiehentie 5, SF-02150, Espoo, 15, FIN
      (Irregular)
      1981? -
      [n14 1981]
NO  - Publication note: Contains some reprints
DT  - Serial: Current Title
LA  - Text in: EN , Summaries in: EN
XR  - Valtion Teknillinen Tutkimuskeskus, Tutkimuksia (Valt. Tek.
      Tutkimuskeskus, Tutkimuksia)
XR  - Technical Research Centre of Finland, Research Reports (Tech. Res. Cent.
      Finl., Res. Rep.)
XR  - Research Reports - Technical Research Centre of Finland (Res. Rep. -
      Tech. Res. Cent. Finl.)
XR  - Statens Tekniska Forskningscentral, Forskningsrapporter (Statens Tek.
      Forskningscent., Forskningsrapp.)
XR  - Forskningsrapporter - Statens Tekniska Forskningscentral (Forskningsrapp.
      - Statens Tek. Forskningscent.)
AV  - Document Supplier: CAS
SS 2 /C?
*TMP* SS 3 /C?
USER:
return ◄─────────────────────────────────── SWITCHING BACK
                                             TO THE ORIGINAL
ELAPSED TIME ON CASSI: 0.05 HRS.             FILE
YOU ARE NOW CONNECTED TO THE CAS82 DATABASE.
ACS COPYRIGHT 1984
COVERS 1982 THROUGH VOL 101 #2 (8414)
```

Fig. 7-5. (Continued from page 72.)

```
SEE ALSO CA77, CA72, AND CA67. LEFT-HAND TRUNCATION AVAILABLE.

SS 2 /C?
USER:
pipes and electron(w)microscopy
```

CONTINUING WITH THE SEARCH IN THE ORIGINAL FILE

Fig. 7-5. (Continued from page 73.)

- The type of the terminal employed by the searcher
- The required visual appearance of the printed results
- The number of unit records retrieved
- The time of the day and day of the week when the search takes place.

The time required to perform an online search generally consists of two parts - the searching time and the printing time. Choices you make concerning decisions such as online versus offline printing, terminal selection, time of day to do the search, and so on are greatly affected by the relative amount of time and resources required in the searching and printing phases.

The online user-computer interaction is not as rapid a process as widely believed by nonsearchers. The computer may be very fast, but interaction between the searcher and computer may be quite slow. Even the best typists cannot be compared with the computer as far as speed and quality of the typing process is concerned (and online searchers are indeed rarely high-class professional typists). In addition, the searching process itself is, on the computer time-scale, fairly slow. Therefore, the duration of the searching phase is not as much reduced by switching from a 300 to a 1200 baud terminal as you might expect.

The situation is quite different regarding the printing phase of the search. The duration of this phase to a great extent depends on the speed of the whole communication process and thus can be greatly increased when the searcher uses a more rapid printer. Selection of a more rapid printer is, however, really significant only when the volume of the search results is quite high.

Unfortunately, with most online services, the speed of the communications process depends to a large extent on the number of searchers simultaneously connected to the computer. Frequently, during the most popular searching hours,

```
??rates

  --Effective Mar. 1, 1985--
For rates for Files 201+ enter ?RATESA.
FILE                       RATE FULL      DISP
NO.   DATABASE             /HR  FMT /PRT  /TYP
  1-ERIC                   $ 25  5  $.10  ---
  5-BIOSIS 81-             $ 75  5  $.28  $.19
  6-NTIS                   $ 48  5  $.20  $.15
  7-SOC SCISRCH(SUBS)$ 75  5  $.15  ---
  7-SOC SCI (NOSUBS) $110  5  $.20  ---
  8-COMPENDEX              $ 99  5  $.47  $.35
  9-AIM/ARM                $ 25  5  $.10  ---
 10-AGRICOLA 79-           $ 35  5  $.10  ---
 11-PSYCINFO               $ 55  5  $.20  $.35
 12-INSPEC 69-76           $ 96  5  $.46  $.36
 13-INSPEC 77-             $ 96  5  $.46  $.36
 14-ISMEC                  $ 84  5  $.40  $.30
 15-ABI/INFORM             $ 73  5  $.30  $.20
 16-PTS PROMT              $114  5  $.58  $.48
 17-PTS ANN RPTS           $114  5  $.68  $.58
 18-PTS F&S                $114  5  $.33  $.28
 19-CHEM IND NOTES         $ 86  5  $.28  $.18
 20-FEDERAL INDEX          $ 90  5  $.20  ---
 21-NCJRS                  $ 35  5  $.15  $.10
 23-CLMS USPATS 50-70$ 95  5  $.50  $.25
 24-CLMS USPTABS71-81$ 95  5
 25-CLMS USPA
 2
```

Fig. 7-6. A portion of an online list of search *rates* for the files accessible on DIALOG online service. (Courtesy of DIALOG Information Services, Inc.)

The column RATE/HR is the hourly cost of online connection to the file, including online printing. The FULL FMT column specifies a command number that displays a full unit record. The /PRT column shows the cost of the offline print of the whole unit record, whereas the DISP/TYP column specifies whether there is a unit cost for printing the record online in addition to the hourly cost of online connection.

the searching process becomes quite slow. Since online print rates usually depend on the duration of the printing process (sometimes, also, on the number of records retrieved), it may be quite expensive to print all the results of a search. This is especially so if the search produces numerous records, and the communication speed at this time of the day is particularly slow.

Figure 7-6 shows the search rates for some files accessible on DIALOG online service. Providing the end-user is able to wait several days for the delivery of results, offline printing is most cost-efficient.

As an example, consider an offline print of 10 records resulting from a search in the relatively inexpensive File 6:NTIS. The cost of such an opera-

```
? t2/6/1

2/6/1
0399966   84127718  AHA
  A hospital energy audit project.


? t2/3/1

2/3/1
0399966   84127718  AHA
  A hospital energy audit project.
  Gleason G
  Aust  Health Rev   ,Nov 1983,    6 (4)  p75-7,   ISSN 0156-5788   Journal
Code: 9GC


? t2/5/1

2/5/1
0399966   84127718  AHA
  A hospital energy audit project.
  Gleason G
  Aust  Health Rev   ,Nov 1983,    6 (4)  p75-7,   ISSN 0156-5788   Journal
Code: 9GC
  Languages: ENGLISH
  Journal Announcement: 8405
  Subfile: Health^
  The project was carried out under the auspices of the  Research
Sub-Committee of the Victorian Branch of the Australian College of Health
Service Administrators. It illustrates the way in which remedial action
based on a thorough, systematic audit of energy losses can yield savings
which are conservatively estimated to be worth tens of thousands of dollars
per annum. While many of the energy saving functions proposed can be
implemented at little or no cost, it is concluded that energy audits must
be thoroughly and competently undertaken and the use of consultants is
considered to have been well justified in this case.
  Descriptors: Australia; *Conservation of Energy Resources--Economics (EC)
;  *Conservation of Natural Resources--Economics (EC); *Maintenance and
Engineering, Hospital--Economics (EC); *MAINTENANCE HOSP--Economics (EC);
*Management Audit; *Organization and Administration; *ORGAN ADMIN
```

Fig. 7-7. Print commands in three various formats (*6*—title, *3*—bibliographic citation, *5*—full record) on DIALOG online service. File 151:Health Planning and Administration.

tion at the specified $0.10 per print is $1. The delivery time for the search results through the ordinary mail service is several days in the USA (at least one week in Canada). The cost of an online print of these records may, however, be as high as $9.20, considering that it may take on average one minute to print out a unit record (the assumption is quite realistic, especially during the most popular operating hours, such as around 10 a.m. or 2 p.m. EST on weekdays).

Of course, outside of peak hours, when the speed of communication may improve rather significantly, searching and printing can be performed at least twice as fast, sometimes even faster, with a corresponding reduction in search costs. Also, during evening hours various discount rates may be in effect. These two factors combined may result in fairly substantial savings for the end-user.

The unit record can be displayed in various *print formats* (see Fig. 7-7). The rate for the shorter print formats is often much lower than the rate for a print in full format. The cost of the shorter prints can be further reduced by the reduction in the required printing time.

DISCONNECTIONS: PLANNED AND ACCIDENTAL

At the end of each online session, a special *disconnection command* (such as logoff, stop, off, end, bye, quit) is issued (see Fig. 7-8). Usually, this command resets the counter that displays the time spent by the searcher online. In many online services, the disconnection command also initiates the printing of an estimate of the direct cost of the searching session and of the additional costs involved. For example, the command may result in a display of the costs for offline prints, for use of the communication network, or for online ordering of original publications.

Disruptions in online sessions can happen fairly often even in the more advanced online services. Users of online services with less-developed software may be literarily plagued by numerous disconnections during the session and have very low reliability of the searching process.

Figure 7-9 shows a typical accidental disconnection that may take place during the online session. Such disconnections can be quite annoying. This is especially so if the online service does not have the capacity to reconnect automatically in a reasonable time; if it does not prompt the searcher that the communication process is reinstated; or if the results of the current searching session are lost after even a brief disruption in the communication process. Also, some online services may charge the user for a session that, due to the communication interruptions, did not result in any useful information.

Often, the typical number of accidental disconnections during a session, that is the reliability of

```
:     ..off

*CONNECT TIME    0:03:35 HH:MM:SS     0.060 DEC HRS     SESSION    53*

EST A400 COST:    C-HRS     DB-ROY   CIT-ROY    COMM     TOTAL

                  $2.10     $2.70     $.04      $.48     $5.32

*SIGN-OFF  20.13.18                       06/08/84:
DATAPAC: call cleared - remote request(272)

DATAPAC: 2040 0079
```

Fig. 7-8. An example of the disconnection command and subsequent logoff procedure. BRS online service. (Courtesy of Bibliographic Retrieval Services.)

```
USER:
file lc/line

PROG:
ELAPSED TIME ON ORBIT: 0.01 HRS.
YOU ARE NOW CONNECTED TO THE LC/LINE DATABASE.
COVERS 1968 TO AUG (8200)

SS 1 /C?
USER:
me
NO CARRIER
```

Fig. 7-9. Example of accidental disconnection. ORBIT online service. (Courtesy of System Development Corporation.)

The user had only started to type the first two letters of a search statement (*me*) when a disconnect occurred. The modem informed the user that the carrier was lost.

the communication and searching processes, is a decisive factor in the user's choice of online service. The user often decides that it does not make much sense to waste too many resources on the retrieval process itself. Since it is highly probable that the online data of interest to the user exists elsewhere, it pays for him to shop around in order to achieve the most efficient online retrieval process.

CONCLUSIONS

This chapter reviews the principal steps involved in performing an online search. These steps are connecting, selecting a file, performing a search, printing out the results, and disconnecting. More complex searches may include some additional steps, such as displaying online parts of the indexes, saving a search, and running a search through several additional files.

Each online service has its own distinctive set of commands (query language) that describes these steps. In general, these relatively simple commands initiate very complex computer actions.

Chapter 8

Records, Files, and Indexes

Just as people organize their data in file folders and filing cabinets, and then index the data, so do online services in their own electronic ways.

FILE STRUCTURE

The majority of online services employ a method known as *inverted-index searching*. This method is similar to searching for a particular subject in an abstract journal.

A secondary publication normally has a special annual issue with a cumulative subject index. In such an index the number following a term indicates which record in the combined annual volume contains information described by the term (see Fig. 8-1). Thus, a user is referred to a specific record in the main publication (see Fig. 8-2).

Just as in a secondary publication, an online file consists of two primary components—a set of unit records and a set of indexes.

UNIT RECORDS

A *unit record* is the basic self-contained unit of a file. A collection of related data items arranged in this unit is intended to convey specific knowledge on a certain subject. The online search is normally intended to detect unit records that are related to a particular topic.

Different examples of unit records were shown in preceding chapters. In reference files, unit records are often called *citations* because they represent descriptions of other documents.

Let us analyze in more detail a sample bibliographic unit record, as shown in Fig. 8-3.

A typical bibliographic unit record contains data that are necessary in order to locate the original publication. It normally describes the publication content and sometimes describes the author's country of origin and organizational affiliation.

General Index of Subjects

Population—*cont.*
control, family planning—*cont.*
methods
contraceptives
oral
and
breast-milk jaundice in infants, 230
cerebral ischaemic lesions, 2810
thromboembolic disease in
Sweden, 2449
U.S.A., 1385
vitamin B6 depletion, 2811
chlormadinone, long-term effects of low dosage, 1710
mestranol and norethisterone, long-term effects, 2809
vaginal, combined with antivenereal preparations, 1822
intra-uterine devices
bacteriology, 749
in Hong Kong, reassurance home visits, 2812
post-partum, in Singapore (book review), 1009
WHO report, 228
programmes
evaluation, (1709)
in developing countries, related to demographic targets, (2447)
post-partum services, 1009
international, 232
WHO report, 480
symposium, 2442
demographic studies in
developing countries (book review), 1708
Mexico, social problems, 3582
U.K., housing and occupancy rates, 1861–1961 trends, 3581
fertility
environmental influences, (2443)

Pseudomonas **spp. infections**—*cont.*
cepacia, in hospital patients in U.S.A., Minnesota, 2956
Pseudotuberculosis *see Pasteurella* infections
Psittacosis
animal, in muskrats and snowshoe hares in Canada, 403
human *see also* Ornithosis
diagnosis, indirect haemagglutination test, 3953
endocarditis, fatal, 668
in U.S.A., 1595
Public health *see also* Medicine
book review, 467
education *see also* Medical
in Europe (book review), 2130
in U.K.
book review, 524
seminar for health education officers, 1411
human development and (WHO report), 1379
in
Africa (book review), 2093
America, Latin, and Caribbean, international aid, 2429
Australia, in Aborigines (book review), 2794
Belgium, statistics, (3200)
Brazil, São Paulo, 4
developing countries (symposium), 1013
Germany, East, (2428)
Ghana, Danfa/Ghana project, 3201, 3202
Hungary, statistics, (3), (3206)
Pakistan (conference), 2430
→ Spain, 2
U.K.
coal mining communities, 532
London, immigrant children, social and cultural factors, 1
pop festivals and, 2128, 2129
1970 report, 474
1971 report, 3578

Numbers refer to abstracts and *not* to pages (unless otherwise shown).

Fig. 8-1. A part of an annual subject index for the U.K.-published *Abstracts on Hygiene*. (Courtesy of Bureau of Hygiene and Tropical Diseases.)

For example, the term "Public Health in Spain" refers to abstract no. 2.

The original document is described by the following *fields* (distinct data elements):

- TITLE: hopefully the shortest description of the article's content.
- ABSTRACT: a summary written by an author, a publication editor, or the online service producer.
- INDEX TERMS (key words, descriptors, identifiers): thesaurus terms normally assigned by the file producer in accordance with a special thesaurus. Another kind of index term, identifiers, may be assigned by the producer freely, without the use of the thesaurus.

Additional fields of the bibliographic record may describe the following:

SOURCE of publication
AUTHORS
ORGANIZATIONAL SOURCE (corporate

1

BUREAU OF HYGIENE AND TROPICAL DISEASES

ABSTRACTS ON HYGIENE

Volume 47, No. 1 — January 1972

Community Medicine

The order in this section is:—General; Vital statistics; Epidemiology; Population; Maternal and child health; Health of students, nurses and hospital staffs; Health of old persons; Dental health; Mental health; Alcoholism, drug abuse, smoking and similar subjects; Organization of medical services; Medical care; Health education.

GENERAL

1 HOOD, C. **Social and cultural factors in health of children of immigrants.** *Arch. Dis. Childh.*, 1971, v. 46, No. 247, 371–5.

This paper, from St. Mary's Hospital Medical School, is based on a presentation given at the 41st Annual Meeting of the British Paediatric Association held at Scarborough on the 22nd–25th April, 1970. It describes a research project undertaken in Paddington, the area served by the St. Mary's Hospital Group, which has a high proportion of immigrants among its population.

The larger groups of these immigrants are from Eire and the West Indies. The study set out to investigate some West Indian children and their families, and the use that they were making of the medical services. Details are provided under the following headings: The 1-year-old children; The Mothers; Follow-up at 2½ to 3 years; Environmental and Cultural Factors; Family Patterns; Working Mothers and Child Minders; and Relationships Outside the Family.

The findings showed that there was some doubt about the quality of the diet of 1-year-old children and that they suffered more from respiratory disease and other minor illnesses. The West Indian mothers were at a disadvantage in employment, in housing and in health. In the follow-up at 2½ to 3 years, the author was disturbed by the developmental attainment of the children. The opinion is expressed that "though the West Indians use the health services at least as often as the non-West Indians . . ., we cannot be certain that they benefit in the same way as a result of these contacts", and it is concluded that "adverse environmental circumstances reinforced by cultural attitudes and patterns, many of which differ from those found in the indigenous population, play a substantial part in explaining these findings".

K. Schwarz

2 GARCÍA ORCOYEN, J. Aspectos de la sanidad española en el año 1970. **[Features of Spanish public health in 1970.]** *Revta Sanid. Hig. Públ.*, 1971, v. 45, No. 1, 1–72. English summary.

The author is the Director General of Health for Spain and gives a summary of some of the work of his department for 1970.

Among special points of interest he mentions that in the summer there was an outbreak of malaria, for which people returning from Spanish Guinea who had settled in a former endemic focus may have been responsible. No autochthonous cases were notified and all were imported or post-transfusional, and he stresses that it is essential to avoid the recruitment of blood donors from malarious areas. Of 26 cases notified 13 were due to *Plasmodium vivax*, 11 to *P. falciparum* and in the 2 remaining patients the diagnosis was clinical because they had previously been given specific treatment. Special attention was devoted to the prevention of cholera in view of the

(L 5253) C

Fig. 8-2. A page from *Abstracts on Hygiene* with the record described by the term contained in the annual subject index from Fig. 8-1. (Courtesy of Bureau of Hygiene and Tropical Diseases.)

source, author's affiliation)
LANGUAGE of original publication
NUMBER OF REFERENCES in the original publication
Different Technical
Data, such as whether the publication is in the publisher's document collection

Usually each unit record includes an *accession number* (record number), which is the unique identifying element of the record in a file. In some files, the accession number of a unit is never changed; in others, an accession number—unit record relationship may be only temporary. A unit record can normally be retrieved by its accession number.

Each file always has its own standard format for unit records. These formats are generally not consistent among different files and online services. An online service may reformat the unit records supplied by the producer for various reasons (see Fig. 8-4). Therefore, the unit records of the same file, created by the same producer but marketed through different online services, may differ in format and even in the data content. This may have serious implications for information retrieval.

A special command prints out unit records or their fields that are of interest to the searcher. The exact combination of data elements retrieved by a particular print command varies from online service to online service and sometimes even from file to file. Especially great variations in the data elements printed through the use of the print command is characteristic of nonbibliographic files.

INDEXES AND FREE-TEXT SEARCHING

Access to the individual unit records in a data processing system can be organized in several different ways.

```
-8-
ACCESSION NUMBER          12240
TITLE                     ECONOMIC AND ENVIRONMENTAL IMPACTS OF A U.S. NUCLEAR
                          MORATORIUM, 1985-2010.
AUTHORS                   WHITTLE CE; ALLEN EL; COOPER CL; EDMONDS FC; EDMONDS
                          JA; MACPHERSON HG
ORGANIZATIONAL SOURCE     INSTITUTE FOR ENERGY ANALYSIS, OAK RIDGE TN. OAK
                          RIDGE ASSOCIATED UNIVERSITIES
SOURCE                    CAMBRIDGE, MA:  MIT PRESS.  381P.
AVAILABILITY              HD 9698 U52 018 1979
INDEX TERMS               NUCLEAR POWER SOCIO ECONOMIC FACTORS; ENERGY
                          ECONOMICS; ENERGY POLICY SOCIO ECONOMIC FACTORS; RISK
                          ASSESSMENT; NUCLEAR POWER ENVIRONMENTAL ASPECTS;
                          NUCLEAR POWER HAZARDS; ENERGY SOURCE DEVELOPMENT;
                          ENERGY DEMAND FORECASTING
ABSTRACT                  STUDY CONCERNS THE ECONOMIC AND ENVIRONMENTAL
                          CONSEQUENCES OF A LIMITED NUCLEAR MORATORIUM IN THE
                          UNITED STATES.  MAJOR TOPICS INCLUDE PROJECTED ENERGY
                          AND ECONOMIC GROWTH, ALTERNATIVE LONG-RANGE ENERGY
                          FUTURES, ECONOMIC AND ENVIRONMENTAL IMPLICATIONS,
                          FUTURE U.S. ENERGY DEMAND, A COST COMPARISON OF COAL
                          AND NUCLEAR PLANTS, INVESTMENT ALTERNATIVES, REGIONAL
                          IMPACTS OF A MORATORIUM, ENVIRONMENTAL IMPLICATIONS
                          OF ALTERNATIVE ENERGY STRATEGIES, AND LONG-RANGE
                          PERSPECTIVES AND SCENARIOS FOR U.S. ENERGY FUTURES.
```

Fig. 8-3. An example of a unit record in the Print full indented format. ORBIT online service. File EBIB (Energy Bibliography & Index). (©1978-1982 by Gulf Publishing Co. Used with permission. All rights reserved.)

In this format, field names are given in full on the left side of the record.

```
    711884   58#21510
  An attempt to construct a logic of constructive mathematics.
  Studies  in  the  theory  of  algorithms and mathematical logic,  Vol.  2
(Russian)
  Markov, A. A.   (Markov, Andrei Andreevich)
  Publ: Vychisl. Centr Akad. Nauk SSSR, Moscow
  1976,    pp. 3 - 31, 157.
  Languages: Russian
  Document Type: Collection
  From the text:  ''This is the Russian version of  an  article  previously
published in French (the author, Rev. Internat.  Philos.  98 (1971),  477 -
507). There are some changes in notation,  and the present paper includes a
new,  shorter variant of the step-by-step semantic system briefly described
in the author's previous papers.''
  (For the entire collection see MR 56 #74.)
  Reviewer: From the text
  Descriptors:    *LOGIC    AND    FOUNDATIONS    -Constructive    mathematics
--Intuitionistic mathematics (02E05)
```

```
AN 7900-041613 7900.
MR 58#21510.
AU Markov-A-A.
AP Markov-Andrei-Andreevich.
TI An attempt to construct a logic of constructive mathematics.
LG RS.
TC Studies in the theory of algorithms and mathematical logic, Vol.  2
   (Russian), pp.  3 - 31, 157.
SO Vychisl. Centr Akad. Nauk SSSR, Moscow, 1976.
YR 76.
PT C.
AB From the text: ''This is the Russian version of an article
   previously published in French (the author, Rev.  Internat.  Philos.
   98 (1971), 477 - 507).  There are some changes in notation, and the
   present paper includes a new, shorter variant of the step-by-step
   semantic system briefly described in the author's previous papers.''
        (For the entire collection see MR 56 #74.).
PC (02E05) LOGIC AND FOUNDATIONS - Constructive mathematics -
   Intuitionistic mathematics.
RE From the text.
```

Fig. 8-4. Examples of format variations in the same unit record supplied by the same producer through different online services. (Courtesy of the American Mathematical Society. Database copyrighted by the American Mathematical Society. No part of this database may be duplicated in hard-copy or machine readable form without written authorization from the database supplier.)

A unit record at the top has been retrieved from File 239:Mathfile on DIALOG online service. The bottom unit record has been retrieved from File Math on BRS online service.

The *sequential access method* (serial or free-text search) is the simplest way to search the records. Searching for necessary data is done in consecutive order, starting from the first unit record in the file. This method is often used in simple computer equipment, such as word-processing machines. The main disadvantage of the sequential method is that individual records cannot be retrieved unless

Postings	Terms	Accession numbers				
18	PORTION	01252	002728	00239	000224	018701 ...
5	PORTIONS	010173	001447	010423	01005	002737
86	PORTLAND	017639	00907	00899	015540	014848 ...
1	PORTLAND CEMENT ASSOCIAT ION (CONCRETE)	00907				
1	PORTLAND GRAIN EXCHANGE (COMMODITY EXCHANG	003190				
4	PORTRAIT	003190	002201	00224	01722	
8	PORTRAITS	014545	014508	013371	005136	00207 ...
1	PORTRAY	001960				
9	PORTRAYAL	01960	010027	00983	00768	014199 ...
4	PORTRAYS	014545	014508	014504	014178	

Fig. 8-5. An example of Basic Index terms with accession numbers (schematic representation). DIALOG online service. File 114:Encyclopedia of Associations.

Only the part of the basic index that is shown in a box can be seen at the request of a searcher.

the whole file is processed. This leads to unacceptable delays when records must be retrieved quickly. Thus the sequential access method is not suited for real-time online retrieval. However, some elements of this method are used in free-text searching (*stringsearch*), which is discussed in more detail later in this chapter.

To retrieve data, online services primarily use the *index sequential access method* (inverted index searching), which is capable of the fast retrieval of individual records. The approach is based on the concept of using an index to retrieve a record by means of a key.

The general organizational principles of major online services and files are similar, even though they may differ substantially in such details as organization and content of their indexes.

Indexes are organized for certain, so-called *searchable fields* of unit records. Thus, in most bibliographic files the *Basic Index* includes words from the titles, index terms and abstracts (see Fig. 8-3). Additional indexes may be created for certain other fields. Some fields are not searchable since no indexes have been created for them.

For example, there are files in which the abstracts in the unit records are not searchable

```
? e portland

Ref  Items  Index-term
E1      18  PORTION
E2       5  PORTIONS
E3      86 *PORTLAND
E4       1  PORTLAND CEMENT ASSOCIAT
              ION (CONCRETE)
E5       1  PORTLAND GRAIN EXCHANGE
              (COMMODITY EXCHANG
E6       4  PORTRAIT
E7       8  PORTRAITS
E8       1  PORTRAY
E9       9  PORTRAYAL
E10      4  PORTRAYALS
                                    -more-
```

Fig. 8-6. An example of an online display of a basic index. DIALOG online service. File 114:Encyclopedia of Associations.

This part of the index has been retrieved online using the *expand* (e) command.

since the abstract terms are not inverted. You cannot search for the unit records in those files with terms that are included only in their abstracts.

In most online services, a special command displays a part of the file's index. This may be especially important when a searcher is looking for different variations and misspellings of the same term.

An *index* (index term file, key term file, inverted file, dictionary file) is normally created by arranging the terms of searchable fields in alphanumeric order (inversion of the fields) and attaching to each term the accession numbers of unit records in which the term may be found.

Set #1 (86 terms)	Set #2 (17 terms)
PORTLAND	**CEMENT**
00907	016104
017639	016089
00899	016083
015540	**00907**
014848	014529
00141	014508
..	..
..	..
..	..

00907
PORTLAND CEMENT ASSOCIATION (Concrete) (PCA)
5420 Old Orchard Rd., Skokie, IL 60077
(312)966-6200
Richard E. Reuss Pres.
Founded: 1916. Members: 40. Staff: 375. Manufacturers of portland cement in the U.S. and Canada. To improve and extend the uses of portland cement and concrete through market promotion, research and development, educational programs and representation with governmental entities. Conducts research on concrete technology and durability; concrete pavement design; load-bearing capacities, field performance and fire resistance of concrete; transportation, building, and structural uses of concrete. Gives lectures and demonstrations for architects, engineers, contractors, and others; provides technical information to schools and colleges; assists with instruction on improved methods of concrete design and construction. Maintains library of 10,000 volumes on cement and concrete technology. Divisions: Construction Technology Laboratories, which conduct contract research and technical services in construction materials, products, and applications. Publications: List of Member Companies Directory, irregular; also publishes a films catalog and publications catalog. Convention/Meeting: annual - always November. 1983 Nov. 14-15, Montreal, PQ, Canada; 1984 Nov. 12-13, New Orleans, LA; 1985 November 18-19, Washington, DC.
Section Heading Codes: Trade, Business and Commercial Organizations (01)

Fig. 8-7. Matching two terms with their own sets of unit record accession numbers. DIALOG online service. File 114:Encyclopedia of Association. (© 1985 Gale Research Company. All rights reserved. Reprinted by permission.)

A common accession number (*00907*, shown at the beginning of the citation) retrieves a unit record that includes both terms.

In addition to high retrieval speed, online organization of indexes for unit records allows for easy access to the records through different routes. Thus, all words in the record become equally accessible, not only a limited number of key words terms selected by an indexer as most important from his own point of view.

Such "uncontrolled" access is feared by many to be dangerous, as it may lead to "information overload" of the end-user, who, after all, can only process a limited volume of raw data. However, access to free-text data just means that the search strategy must be organized highly effectively. Providing that proper and more stringent criteria for information retrieval are selected by the searcher, the quality of the results obtained during a free-text search should generally be higher than the results of index-term searching.

In the computer's memory, an index term has *pointers* that refer the computer to the corresponding unit records. For example, such a pointer could be the accession number that uniquely identifies a unit record (see Fig. 8-5).

However, the unit record accession numbers for a term are normally not seen by the searcher when the index is displayed online. Instead, the computer may show the number of postings, or *hits*, (that is, the total number of unit records that include the term), as shown in Fig. 8-6.

In many online services, a record can also be retrieved by keying in its accession number.

If the task is to find the records which include two desirable terms, the computer does it by finding the accession numbers common to both terms (see Fig. 8-7).

In addition to the Basic Index, a bibliographic file may also have some other indexes, such as an author index, a language index, and a publication's country of origin index. The terms in these indexes are normally distinguished with special identifiers (*mnemonics*) (see Fig. 8-8).

It is useful in information retrieval to have at least a general knowledge of which fields of a unit record are represented in the Basic Index, which are in additional indexes, and which are not directly searchable. This information may help in composing a search strategy and in the choice of the terms, files, and online services.

Some files have a *word addressing* feature. They include additional information on the precise position of a word within the unit record (see Fig. 8-9).

```
? e au=doe j.e.

Ref  Items   Index-term
E1       3   AU=DOE B.
E2       1   AU=DOE DE MAINDREVILLE
                 M.
E3       3  *AU=DOE J.E.
E4       1   AU=DOE P.W.
E5       3   AU=DOE R.P.
E6       1   AU=DOE T.
E7      10   AU=DOE W.F.
E8       1   AU=DOEBBELIN W.
E9       2   AU=DOEBBER T.W.
E10      1   AU=DOEBEL K.J.
E11      1   AU=DOEBERT U.
                                          -more-

? e la=dutch

Ref  Items   Index-term
E1    3418   LA=CZECH
E2    2614   LA=DANISH
E3    5549  *LA=DUTCH
E4     252   LA=FINNISH
E5   51674   LA=FRENCH
E6   71946   LA=GERMAN
E7     639   LA=GREEK
E8     925   LA=HEBREW
E9    1650   LA=HUNGARIAN
E10     37   LA=INDONESIAN
E11  24852   LA=ITALIAN
E12  25628   LA=JAPANESE
                                          -more-
```

Fig. 8-8. Examples of online displays from non-basic indexes. DIALOG online service. File 72:EMBASE (Excerpta Medica).

These indexes have been retrieved using corresponding mnemonics (AU = for the Author Index and LA = for the Language Index). An author index is an indispensable feature for almost all the bibliographic files. However, the language identification of an original document is not always organized as a separate language index and, in many cases, is not consistent throughout a file.

```
                Set #1                              Set #2

          acid                                rain
           ..                                  ..
           ..                          1312085(004)
    1312085(003)                               ..
           ..                                  ..
           ..                                  ..
           ..                                  ..

1312085
  Effects of Acid Rain on Water Supplies in the Northeast
  Taylor, Floyd B.; Symons, George E.
  American Water Works Association Journal,   1984 VOL. 76, NO.  3 (March),
p. 34
```

Fig. 8-9. A comparison of two terms in the *basic index* that have common accession numbers with different word positions (posted here in brackets) shows that these terms are adjacent in the original unit record. DIALOG online service. File 68:Environmental Bibliography. (Courtesy of Environmental Studies Institute.)

This information can be used for *proximity searching*, or *adjacency searching*. Adjacent terms can be retrieved by locating accession numbers that are common to both terms and calculating the difference in their word positions.

Proximity searching can greatly increase the search effectiveness. It is instrumental in retrieving commonly used word combinations such as "management-by-objective" or "open-plan office." Since proximity searching requires highly sophisticated software and increased computer capabilities, it is characteristic of the more advanced retrieval systems.

In online services with simpler software, search effectiveness can sometimes be increased with the help of the *stringsearch* feature, which employs elements of the previously mentioned sequential access method.

In stringsearch, a computer cannot use indexes but instead searches for a string of characters by consecutive scanning of a subset of unit records.

```
SS 1 /C?
USER:
funds and transfer

PROG:
SS 1 PSTG (236)

SS 2 /C?
USER:
strs : funds transfer :

PROG:
(81) SEARCHED (3) MATCH.  CONT? (Y/N)

USER:
y

PROG:
(161) SEARCHED (4) MATCH.  CONT? (Y/N)

USER:
y

PROG:
SS 2 PSTG (6)
```

Fig. 8-10. A stringsearch for two adjacent words performed on the previously formed subset of unit records. ORBIT online service. File Banker.

Such a scanning process is very slow and would not be practical if a search was to be performed on the

```
SS 1 /C?
USER:
paraffin and refining

PROG:
SS 1 PSTG (62)

SS 2 /C?
USER:
strs :ane:

PROG:
(53) SEARCHED (2) MATCH.  CONT? (Y/N)

USER:
y

PROG:
SS 2 PSTG (2)

SS 3 /C?
USER:
prt ti

PROG:

-1-
TI  - API REFINING REPORT/NEW LOOK AT CETANE--1. DIESEL TRENDS PUT NEW
EMPHASIS
      ON ECONOMICS AND FUEL QUALITY

-2-
TI  - AN HP/PR SPECIAL REPORT ON REFINING PROCESS DEVELOPMENTS/PROPANE
      EXTRACTION' A WAY TO HANDLE RESIDUE
```

Fig. 8-11. A stringsearch for chemicals in a paraffin refining process that includes the name fragment *ane* describing saturated carbon-hydrogen compounds. ORBIT online service. File Aplilit. (Courtesy of American Petroleum Institute.)

whole file. Therefore, in practice, a stringsearch is performed only as a secondary search on a previously retrieved subset of unit records (see Fig. 8-10). Usually, a subset of not more than 300 unit records is recommended for a stringsearch.

Besides finding more precise combinations of terms, a stringsearch can be used to search for *word fragments* in chemical names that are not listed as separate entries in their indexes (see Fig. 8-11) or to *locate terms in fields that are not directly searchable.*

CONCLUSIONS

The structure of an online file is similar to the structure of a secondary publication. It consists of two primary components, a set of unit records and a set of indexes.

A unit record is the basic self-contained unit of a file. A collection of related data items arranged in this unit is intended to convey specific knowledge on a certain subject. An online search is normally organized to detect unit records that are related to a particular topic.

Online services primarily use inverted index searching, which is capable of the fast retrieval of individual records. The approach is based on the concept of using an index to retrieve a record by means of a key.

Chapter 9

Elements of Online Retrieval

Various features of online systems are powerful tools in information retrieval.

COMBINATORIAL LOGIC

Online information retrieval systems primarily utilize *Boolean logic* (named after the 19th century British mathematician George Boole) in order to describe the relationship between the terms selected.

Different online services may use up to a dozen *logical operators* (*Boolean operators, combinatorial operators*) to combine the terms in logical order. However, there may be slight variations in how different online services handle particular logical operators. Therefore, running the same search strategy on different online services may produce different results.

In our Subject Expert Searching Technique we use only a limited number of logic operators in such a way as to reduce the ambiguity of the search results. These operators are:

AND
OR
NOT
(w) (Proximity)
( ) (Parentheses)

The logic of Boolean operators is often illustrated with the help of Venn diagrams (introduced by John Venn).

OR Logic

Two terms combined with the OR operator retrieve a joint set of unit records that include either of the terms, as shown in Fig. 9-1.

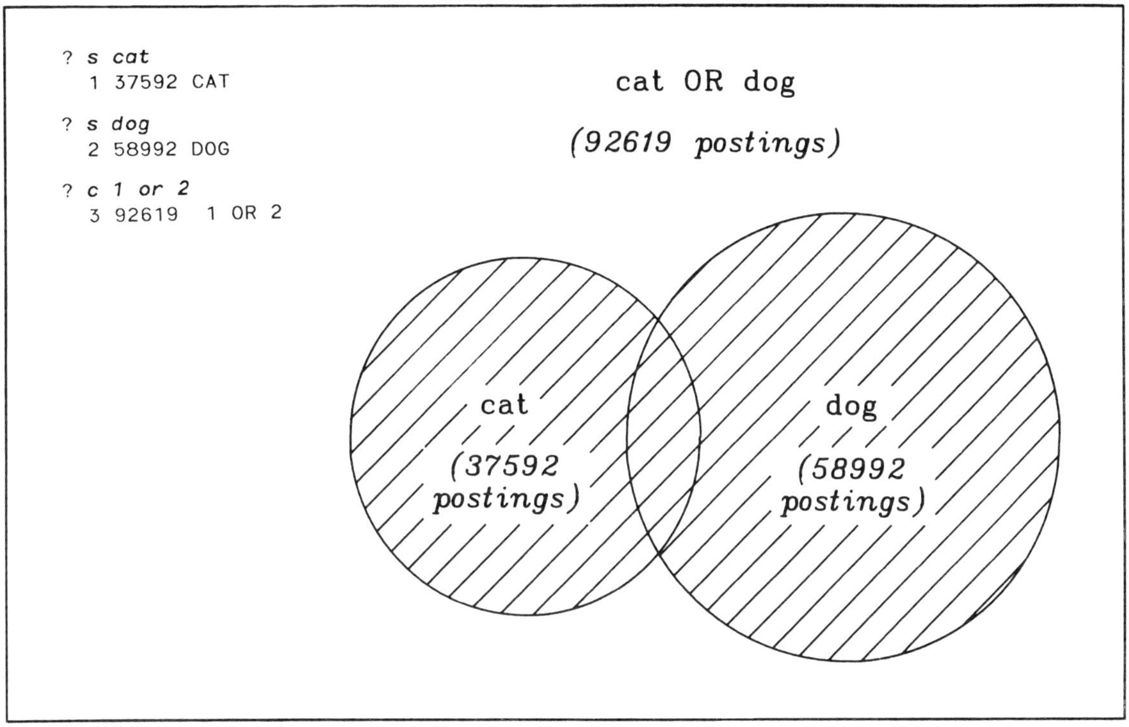

Fig. 9-1. Combining two terms with OR logic. ESA online service. File 07:BIOSIS.

(The diagram is in scale).

AND Logic

The AND operator reduces the sets of unit records to only those that include both terms as shown in Fig. 9-2.

NOT Logic

The NOT operator locates the unit records which include one term but not another term, as shown in Fig. 9-3.

The NOT operator should be used extremely cautiously because, in some cases, it may eliminate fully relevant unit records that include both desirable and undesirable subjects. Such elimination, for example, may occur when a review consists of two separate parts, one dealing with desirable and another with undesirable topics.

Proximity

A proximity search can be used to retrieve standard terms that consist of two or more separate words. Proximity may also be useful when a term could be fragmented due to the differences in spelling (see Fig. 9-4).

A proximity search can be performed for two immediately adjacent terms or for two terms that may be separated by one, two, or three separate words (see Fig. 9-5).

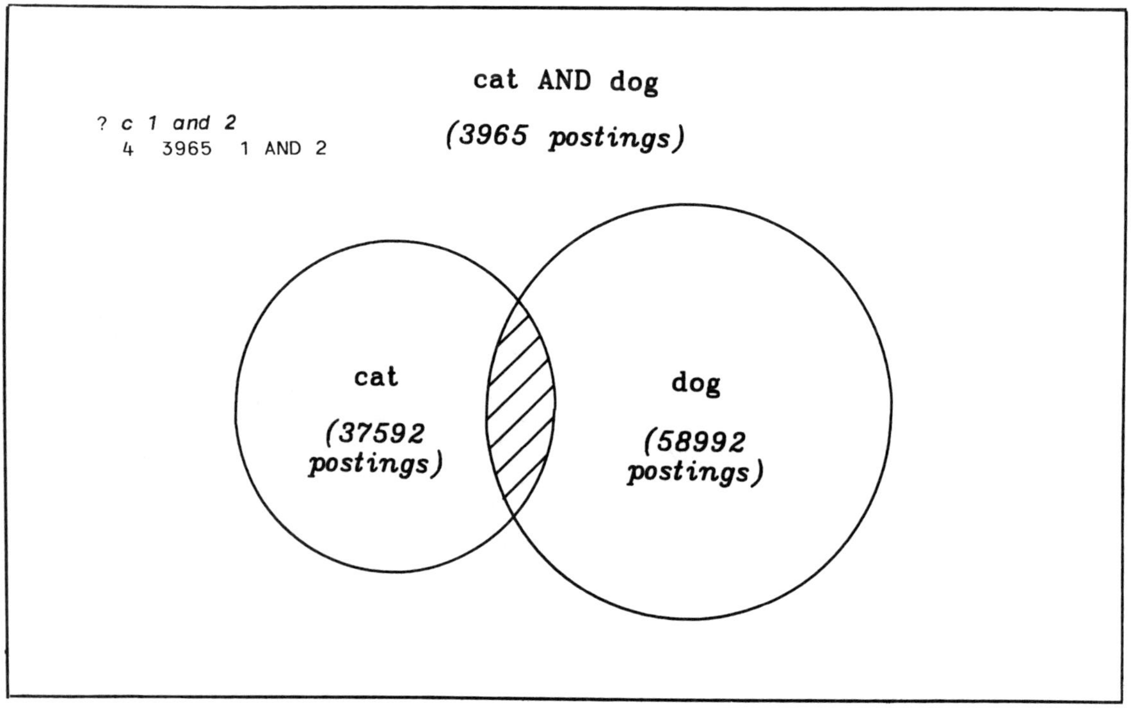

Fig. 9-2. Combining two terms with AND logic. ESA online service. File 07:BIOSIS.

The combine (*c*) command in DIALOG allows one to operate with the previously formed sets of unit records. An *AND* result is equal to the difference between the number of postings in two sets and the "OR set" of postings (that is, *37592 + 58992 − 92619 = 3965).*

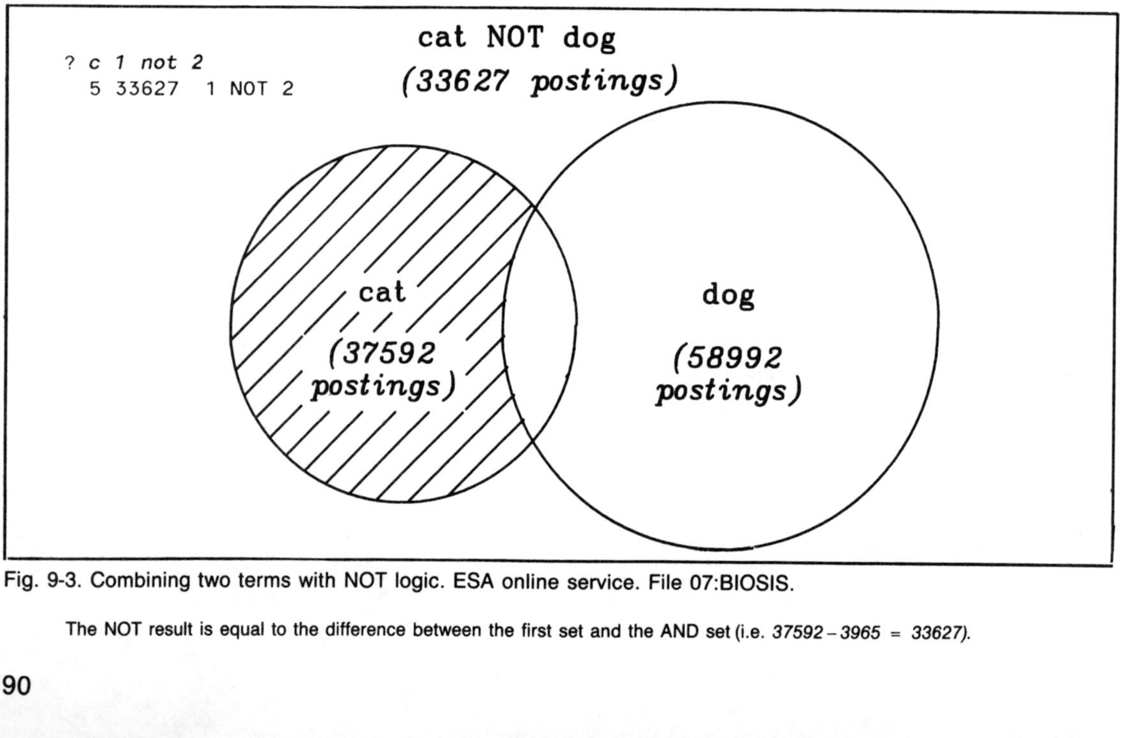

Fig. 9-3. Combining two terms with NOT logic. ESA online service. File 07:BIOSIS.

The NOT result is equal to the difference between the first set and the AND set (i.e. *37592 − 3965 = 33627).*

```
         Set Items Description
         --- ----- -----------
? s online
           1   960 ONLINE

? s on(w)line
           2  4540 ON(W)LINE

? c 1 or 2
           3  4654 1 OR 2
```

Fig. 9-4. A search for a one-word term and for a two-adjacent-word term. DIALOG online service. File 61:LISA (Library and Information Science Abstracts).

The search retrieves different spellings of the same term (online; on line; on-line). A computer normally regards a dash (-) and similar signs as a space, and such terms can be retrieved with a proximity search.

Parentheses

Parentheses are auxiliary logic operators that help to organize the priority of the logic statement components.

In our searching technique, parentheses are used for several reasons:

- They make a logic statement more clear for the user by identifying the priority of its separate components.

```
         Set Items Description
         --- ----- -----------
? s open(w)plan(w)office
           1    24 OPEN(W)PLAN(W)OFFICE

? s open(2w)office
           2   110 OPEN(2W)OFFICE
```

Fig. 9-5. A proximity search for commonly used word combinations. DIALOG online service. File 15:ABI/Inform.

The second statement retrieved such combinations of the term *open-plan office* as "open plan office", "open-space office", "open-spaced office", "open office", "open plan of office organization", and "open, flexible office layout".

- They may be useful in future modifications of a search.
- They help to avoid the ambiguity that is caused by the variations in meaning of the OR, AND, and NOT operators in different online services. These variations are due primarily to differences in execution priorities of particular operators in different online services.

Figure 9-6 illustrates the ambiguity that may result from the variation in the placement of parentheses.

THE USE OF COMBINATORIAL LOGIC

The online use of combinatorial logic is the most important characteristic of online information retrieval systems. In order to reproduce some logical operations that may take only seconds of

```
SET ITEMS DESCRIPTION (+=OR;*=AND;-=NOT)
--- ----- ------------------------------
? s cat
  1 37592 CAT

? s dog
  2 58992 DOG

? s mouse
  3139212 MOUSE

? c 1 or 2 not 3
  4 90380   1 OR 2 NOT 3

? c (1 or 2) not 3
  5 88530   (1 OR 2) NOT 3

? c 1 or (2 not 3)
  6 90380   1 OR (2 NOT 3)
```

Fig. 9-6. Examples of ambiguity resulting from certain execution priorities of the logic operators. ESA online service. File 07:BIOSIS.

In ESA online service the logic operator NOT has priority over OR. Other online services may differ in their logic operator execution priorities.

computer time, a subject specialist would be required to spend many man-hours of manual work examining secondary publication and primary literature. Moreover, many of the searches performed online would not be feasible using the manual information gathering process.

Thus, to make even the simple search comparable to one shown in Fig. 9-2, you would have to scan at least 37,592 records in the bibliography with the word *cat*, looking for those which also include the word *dog*. This would take many man-days of manual work. Manual searches that use more complex logic, word proximity, or stringsearch for word fragments maybe not feasible at all.

You should also understand that no logic operators can guarantee that only the unit records that are considered relevant by the user will be retrieved.

This may happen for several reasons:

- The meaning of a sentence depends on the combination of words used and the sentence structure. It does not depend exclusively on the words that make up the sentence. Thus, a search on the term "economic model" could retrieve a unit record whose abstract states that "economic models are not discussed in our article" (see also Fig. 9-7). A "false drop" may also be caused by an unfavorable word sequence (see Fig. 9-8).
- Scientific and professional terminology is ambiguous and there may be many meanings for the same terms. Therefore, a term with an undesirable meaning may be retrieved during a search session (see Fig. 9-9).
- A user is subjective in his definition of relevancy. What is considered relevant by one may often be considered irrelevant by another, depending

```
AN EI 8106-046073.
AU Filippi-M.  Pompoli-R.
IN Politec di Turin, Italy.
TI EVALUATION OF NOISE FROM AIR-CONDITIONING SYSTEMS--A DRAFT PROPOSAL.
SO Appl Acoust v 13 n 6 Nov-Dec 1980 p 433-440.
MJ AIR-CONDITIONING.
MN Noise.
IS 0003-682X.
CC A643.  A751.
CD AACOBL..
AB This paper discusses the practical evaluation of noise levels
   generated by air-conditioning and ventilating systems inside
   buildings.  The results of this work are incorporated in a Draft
   Italian Standard.  The criterion for evaluation is based on the
   difference between the total sound pressure level in the room where
   the noise source is working, and the background noise level.  The
   allowable difference must decrease with the value of the background
   noise level.  The measured sound pressure level is corrected
   according to the type of noise and to the acoustical characteristics
   of the room; impulsive noises should not be present in the system.
   13 refs.
LG EN..
```

Fig. 9-7. A search for BUILDING SYSTEMS GENERATING IMPULSE NOISE produces a record that states that this kind of noise is not characteristic of the air-conditioning system. BRS online service. File COMP (Compendex). (Courtesy of Engineering Information, Inc. No part of this work may be reproduced or transmitted in any form or by any means, electronic or mechanical, including photocopying or by any information storage & retrieval system, without permission in writing from Engineering Information, Inc.)

```
-1-
AN  - 75-07762
TI  - THE OSHA SCENE IN 1975: SMALL BUSINESS CONSULTATION,
      ECONOMIC-PRODUCTIVITY IMPACT, NOISE STANDARDS
AU  - HEYMAN, MATTHEW
SO  - PROFESSIONAL ENGINEER, MAR 75, V45, N3, P14 (4)
CC  - GENERAL
DT  - SURVEY REPORT
IT  - *OCCUPTN SAFETY HEALTH ACT 70; *SMALL BUSINESSES; LEGISLATION, ENV-FED;
      ECON IMPACT-POLL CONT; NOISE CONTROL STANDS; HEARING PROTECTION; U S
      OCCUPTN SAFETY HTH ADMIN
AB  - THE OCCUPATIONAL SAFETY & HEALTH ACT WILL CONTINUE TO CONCERN CONGRESS,
      LABOR, BUSINESS, AND ENGINEERING PROFESSIONS. THE DOMINANT ISSUES WILL BE
      ECONOMIC AND PRODUCTIVITY IMPACT, SMALL BUSINESS HARDSHIPS, ENGINEERING
      CONTROLS VS. PERSONAL PROTECTIVE DEVICES, THE STANDARDS-SETTING PROCESS,
      CONSULTATION PROGRAMS, AND PROBLEMS RELATED TO ENFORCEMENT AND
      ADMINISTRATION. PLANS EXIST TO ENLARGE THE $5 MILLION CONSULTATION
      PROGRAM FOR SMALL FIRMS IN STATES WHERE SAFETY AND HEALTH PROGRAMS ARE
      UNDER DIRECT CONTROL OF THE ACT. TOPICS INVOLVING THE ACT THAT ARE UP FOR
      DEBATE IN CONGRESSIONAL HEARINGS ARE REVIEWED. (1 DRAWING)
```

Fig. 9-8. A "false drop" in a search for the terms "impact(w)noise" and "standards" caused by unfavorable word sequence. ORBIT online service. File Enviroline. (Reprinted from Enviroline© EIC/Intelligence, Inc. with permission from EIC/Intelligence, Inc.)

```
File 148:TRADE AND INDUSTRY INDEX
(COPR. IAC) ** FMT 9 = $7.00 **

         Set  Items  Description
         ---  -----  -----------
         S1     212  BLIND
         S2   41451  COMPUTER?
         S3      24  BLIND AND COMPUTER?
?t3/5/1-2

 3/5/1
1148819    DATABASE: TI File 148
  Talking computers open career doors for blind
  Baltimore Business Journal  p7B  March 12  1984
  DESCRIPTORS: Computers; Private companies; Handicapped workers; Maryland
Computer Services Inc.

 3/5/2
0495338    DATABASE: MI File 47
  Laser drills 5-mil blind vias.
  Lyman, Jerry
  Electronics   v55  p48(1)  June 2  1982
  CODEN: ELECA
  SIC CODE: 3573; 3546; 3811
  DESCRIPTORS: IBM 3081 (computer)-design and construction; International
Business Machines Corp.-manufactures; lasers-industrial applications;
printed circuits-design and construction; drilling and boring
machinery-miniaturization
```

Fig. 9-9. The second record retrieved illustrates a "false drop" in a free-text search on the subject *computers and blind (persons).* DIALOG online service. File 148:Trade and Industry Index. (Courtesy of Information Access Company. ©Information Access Company.)

The false drop here occurs due to the ambiguity of scientific and technical terminology. The *blind via* in the second record is obscure technical jargon for a very small diameter hole in a printed circuit computer board. A blind via is drilled and plated through only a few of the many layers that a typical board is made of.

on educational background, experience, professional objectives, and resource limitations.

Thus, even a well-organized search will always produce a certain degree of irrelevancy in its results. With our Subject Expert Searching Technique, this should not cause significant problems because the subject expert, being involved in the different stages of a searching process, can easily distinguish between the relevant and irrelevant postings.

From another point of view, it is safe to assume that a search statement that produces only relevant results does not retrieve all the available information on the specified subject.

SAVESEARCH AND CROSS-FILE SEARCH

Savesearch and *Cross-file search* are amongst the most powerful features of modern online services. They are primarily characteristic of online services that include many files. A search performed in one file can be saved and later executed in any other file of the same online service. This could save the searcher a considerable amount of time and resources (see Fig. 9-10).

Switching from one file to another with the "prefabricated" saved search can be very fast and efficient. It is a well-known fact that most searchers are inexperienced typists. Keying in the same search again and again may be a very slow and frustrating procedure, especially if you take into account the high probability that scientific and technical terms will be misspelled.

The differences in the contents of various files may be another reason for using cross-file searching. Any one file, however large, does not represent all the information available on a given subject. Some information may be presented in various online files from different angles. Also, file contents often represents the priorities of its producers.

There are two kinds of postings that may be retrieved during a cross-file search:

- *Core information.* There is a high degree of correlation between the core documents retrieved with a cross-file search from different files.
- *Noncore information.* The correlation between different files, when a cross-file search is performed, is very low.

A search that is intended to retrieve only the core information on a given subject is indeed very poor from the point of view of the subject expert who is most interested in new unconventional ideas. Such a search does not sufficiently use the potential of online retrieval systems because the core information may, in fact, be easily accessible through more traditional routes.

Noncore information does not imply second-rate research publications. This category may include the descriptions of uncommon applications for familiar topics; the results of foreign studies that do not readily find their ways into the dominant bibliographic publications; the results of studies devoted to applications and technological know-how; and the contents of publications such as reports, theses, books, standards, and conference proceedings.

In reality, core publications do not have the inherent superiority that the term often implies. The use of nothing but core publications reflects only the experts' narrow approach. Such narrowness is unacceptable at a time when the integration of different scientific and technical disciplines is rapidly developing. Nowadays, not many professionals or scientists can afford the luxury of ignoring information available beyond a limited circle of chosen publications and scientific laboratories.

The newest and most effective way of organizing your information activity is in an "open" fash-

```
? b470;s business and law;t1/3/1

          25jun84 17:24:54 User12345
    $0.38 0.017 Hrs File1
    $0.14 Tymnet
    $0.15 1 Types
    $0.67 Estimated Total Cost

File470:Books in print - 1490-1984/MAY
(Copr. R. R. Bowker Company 1984)
        Set Items Description
        --- ----- -----------
              1296 BUSINESS
               943 LAW
           1   102  BUSINESS AND LAW
1/3/1
1018955   1058104XX
  Japanese Business Law & the Legal System
  Hahn, Eliott J.
  Quorum
  Greenwood  Date not set
  Trade price not set
  ISBN: 0-89930-047-2
  Status: Active entry
```

SELECTING THE FIRST FILE; PERFORMING A SEARCH; PRINTING THE RESULTS

```
? end/savetemp

Serial#T19P
          25jun84 17:25:15 User12345
    $0.36 0.005 Hrs File470 2 Descriptors
    $0.06 Tymnet
    $0.42 Estimated Total Cost
```

TEMPORARILY SAVING THE SEARCH

```
? b137;.exs t19p;t1/3/1

          25jun84 17:26:07 User12345
    $1.04 0.016 Hrs File470
    $0.26 Tymnet
    $1.30 Estimated Total Cost

File137:Book Review Index = 1969-83/dec
        Set Items Description
        --- ----- -----------
              3176 BUSINESS
              3614 LAW
           1    42  BUSINESS AND LAW
```

SELECTING A NEW FILE; AUTOMATICALLY EXECUTING A SAVED SEARCH; PRINTING THE RESULTS

Fig. 9-10. An example of a cross-file search with the *Savesearch* command. DIALOG online service. (Citation from File File 470 is courtesy of R.R. Bowker Company. © of R.R. Bowker, a Xerox Information Company, 1985. Citation from File 137 is © 1985 Gale Research Company. All rights reserved. Reprinted by permission. Citation from File 425 is courtesy of Carrollton Press, Inc. REMARC is a registered Trade Mark of Carrollton Press, Inc. Citation from File 90 is courtesy of Netherland Foreign Trade Agency EVD.) (Continued on page 96.)

After performing each search in a particular file, the resulting unit records can be retrieved. Note the "stacking" of the commands on one line using the semicolon.

```
1/3/1
 1281682
  Prentice-Hall Dictionary Of Business, Finance And Law
  RICE, Michael D
  Reviewed in : Choice   v21    p256   Oct 1983

? b425;.exs t19p;t1/3/1 ◄──────────────────  A NEW STEP,
                                              SIMILAR TO
          25jun84 17:27:43 User12345          THE ABOVE
    $0.42  0.009 Hrs File137 2 Descriptors
    $0.10  Tymnet
    $0.52  Estimated Total Cost

 File425:REMARC - 1970-1980 (to Z) 1984/Apr
 (Copr. Carrollton Press 1984)
          Set Items Description
          --- ----- -----------
                 781 BUSINESS
                 793 LAW
            1     11  BUSINESS AND LAW
 1/3/1
 0158070   LCCN: unk83063577
   US business law
   Treumann, Walter.
   1.- Aufl   Koln : O. Schmidt, 1978  424 p.  :  21 cm.
   LC Call No.: KF889.9.G4T73

 ? b90;.exs t19p;t1/3/1 ◄──────────────────  A NEW STEP
          25jun84 17:28:16 User12345
    $0.65  0.009 Hrs File425 2 Descriptors
    $0.08  Tymnet
    $0.25  1 Types
    $0.98  Estimated Total Cost
File90:Economic Abstracts International - 74-84/Apr
          Set Items Description
          --- ----- -----------
                8295 BUSINESS
                3871 LAW
            1    406  BUSINESS AND LAW
1/3/1
 7690191   841000191
  Dutch business law; legal,  accounting and tax aspects of business in the
Netherlands
  Schuit, S.R.;  Beek, J.M. van der;  Raap. B.K
  EDITION: 2nd ed.
  Netherlands,  Deventer,  KLuwer,  1983.  ,    592p.A5 Bibl.   Ref   ISBN:
90-6544-122-0  CATALOG NO.: 3-8769
? logoff ◄─────────────────────────────────  DISCONNECTING

          25jun84 17:28:58 User12345
    $0.68  0.009 Hrs File90 2 Descriptors
    $0.10  Tymnet
    $0.13  3 Types
    $0.91  Estimated Total Cost
 LOGOFF 17:28:59
```

Fig. 9-10. (Continued from page 95.)

ion. This means dealing as much as possible with the whole flow of scientific and technical information. This is in contrast to the more traditional "closed" organization of information activity in which only a limited number of "authoritative" sources are dealt with. Such an open organization of information activity allows the subject expert to constantly learn something new during the retrieval process and to use the associative potential of online information retrieval.

> Our searching technique, being oriented towards the cross-file search as a primary tool of information retrieval, allows you to greatly increase the efficiency and information output of online searches. It also allows you to effectively use the information from various sources that examine the problem from different angles.

> The savesearch command is very useful at various stages of the search strategy development. A strategy is not a static thing. Rather, it changes during the process of interaction between the subject expert, his professional environment, the task, his knowledge, and the system. You cannot expect that the first version of any search strategy will be successful immediately and forever.

In order to develop a successful search, it may be necessary to temporarily save an unsatisfactory search. Later only those parts of it that are useful will be executed. These useful parts of the old search supplemented with new terms and logical statements will constitute a new search statement. This new version of a search can, in turn, be saved as a *clean* search.

> In our technique, the process of developing a clean search statement from the first inadequate version is called *online adaptation* of the search strategy.

There are numerous reasons to carry on an online adaptation, including the following:

- A search strategy as a whole may be unsuccessful (not enough or too many postings may be retrieved with it).
- Some terms in the initial search strategy statement may be misspelled.
- A successful search strategy may result in finding new terms or new concepts that should be incorporated into the strategy.

The use of the savesearch command in the online adaptation of a search strategy is demonstrated in Fig. 9-11.

TRUNCATION

Truncation is one more powerful feature that is characteristic of the computerized information retrieval systems. Truncation saves significant time and allows the searcher to retrieve different variations of the same term, some of which may neither be apparent nor expected by him. Truncation allows the searcher to retrieve all those words that include common fragments. All the unit records that include these common word fragments are automatically ORed during the retrieval process.

The term *truncation* normally refers to right hand truncation when the search is performed on the initial part of a word and retrieves terms with any number of characters following the truncation sign (see Fig. 9-12).

Sometimes truncation leads to retrieval of unnecessarily long terms. Therefore, some systems allow the searcher to specify how many characters to the right are to be included in the retrieved terms. This kind of truncation is primarily done with short words that constitute the initial part of irrelevant terms (see Fig. 9-13).

```
? b10 <------------------------------------------------    SELECTING THE
                                                           FIRST FILE
           30jun84 16:45:18 User12345
     $0.49  0.046 Hrs File1 1 Descriptor
     $0.37  Tymnet
     $0.86  Estimated Total Cost

File10:AGRICOLA - 1979-84/May & 1979 Supplemental
See File 110(thru 1978)
         Set Items Description
         --- ----- -----------
? s seeding? <-----------------------------------------    RETRIEVING WITH
                                                           THE FIRST TERM
           1    787 SEEDING?

? s sowing? <------------------------------------------    RETRIEVING WITH
                                                           THE SECOND TERM
           2   1831 SOWING?

? s imlanting <----------------------------------------    THE TERM IS
                                                           MISSPELLED
           3      0 IMLANTING                              BY THE SEARCHER

? s implanting? <--------------------------------------    RETRIEVING WITH
                                                           PROPERLY
           4     15 IMPLANTING?                            SPELLED TERM

? c1-4/or <--------------------------------------------    COMBINING
                                                           TERMS WITH THE
           5   2617 1-4/OR                                 OR OPERATOR

? end/savetemp <---------------------------------------    TEMPORARILY
                                                           SAVING
Serial#T021 (T-ZERO-2-1)                                   THE SEARCH
           30jun84 16:46:47 User12345
     $0.91  0.026 Hrs File10 3 Descriptors
     $0.21  Tymnet
     $1.12  Estimated Total Cost

? pr 5/5/1-10 <----------------------------------------    PRINTING
                                                           THE RESULTS
Printed5/5/1-10 Estimated Cost: $1.00 (To cancel, enter PR-)   OFFLINE



? b110;.exs t021/1-2 <---------------------------------    EXECUTING THE
                                                           SAVED SEARCH
           30jun84 16:48:17 User12345                      IN A NEW FILE
     $0.91  0.026 Hrs File10                               (ONLY 2 FIRST
     $0.21  Tymnet                                         LINES OF THE
     $1.12  Estimated Total Cost                           SAVED SEARCH
                                                           ARE EXECUTED)
File110:AGRICOLA - 70-78/Dec
See File 10(Current)
         Set Items Description
         --- ----- -----------
           1   1129 SEEDING?
           2   2066 SOWING?
```

Fig 9-11. An example of the use of *savesearch* in the online adaptation of a search strategy. DIALOG online service. Files 10, 110:Agricola. (Continued on page 99.)

```
? .exs t021/4-4  ◄——————  EXECUTING THE FOURTH LINE OF THE SAVED SEARCH

            3    20 IMPLANTING?

? s farming?  ◄——————  RETRIEVING WITH A NEW TERM NOT USED IN THE PREVIOUS SEARCH

            4  5405 FARMING?

? c1-4/or  ◄——————  COMBINING A NEW SET WITH THE OR OPERATOR

            5  8579 1-4/OR

? end/save  ◄——————  PERMANENTLY SAVING THE SEARCH

Serial#8Y35
            30jun84 16:50:07 User12345
     $1.12  0.032 Hrs File110 4 Descriptors
     $0.26  Tymnet
     $1.38  Estimated Total Cost
```

Fig. 9-11. (Continued from page 98.)

```
? e electromechanic  ◄——————  DISPLAYING NEIGHBOURING TERMS FROM THE BASIC INDEX

Ref  Items  Index-term
E1       1  ELECTROENCEPHALOGRAPHIC
E2       1  ELECTROENCEPHALOGRAPHY
E3         *ELECTROMECHANIC
E4      25  ELECTROMECHANICAL
E5       3  ELECTROMECHANICAL AIDS
E6       1  ELECTROMECHANICAL
              TECHNICIANS
E7      22  ELECTROMECHANICAL
              TECHNOLOGY
E8       1  ELECTROMECHANICS
E9       1  ELECTROMECHANISMS
E10    199  ELECTRONIC
                                    -more-

? s e4-e8  ◄——————  RETRIEVING AND COMBINING WITH THE OR OPERATOR ALL THE TERMS LISTED UNDER CERTAIN NUMBERS

 1     25 E4-E8
          E3: ELECTROMECHANIC

? s electromechanic?  ◄——————  TRUNCATION AUTOMATICALLY COMBINES THE TERMS WITH THE OR OPERATOR

           2     25 ELECTROMECHANIC?
```

Fig. 9-12. An example of (right hand) truncation. DIALOG online service. File 9:AIM/ARM (1967-76 file on vocational and technical education).

In DIALOG online service a truncation sign is signified by a question mark. The online display of the basic index shows which words or multi-word terms are included in single word postings.

```
? e dog

Ref  Items    Index-term                          RT
E1       1    DOFLEINIA
E2       1    DOFTANAE
E3   21270   *DOG                                  1
 .
E11    271    DOGFISH
E12      1    DOGFISHES
                                              -more-

? p

Ref  Items    Index-term
E31      3    DOGO

E37  11341    DOGS
E38      1    DOGSTAIL

                                              -more-

? s e3 or e37

                  21270 DOG
                  11341 DOGS
              1 26049   E3 OR E37

? s dog? ?

              2 26052 DOG? ?

? s dog?

              3 26542 DOG?
```

Fig. 9-13. An example of truncation of a limited number of characters. DIALOG online service. File 55:BIOSIS Previews (1969-76).

In this online service, the searcher can specify the desired number of truncated characters by placing the necessary number of question marks after the initial word fragment followed by a space and a single question mark. The online display of the basic index shows that only terms *e3*, *e31*, and *e37* are included in the selected set *2*.

Internal truncation is the main way of retrieving different spellings of the same term. Some online services permit internal truncation to substitute for any number of characters or even for a lack of characters (see Fig. 9-14); others substitute a truncation sign only for one character (see Fig. 9-15).

Some systems or files also allow *left-hand truncation.* This may be done either through index words (see Fig. 9-16) or with the help of a stringsearch command (as was previously shown in Fig. 8-11). Left-hand truncation can be used to search for term fragments or to study certain linguistic patterns.

Different kinds of truncation can sometimes be used together at the same time. This gives additional possibilities to online searching.

In our Subject Expert Searching Technique, truncation plays a prominent part. However, it should be used

```
SS 1 /C?
USER:
labo:r

PROG:
MM (LABO:R) (6)
     1      2224     LABOR/BI
     2         1     LABOR/IW
     3         1     LABORER/BI
     4     23841     LABOUR/BI
     5     22104     LABOUR/IW
     6         5     LABOURER/BI
SPECIFY NUMBERS, ALL, OR NONE

USER:
all

PROG:
SS 1 PSTG (24558)

SS 2 /C?
USER:
labor or labour

PROG:
SS 2 PSTG (24557)
```

Fig. 9-14. An example of internal truncation. ORBIT online service. File Labordoc.

In this online service, the internal truncation sign *:* substitutes for several characters or for a lack of characters.

```
SET ITEMS DESCRIPTION (+=OR;*=AND;-=NOT)
--- ----- ------------------------------
? s wom?n
  1   494 WOM?N

? s woman
  2    31 WOMAN

? s women
  3   470 WOMEN

? c 1 or 2 or 3
  4   494  1 OR 2 OR 3


? s labo?r
  5   707 LABO?R

? s labor
  6    29 LABOR

? s labour
  7   707 LABOUR

? c 5 or 6 or 7
  8   729  5 OR 6 OR 7
```

Fig. 9-15. Examples of internal truncation. ESA online service. File 40:CISDOC.

In this online service, the internal truncation sign *?* substitutes for any one character *but not* for the lack of characters.

```
SS 1 /C?
USER:
:photometry

PROG:
MM (:PHOTOMETRY) (16)
     1       3    CHROMATOSPECTROPHOTOMETRY/BI
     2       5    CHRONOPHOTOMETRY/BI
     3     101    CYTOPHOTOMETRY/BI
     4       4    CYTOSPECTROPHOTOMETRY/BI
     5       8    FLUOROPHOTOMETRY/BI
     6       3    HISTOPHOTOMETRY/BI
     7       3    ISOPHOTOMETRY/BI
     8      29    MICROPHOTOMETRY/BI
     9      33    MICROSPECTROPHOTOMETRY/BI
    10    4417    PHOTOMETRY/BI
    11       3    SEPCTROPHOTOMETRY/BI
    12       3    SPECTOPHOTOMETRY/BI
    13    7118    SPECTROPHOTOMETRY/BI
    14       3    SPECTRPHOTOMETRY/BI
    15       3    SPETROPHOTOMETRY/BI
    16       4    THERMOPHOTOMETRY/BI
SPECIFY NUMBERS, ALL, OR NONE

USER:
all

PROG:
SS 1 PSTG (9721)
```

Fig. 9-16. Left hand truncation performed in indexes. ORBIT online service. File CAS77.

Note that terms *11, 12, 14,* and *15* represent various misspellings of term *13.*

cautiously since truncation may lead to the retrieval of irrelevant terms and cause ambiguity of search results. This can be avoided through the proper use of search logic and the cautious application of truncation procedures.

CONCLUSIONS

This chapter describes the steps involved in the organization of online searching. Also described are such important features of modern information retrieval systems as proximity searching, stringsearch, use of logical operators, cross-file searching, and truncation. The information that is given relates primarily to the effective use of these features in our Subject Expert Searching Technique.

Chapter 10

The End-User, The Intermediary, and Information Evaluation

The first information retrieval systems were brought online with the expectation that this new medium would be widely used by subject experts themselves without the use of intermediaries. The benefit of such a wide use of online systems would be threefold:

1. It would greatly increase the effectiveness of information gathering.
2. It would enhance the role of information materials in the everyday activity of professionals and scientists.
3. Computerized information systems would become a truly mass information medium with significantly reduced search costs and improved quality of service. This would result from a greatly increased demand for such services and further advancements in online information retrieval systems.

END-USERS ONLINE

Unfortunately, this potential of online retrieval has not yet fully materialized. According to some studies, only 10 percent of all searches are being performed by the end-users themselves.

> One of the main reasons for such a situation is that the existing online searching techniques were primarily developed by and for the *intermediary* (delegated user, information specialist, reference librarian, information broker). These techniques are generally unsuitable for use by subject experts themselves.

A contributing factor is that the evaluation of the results of an online search is primarily conducted by the intermediaries or according to some criteria developed by intermediaries. These criteria, in general, do not represent the real needs of the end-users well; neither do they reflect the objective nature of the information retrieval process.

Below we examine how the evaluation of search

results is presently organized, and why such an organization is not effective in the online retrieval of useful information.

PRECISION AND RECALL

Various criteria are used to evaluate the quality of an online search. Most popular among them are *precision* and *recall* ratios.

Precision is a measure of the search's success in not retrieving irrelevant unit records.

Recall is a measure of the search's success in retrieving relevant unit records.

For the moment, let us not consider what "relevant" means, or who determines if a record is relevant.

Suppose that a search resulted in retrieval of k records, m of which were somehow recognized as being relevant to the subject of the search. Also somehow it is known that the total number of relevant records in the file is n (see Fig. 10-1). Then the *precision ratio* is determined as:

$$P = \frac{m}{k} \bullet 100\%;$$

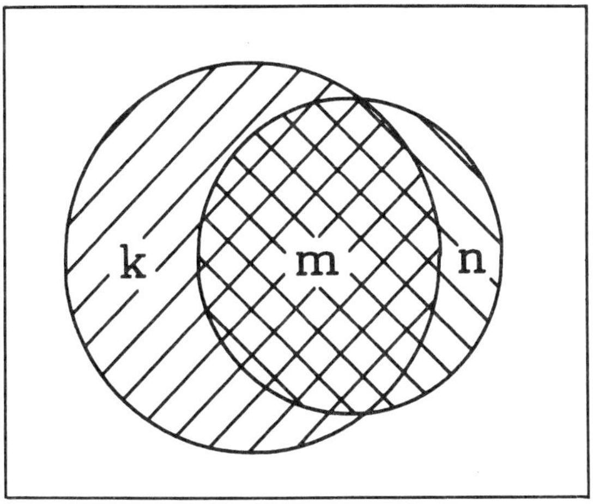

Fig. 10-1. Venn diagram illustrating the meaning of recall and precision ratios.

The circle k represents the number of records retrieved by the search; the circle n represents the number of relevant records in the file; the cross-hatched area m represents the number of relevant records retrieved by the search.

and the *recall ratio* is determined as

$$R = \frac{m}{n} \bullet 100\%.$$

Thus, if a search resulted in the retrieval of k = 50 unit records, m = 30 of which are found to be relevant, but in reality the file includes n = 40 relevant unit records, the precision ratio of such a search is:

$$P = \frac{m}{k} \bullet 100\% = \frac{30}{50} \bullet 100\% = 60\%;$$

that is, 60% of the unit records retrieved were found relevant; whereas, the recall ratio is:

$$R = \frac{m}{n} \bullet 100\% = \frac{30}{40} \bullet 100\% = 75\%;$$

that is, only 75% of the relevant unit records were retrieved from the file.

> In practice, precision and recall are inversely related. This means that improvements in precision tends to deteriorate recall.

Precision is sometimes increased by either of the following methods:

- Artificially increasing the number of unit records considered relevant (increasing n, so that m tends to cover k fully). As a result, all the retrieved postings could be considered relevant to the subject of a search. This approach is characteristic primarily of the inexperienced user who does not know the information potential of online retrieval systems. As an example, such a searcher may be willing to accept as relevant many thousands of postings as the result of a search on the term "computer," when in fact he only needs information on the "new operating system for IBM PC."

- Artificially narrowing a search strategy (reducing k) by limiting it only to the terms that are known beforehand to be in the file, and that are known to be exclusively used in that subject area. In most cases, this approach does not permit the retrieval of all the relevant information on the subject. Many terms have various technical meanings that are clear only in the context of a particular subject area. Choosing too narrow a search strategy is often characteristic of the nonsubject specialist who does not know the field he is searching and therefore relies exclusively on the index terms from the file thesaurus.

In both cases, recall would probably suffer as it is unlikely that all necessary information would be retrieved.

Conversely, recall ratio may be increased by either of the following methods:

- Artificially decreasing the number of unit records considered relevant (decreasing n). This may actually happen when there is no deep exploration of the search subject, and only the "core" information is sought online and everything else is assumed to be of low value.
- Widening a search strategy (increasing k) to include as many terms as possible, even if it means a lot of additional "noise" and as a result sharply reduced precision.

It is easy to see that the concepts of recall and-precision are related to the cost structure of an online search. Generally speaking, the direct cost of a search is increased with higher recall and lower precision and is decreased with lower recall and higher precision.

> **The evaluation of the success of a search exclusively in precision-recall terms is being criticized more and more often as being inadequate.**

Inappropriate use of precision and recall ratios can be illustrated by a search performed by an intermediary at the request of a subject expert that results in retrieval of only the articles written by the end-user himself. Such a search would have a precision ratio equal to 1. However, the information value of such a search to the end-user is nil since no new knowledge is created in this case.

This example, of course, is not in conflict with the fact that the retrieval of known articles is sometimes desirable as a means of evaluating a new search strategy. Lack of retrieval of any articles but the author's own proves either that no other work has been published in this area of knowledge or that the author uses nonstandard terminology.

INFORMATION AND THE INTERMEDIARY

The main thrust of existing searching techniques seems to be to increase the formal precision of a search without the necessity of making the hard decision whether the data retrieved are really relevant to the end-user's problem. This is important for those intermediaries who cannot distinguish between the relevant and irrelevant postings in a particular subject area. As a result, online retrieval systems, query languages, file contents, retrieval techniques, training, and various reference manuals are organized around the concept of increasing precision.

Of course, an intermediary who is himself an expert in the subject area would search in a far more flexible fashion, and for him, a decision on the relevance of retrieved data is much easier to make. Such a specialist could bring his own expertise and knowledge of the subject to the development of the search strategy. He can usually be expected to conduct information gathering on his own including, if necessary, abandoning a losing search strategy or choosing a different area of searching. Such an expert in the search subject should not, strictly speaking, be considered to be a delegated searcher.

Unfortunately, a classical intermediary by definition cannot be expected to be an expert in all of the areas that he searches online. A good intermediary is usually expected to be acquainted with the terminology of the searches that he performs; however, familiarity with the terminology is not always sufficient for the development of a winning search strategy and especially for the retrieval of data with high information value to the end-user.

Historically, the use of intermediaries may have resulted from the following situation. The traditionally printed secondary publications (abstract journals) were accumulated mainly in special and public libraries rather than in the private library of a subject expert himself. The subject expert was expected to visit the library in order to get this kind of information.

Online information retrieval systems were introduced in the 1960's by the publishers of secondary publications, primarily to expedite their compilation, typesetting, and printing. For example, MEDLARS, one of the first widely used online services, was developed for the United States National Library of Medicine in 1963 chiefly as a publishing system. Machine readable tapes were created to produce the monthly *Index Medicus*. It was logical that these tapes were subsequently used to perform online searching.

However, the tradition of marketing this important new service through libraries has remained, even though the objective reasons for such an intermediary role have long since disappeared. Unlike abstract journals, online information does not need storage space on library shelves.

INFORMATION AND THE END-USER

A number of studies on the criteria by which a user selects a source of information when faced with a question to answer were described by Lancaster (F.W. Lancaster. *Information Retrieval Systems: Characteristics, Testing and Evaluation*. J. Wiley & Sons, Inc, New York, 1979). These studies highlight the principal drawbacks to gathering information in the traditional way. These drawbacks include the following:

- Selection of an information source by the professional is based almost exclusively on its accessibility.
- Accessibility of personal files and informal information channels was ranked very high over the accessibility of library materials. This is primarily due to convenience and ease-of-use factors, but also because the libraries were judged difficult to use and "generally unpleasant to work in . . .."
- Many professionals feel that more information reaches them than they can possibly handle. Thus they emphasize the need for more selectivity in information services.
- Information services need to be more up-to-date, especially in the sciences.

In addition, Lancaster noted that large segments of the population are completely unaware of many currently existing information services.

> The main advantages of the introduction of modern online information retrieval systems for the end-user lie in their capability to overcome the two main problems Lancaster and other scholars noted, namely accessibility and selectivity.

Even today, online searching and ordering allow the user access to a significant portion of the world's literature. *Its accessibility compares favorably with traditional methods of information gathering through a library or an archive*. Ironically, accessibility to outside materials is in reality comparable to and sometimes even better than accessibility to the materials in the user's own private library.

> The existing intermediary-oriented organization of online information activities does not have any objective basis. In fact, the most attractive feature of computerized information services is that, if properly organized, online information activities considerably reduce the dependence of the subject expert on traditional library services.
>
> Thus, the wider availability of information about online services can also greatly facilitate their active use by sub-

ject experts and the general public. The direct involvement of subject experts in online retrieval may be encouraged by the development of online searching techniques that are specially suited for their use.

ARGUMENTS AGAINST DIRECT INVOLVEMENT

Various arguments have been raised against the direct involvement of end-users in online searching. Below, we examine the validity of some of these arguments.

1. **The time of the subject expert is valuable, and he can spend it in a more efficient way by delegating his information gathering activities to an experienced intermediary.**

There are several reasons for which direct involvement of the subject expert in computerized information gathering is not only desirable, but really necessary.

First, information gathering has always been considered an integral part of the subject expert's activities. For example, generations of European-trained scientists were brought up on the notion that at least the first year of work on a PhD dissertation has to be spent in the university library, gathering and analyzing information.

The habit of keeping track of everything that is going on in a particular area would remain with a scholar, however prominent, during his scientific career. Thus, Einstein read most of the physics papers that were published in languages he knew up to the time that the information explosion made such an activity impossible to carry on.

Even though work in the traditional library usually constitutes only a part of the subject expert's information gathering effort, this part was always considered to be vitally important. Online information gathering permits the subject expert to conduct such work much more effectively, regardless of his physical location. It also allows him to gather various data that are not usually found in the traditional library.

Second, in today's world it is not easy to find an experienced intermediary who knows the subject of research well, whose services are affordable to the subject expert, and who is readily available at any time when there is a need.

The subject expert, of course, usually has a desire to gather as many resources and sources of outside help as is possible. The reality of life, however, rarely permits the modern professional the luxury of using all the support that his work requires. More often than not, he has to settle for what he can afford. This frequently means that a modern subject expert is forced to conduct on his own many support tasks that were traditionally performed by intermediaries.

A more competitive environment in many subject areas means that the expert cannot afford to overlook important information. Many shorter projects mean that a mistake made by supporting staff may not be easily spotted. With the help of computers it may be as fast and even more effective for a subject expert to perform a task properly himself than to fix somebody else's faulty work.

Unfortunately, it looks like the classical information gathering intermediary, a research librarian, is going to be included in the list of endangered species in the very near future; the same list that already includes representatives of white-collar professions such as secretaries, mail carriers, and bank tellers. At best, the number of research librarians will decrease; their role will be redefined to that of consultants on the use of computerized services; and many of their present day duties will be taken over by others, mainly by subject experts and by EDP specialists.

2. **The use of intermediaries normally cuts the direct cost of online searching.**

This argument, of course, does not take into account the fact that the information activities of a subject expert are only a part of a much more complex task. A "cheap" search by an intermediary is almost always done at the expense of quality of the information retrieved. The cost of not retrieving a document that would significantly advance the user's work and eliminate duplication of other specialist's efforts may indeed be very high in comparison with the direct cost of an information search.

In information gathering, both the direct and indirect costs should be taken into account. Evaluation of indirect costs requires taking into account the involvement of the end-user. It is in principle impossible to skip all end-user involvement in information gathering. Regardless of whether the end-user is physically present during the searching process, he inevitably has to be involved at the information-creation stage, when the data obtained during the search are accepted and become information or are rejected and sent to the garbage bin.

Unfortunately, a familiar picture is one of an end-user screening a pile of useless references resulting from a search performed by an intermediary. Sometimes, being impressed with the size of an "information file" that he obtained in response to his request, the user may not realize that he has to spend considerable time and effort in order to retrieve something useful from this file. The final results frequently do not merit the effort.

However, since the library usually provides "free service," professionals or scientists often tend to be quite tolerant about the results that they get from it. After all, the search was performed "for free." One does not expect too much from a giveaway in any case . . .

The end-user may not realize that such a search is always very expensive for him, who, in most cases, has to pay the final bill. In profit-oriented organizations the funds for the library service are coming from the overhead necessitated by the very same professionals who are the users of information. In nonprofit organizations, the library is amongst the services that compete for a share of the budget pie. An unproductive search requires spending of resources that can be more effectively used elsewhere.

It is quite ironic that for an average professional user computerized data retrieval may actually result in decreased quality of gathered information. At the same time, this information is frequently obtained at a cost that has skyrocketed compared with the cost of old-fashioned manual data retrieval.

Such a situation, however, is not inevitable. It could be changed by organizing the overall information gathering activity in a fashion that is productive and takes into account the objectives and working habits of the end-user.

When both direct and indirect costs are taken into account, as well as the costs of duplicating results published elsewhere, it is clear that the active involvement of the end-user in searching activities may well be one of the best expenditures of his time, efforts, and resources.

3. **A subject expert should not be allowed to deal directly with online services because he may not know how to deal with sophisticated computers and thus could make expensive mistakes.**

This argument does not withstand any serious criticism. The subject expert more and more often deals with computers in his primary activities. For example, data analysis and presentation, programming, and the use of electronic mail are no less sophisticated or expensive tasks than online searching. A professional is usually a mature enough individual to make the necessary judgments concerning the cost of a planned search and to handle relevant search expenses. In most cases the cost of a search is but a small fraction of the subject expert's overall budget.

4. **With the rapid changes in computerized services, only a frequent user can keep abreast of new developments and correspondingly adjust his search strategies.**

This argument is essentially valid. In practice, however, due to wide proliferation in online services and to their rapid changes, even the intermediary who frequently uses online systems may not be as up-to-date on recent online developments as is desirable. Furthermore, an intermediary may have a number of biases limiting the information value of his search. He may choose one online service over another because of any of the following reasons:

- Its online rate may be lower and thus the search may be marginally cheaper.
- He is accustomed to the query language of a particular online service.
- He is not sufficiently informed on the topic of the search, and he does not realize that a particular file may have useful information on the subject.

Often, a commercial information broker has established a business relationship with a particular online information service, which he would automatically choose over any competitors.

ARGUMENTS IN FAVOR OF DIRECT INVOLVEMENT

The main arguments for the active participation of the subject expert in online searching relate to the objective qualities of information. These arguments include the following:

- The transformation of information into new knowledge is impossible without the active participation of a subject expert in information retrieval.
- There is an interdependence between the primary professional activity and its supportive information gathering process. Information gathering is not a truly independent process.
- In any kind of creative activity, the final results are not determined before the creative act starts. Even if a person who is going to create a new document is fairly certain what kind of text he is going to create, life invariably introduces some changes to his preliminary plans. The resulting document almost always constitutes a compromise between the original idea and the existing resources or other external factors. Thus, end-user's needs cannot always be explicitly expressed beforehand. Indeed, his expressed demands may significantly differ from his real or latent needs. Frequently, the expressed demands of the end-user are much narrower than his real needs. Often this is because the end-user does not really know the information potential of existing information retrieval systems until the moment of his personal involvement in the search.
- The use of an intermediary does not allow the subject expert to realize and effectively use the associative, educational, and scientific potential of the information gathering process.
- An effective search strategy development process is, in principle, iterative. During an online session, a searcher has to revise and adjust his criteria concerning the relevancy and information value of the results obtained a number of times. Sometimes it means selecting a wider subject in order to find at least some information. On the other hand, limiting the scope of a search brings down the number of unit records retrieved. In some cases, a search subject has to be shifted into a new area because no information was found. In other cases, information found online prompts the examination of the same problem from a different angle. Of course, an intermediary cannot be expected to evaluate the information potential of data obtained during a search session.

The evaluation of search results exclusively in terms of precision, recall, and search cost only exaggerates these problems. These terms may, with certain reservations, be suitable to evaluate only searches performed by an intermediary. Such characteristics are not suitable to evaluate the searches performed by the subject expert himself as a part of his wider professional or scientific activities.

> The direct involvement of the subject expert in online searching allows a great improvement in information quality and time response, and a significant reduction in overall costs.

INTERMEDIARIES AND CONTROLLED VOCABULARY

Existing searching techniques are often geared to the use of controlled vocabulary obtained by searching through index terms. The supposed justification for such a procedure is that it increases search precision, even if it results in a deterioration in search recall.

In practice, the following basic steps in a searching procedure are usually followed:

1. The end-user formulates his request to an intermediary, often in a written form.
2. The intermediary chooses several files that he believes are relevant to the problem.
3. Using a file thesaurus, the intermediary composes a search for this file and runs it. This search cannot be effectively used in any other file unless it shares a common thesaurus with the original file for which the search was created.
4. Results of the search are submitted to the end-user.

When an intermediary conducts an online search himself, he has to decide on his own whether or not a retrieved record is relevant. Unless an intermediary is an expert in the search area, he has to rely heavily on index terms (keyword searching) in order to achieve a satisfactory precision ratio. Nevertheless, the results of such index term searching are often poor and do not sufficiently contribute towards the direct task or long-term objectives of the subject expert.

In defining both precision and recall ratios, the term *relevant records* is used. For example, the use of a recall ratio implies that a set of relevant records in the file can be easily identified and that the total number of these records can be easily determined. Such an approach can only be realized when an individual unit record is identified by somebody as being relevant. This identification is presumably based on common, undisputed knowledge.

This, in practice, is often done using standard index terms (subject headings, controlled vocabulary terms, descriptors, keywords) taken from a standardized thesaurus and attached by the producer's indexers to each record. The deficiencies of the controlled vocabulary method are frequently discussed in the special literature and will be illustrated further.

In many cases index terms inadequately describe the information contents of the original documents or are not sufficient for retrieval of useful information. This may happen for a number of reasons:

- Index terms are often attached by bibliographers or other information specialists with insufficient knowledge of the subject being indexed. It also seems that in many cases the indexer does not scan the whole document when he assigns controlled terms. According to data first produced by C. Montgomery and D.R. Swanson (*American Documentation*, October 1962, v.13, no.4, p.359-366) and later confirmed by several other scholars, the controlled terms are often assigned based on the title words of the original publication only. This may lead to misindexing of the article—not such an infrequent phenomenon, illustrated well in Figs. 10-2 and 10-3).
- Even an experienced literature analyst who is employed as an indexer may miss quite important points of discussion. After all, even for the expert working in the same scientific area, it is difficult to comprehend a new idea at a first glance. The history of science knows many examples in which important discoveries were misunderstood by contemporaries, and rediscovered only years later.
- Often, a standardized thesaurus is itself inadequate—either too primitive or lacking the terminology to describe a new concept. Thus, even if a file covers a relatively narrow and specialized area of knowledge, its subject indexes may be imprecise, inconsistent, or incomplete. Also, no index terms can totally substitute for all text words from the original document (or even the words from a title and an abstract), but they can only compliment the text words. After all, the title and the abstract are created by the authors themselves who in most cases are quite capable of realizing what the highlights of their publications are.
- Index searching effectively restricts a searcher to a meaningful use of only those files for which he has thesauri. The number of such files is always limited because, with the exception of a

```
77003221
  DEAF  LEADING THE DUMB A DIRECTIVE INTERVIEW FOR HELPING THE NAIVE PERSON
IDENTIFY IMPAIRMENTS IN SPEECH TRANSMISSION SYSTEMS
  DUNCANSON J P; LAHDER D Z
  J ACOUST SOC AM   58 (SUPPL 1). 1975 S129   CODEN: JASMA
  Descriptors: ABSTRACT TELEPHONE
  Concept Codes: BIOPHYS-BIOENGINEERING(*10511); EXTERN EFF-SONICS,ULTRASO-
NICS(10608); SENSE ORGANS-PATHOLOGY(*20006); SENSE ORGANS-DEAFNSS,SPEECH,H-
EAR(*20008)
  Biosystematic Codes: HOMINIDAE(86215)
```

Fig. 10-2. An example of blatant misindexing of the original document. DIALOG online service. File 55:BIOSIS Previews 77-80. (Courtesy of BioSciences Information Service. © 1984 BioSciences Information Service.)

Index terms included in a citation to a conference presentation identify its subject as having something to do with the *hard of hearing.* A brief examination of the conference proceedings showed that the original publication is devoted to telecommunications and its contents have absolutely nothing to do with the assigned controlled vocabulary terms.

```
924669   DA
  SELF-LEVELLING HEADLAMPS.  A SIMPLIFIED SYSTEM IN PROTOTYPE FORM
  Scott, David; Scott , David
  Motor n3467 p41 (30 Nov 1968)  1968 Monograph HS-004 424
  AVAILABLE FROM: see publication see publication
  SUBFILE: HSL
  System  holds  the beams on the road regardless of weight in trunk of car
or number of back-seat passengers.  It also controls aim of the lamps.   It
is constructed of levers, springs, piano wire, and pendulums.
DESCRIPTORS:
  HEADLIGHTS
  LEVELING
  LEVERS
  PENDULUMS
  REAR COMPARTMENTS
  REAR SEATS
  SPRINGS (ELESTIC)


220625   DA
  SELF-LEVELLING HEADLAMPS-A SIMPLIFIED SYSTEM IN PROTOTYPE FORM
  Scott, D
  Motor /UK/  Nov 1968 No 3467, P 41
  SUBFILE: HRIS; HSL
  SYSTEM  HOLDS  THE BEAMS ON THE ROAD REGARDLESS OF WEIGHT IN TRUNK OF CAR
OR NUMBER OF BACK-SEAT PASSENGERS. IT ALSO CONTROLS AIM OF THE LAMPS. IT IS
CONSTRUCTED OF LEVERS, SPRINGS, PIANO WIRE, AND PENDULUMS. /HSL/
DESCRIPTORS:
  CONTROL SYSTEMS
  HEADLIGHTS
  HUMAN FACTORS
  LEVELING
  SAFETY
```

Fig. 10-3. An example of inconsistent indexing of the same document in the same file. DIALOG online service. File 63:TRIS (Transportation Research Information Service).

Duplicate records from the same file with numerous variations in the title, index terms, listed subfiles, and even the author's name and publication source. Apparently, both unit records found their way to the online file from different secondary publications.

```
Ref Items   Index-term
E1       3  TELECOMMUNCATION SYSTEMS
E2       4  TELECOMMUNCATION SYSTEMS
              , SATELLITE RELAY
E3       2 *TELECOMMUNCATIONS
E4       1  TELECOMMUNCATIONS
              SECURITY
E5       1  TELECOMMUNIC
E6       1  TELECOMMUNIC; ATION
              CABLES
E7       2  TELECOMMUNICAITON
E8       1  TELECOMMUNICAITON SYSTEM
              S, SATELLITE RELAY
                                  -more-

? p

Ref Items   Index-term
E9    1597  TELECOMMUNICATION
```

Fig. 10-4. Examples of various misspellings amongst index terms. DIALOG online service. File 165:Ei Engineering Meetings.

few leading producers, published thesauri of the several hundred files currently available online are not easily accessible. The list of index terms that a searcher eventually gets from the producer is often outdated, not sufficiently developed, or not comprehensive enough.

- Misspellings are frequent among the index terms as well as free-text words. According to data from different sources cited by J. Fedorowicz (Journal of the American Society of *Information Sciences*, July 1982, p.223-232):
  - An estimated 80 percent of all text words that occur only once or twice in the Medline database are misspelled.
  - On average, the proportion of misspellings amongst Medline text words and index terms listed in the inverted files is about 31-38 percent.
  - One study showed that the average misspelling rate for index terms listed in the inverted file varied from 0.5 to 23 percent among eleven different files (see Figs. 9-16 and 10-4 for illustrations of this point).

However, misspellings among free-text words may not be as critical during the searching procedure as they are for the standard index terms. This is because the most important words in many unit records are repeated several times. In contrast, index terms taken from a controlled vocabulary do not have such a high degree of redundancy. This fails to provide the additional assurance that a relevant unit record will indeed be retrieved.

Figure 10-5 shows that redundancy in important concept terms allows retrieval of records even with misspelled free-text words. Despite the fact that the misspelled word *telecommunications* in the title is very important for tracking down the unit record, its misspelling is not very critical for the record's retrieval. This is because a similar term *communication devices* is also listed as a descriptor.

However, if a word in a descriptor were misspelled as in Fig. 10-6, the unit record would be difficult to track down with a search limited to the controlled vocabulary only.

The most fundamental problem with the use of controlled vocabulary both for the search and for relevancy decisions is, however, that it does not work well with *problem solving by association.*

Problem solving by association means the capability of a subject expert to associate two seemingly unrelated pieces of information, producing something totally new. This characteristic may well be the most valuable and sought after skill in the expert.

By using only controlled terms, a subject expert inevitably limits his capability to gather information. A critical factor is the ability of the producer's indexer (information analyst) to appreciate the information contents and value of the document and to express them with the use of a limited number of prescribed terms.

Furthermore, exclusive use of controlled terms in searching also tends to narrow the subject ex-

```
0184010          Y 3.T 22/2-2 T 22/6/no. 2
  Selected teleco,mmunicationd devices for hearing-impaired persons
/.Virginia W. Stern, Martha Ross Redden
  Stern, Virginia W.
  Redden, Martha Ross.
  Corporate Source: United States. Congress. Office of Technology
Assessment. Project for the Handicapped in Science (American Association
for the Advancement of Science)
  Series: Technology and handicapped people ; background paper #2
  Washington, D.C. : Congress of the U.S., Office of Technology Assessment
: For sale by the Supt. of Docs., U.S. G.P.O., 1982. vii, 20 p. ; 26 cm.
  Publication Date(s): 1982
  LCCN: gp 83016478
  Price: $3.50
  Place of Publication: District of Columbia   GPO Item No.: 1070-M
  Stock No.: 052-003-00898-0; GPO
  Technical Report No.: OTA-BP-H-16
  Languages: English
  Document Type: Monograph
  "Project on the Handicapped in Science, Office of Opportunities, American
Association for the Advancement of Science." "December 1982."
Bibliography: p. 19-20.
  Descriptors: Aged, Deaf; Children, Deaf; Deaf-Means of communication;
Communication devices for the disabled
```

Fig. 10-5. An example of misspelling of a word in the title of a unit record. DIALOG online service. File 66:GPO Monthly Catalog.

```
AN   - 82-062414
CN   - 01255
TI   - RANDOM TDMA ACCESS PROTOCOL WITH APPLICATION TO MULTI BEAM SATELLITES
AU   - KAWAI, M; SAADAWI, T. N; SCHILLING, D. L
OS   - NIPPON TELEGR & TELEPH PUBLIC CORP, KANAGAWA, JPN
SO   - CONFERENCE RECORD - INTERNATIONAL CONFERENCE ON COMMUNICATIONS V 3. PUBL
       BY IEEE, NEW YORK, NY, USA. AVAILABLE FROM IEEE SERV CENT (CAT N
       82CH1766-5), PISCATAWAY, NJ, USA P 7F. 3. 1-7F. 3. 5; 1982
LA   - ENGLISH
JC   - CICCDV
CONF- CONFERENCE RECORD - IEEE INTERNATIONAL CONFERENCE ON COMMUNICATIONS:
       ICC'82, THE DIGITAL REVOLUTION, PHILADELPHIA, PA, USA 1982 JUN 13-17
SP   - IEEE COMMUN SOC, NEW YORK, NY, USA; IEEE PHILADELPHIA SECT, PA, USA; IEEE
       AEROSP AND ELECTRON SOC, NEW YORK, NY, USA; IEEE GEOSCI AND REMOTE SENS
       SOC, NEW YORK, NY, USA
IT   - *TELECOMMUNICAITON SYSTEMS, SATELLITE RELAY
ST   - RANDOM ACCESS TDMA PROTOCOL; MULTIBEAM SATELLITES; AVERAGE PACKET
       QUEUEING DELAY; ON-BOARD DELAY; AVERAGE NUMBER OF RETRANSMISSIONS
CC   - 716
```

Fig. 10-6. An example of the misspelling of a word in the descriptor of a unit record. ORBIT online service. File EIMET (Ei Engineering Meetings). (Courtesy of Engineering Information, Inc. No part of this work may be reproduced or transmitted in any form or by any means, electronic or mechanical, including photocopying or by any information storage & retrieval system, without permission in writing from Engineering Information, Inc.)

pert's professional horizon by filtering out a potential for achieving associative results during the information retrieval process.

Thus, the use of an intermediary involves not just one, but several "filters" in the information retrieval process (see Fig. 10-7):

1. The only records retrieved from a file with the help of controlled vocabulary may be the ones that were assigned the proper index terms in the first place. Thus, the qualifications of the producer's indexer who assigned the index terms to the records in the file, his knowledge of the subject, and his conceptual analysis of the original record are crucial for the success of the information retrieval process. These characteristics of the indexer are thus indirectly involved in the online information retrieval process.
2. Since in most of the cases the intermediary's knowledge of the subject area is at best very general, he has to rely exclusively on the index terms that are found in the thesaurus of the file that he is going to search. This thesaurus may not be well enough developed to express the subject of the search.
3. Characteristics of an online system, such as the power of the query language, the versatility of the software, and the user-friendliness of the interaction process, may greatly enhance the searching. On the other hand, outdated software and a poor query language may be major obstacles to an effective information retrieval process, both for a delegated searcher and for an end-user, albeit in different fashions. Sometimes, a particular file is worth searching, but the recommended searching procedure encourages use of esoteric commands, mnemonics, and tags. To master the knowledge sufficient to search such a file requires extended time and effort, a rare luxury even for the intermediary who is frequently involved in the searching process and is familiar with dozens of files.
4. When building a strategy of information retrieval, an intermediary limits retrieved data

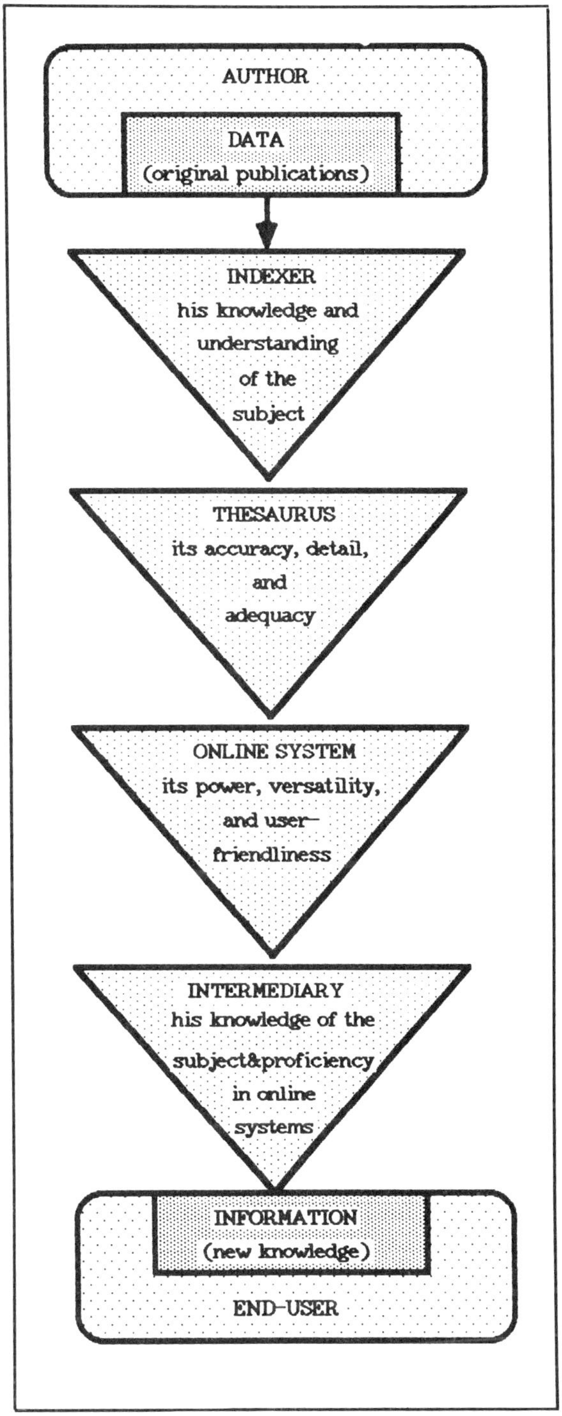

Fig. 10-7. Various "filters" involved in the information retrieval process.

to his understanding of the request of the end-user, his knowledge of the search subject, and his abilities to establish associative relationships between the various concepts that constitute a search request.

In contrast, by performing the search himself and actively using information provided by the author, the subject expert is able to establish important direct links with the state of knowledge in a particular subject area, as well as with the author's original thoughts. The index terms in this case may add some important dimensions to the original publication, but cannot substitute for its meaning.

THE END-USER AND FREE-TEXT SEARCHING

The use of *free-text searching* (natural language, text-word searching) is given preference in our searching technique for the following reasons:

- Free-text searching allows full realization of the potential of computerized information retrieval systems. As was noted above, it is often not feasible to search for nonindexed text words in traditionally printed secondary publications. Computerized information retrieval allows you to perform logical operations that are unthinkable with traditional bibliographies. This is especially important at a time of rapid proliferation of scientific and technical knowledge and development of new multidisciplinary fields.
- Free-text searching permits effective cross-file searching. Cross-file searching may save considerable time for a subject expert, whereas the development of individual searches for each separate file may be long and expensive. Also, typing in a search only once is preferable to typing in individual searches one-by-one.

The use of free-text searching does not mean that index terms are totally ignored. On the contrary, in most online services the basic index includes all the text words and index terms. In such a case, free-text searching also retrieves index terms. The resulting increase in recall may be quite significant, especially in new areas with insufficiently established terminology (see Fig. 10-8).

On the other hand, the searcher does not have to rely totally on index terms, as they constitute only a part of the basic index used in the search.

It is sometimes claimed that exclusive use of controlled vocabulary may increase the recall ratio to a significant degree; however, such claims do not have any objective basis. In numerous comparative tests, such as those described by C. Cleverdon (*Journal of Documentation*, March 1970, v.26, no.1, p.55-67) or E.M. Keen (*Journal of Documentation*, March 1973, v.29, no.1, p.1-35), free-text searching performed at least as well, and sometimes better, than searching with any controlled vocabulary.

The sole reliance on index terms increases the probability of missing relevant unit records; whereas in the cases of free-text cross-file searching with the same search strategy, there is a reasonable chance that a unit record misspelled in one file will be retrieved in another file. Thus, the overall reliability of cross-file searching should be higher than the reliability of separate searches performed on a limited number of files.

INFORMATION VALUE AND THE SUBJECT EXPERT'S OBJECTIVES

As was noted previously, a particular search may formally have high precision and recall ratios, but its true information value for a subject expert could be negligible. Thus, information value is a highly subjective term. The information value of the search results cannot be evaluated by anyone but the end-user himself. As is well-known, one person's garbage is another person's treasure (and vice versa)! The results are also individual because the work of a subject expert is highly individual and cannot be fully reproduced by any other expert even

```
ENTER DATA BASE NAME:     rbot

* THIS DATABASE IS OWNED BY CINCINNATI MILACRON MARKETING CO.
* COPYRIGHT 1984. *

BRS/RBOT/JUL 1984
BRS - SEARCH MODE  - ENTER QUERY

     1:     flexible-manufacturing
     RESULT         5

     2:     flexible adj manufacturing
     RESULT       419

     3:     2 not 1
     RESULT       414

     4:     ..print 3 all/doc=1

      1

 AN R84060127.
 AU KOENIGSAECKER, GEORGE J.
 TI ROBOT CELLS FORM FLEXIBLE WELDING SYSTEMS.
 IN ADVANCED ROBOTICS CORPORATION.
 SO PRODUCTION ENGINEERING, VOLUME 31, NUMBER 6, JUNE 1984, PP 68-73.
 CD PENGDA. ISSN: 0146-1737.
 LG EN.
 PT J.
 PD 1984.
 DE INDUSTRIAL ROBOTS.  WELDING.  ARC WELDING.  MANUFACTURING SYSTEMS.
 ID CELLULAR MANUFACTURING.  FLEXIBLE MANUFACTURING SYSTEMS.  FMS.
 AB THE FULLY INTEGRATED ROBOT WORK CELL IS A FLEXIBLE MANUFACTURING
    SYSTEM THAT CAN CUT COSTS AND BOOST PRODUCTIVITY IN PRODUCTION ARC
    WELDING.  BUT A SYSTEMS ORIENTED MANUFACTURING PHILOSOPHY IS NEEDED
    TO APPLY ROBOT WORK CELLS EFFECTIVELY.
 LN CIC.

                END OF DOCUMENTS
```

Fig. 10-8. An example of free-text searching versus index term searching. BRS online service. File RBOT. (Courtesy of Cincinnati Milacron Industries, Inc.)

Out of *419* records that include the terms FLEXIBLE MANUFACTURING somewhere in the text, only 5 records were explicitly assigned this term as a descriptor. Note that in this record FLEXIBLE MANUFACTURING is also assigned as an *identifier* (ID). Identifiers are usually not controlled vocabulary terms. Being assigned by the indexers more freely than the descriptors are, they may better represent nonstandard terminology that is characteristic of new ideas.

with a comparable knowledge of the subject.

Being a part of an expert's primary professional activity, the information gathering process should be evaluated based on the following:

- The *immediate task* of the subject expert, that is, what kind of a search on a particular topic is needed in order to solve a particular problem.
- The *long-term objectives* of the subject expert himself, that is, to what extent the strategy and results of the particular search could be useful in the future to the subject expert. If a search

has a high long-term potential from the subject expert's point of view, and the first results of the topic search are highly encouraging, there may be merit in performing a wider or deeper search in that particular subject or moving into a related area to broaden a search.

- The *resource limitations* that only the subject expert himself can evaluate. The subject expert must balance the immediate task and the long-term objectives against the search cost in order to decide whether a search should be aborted, modified, or further developed.

The Subject Expert Searching Technique allows the immediate task of a particular project to conform with the long-term objectives of a subject expert, taking into account the usual resource limitations.

It is clear that the end-user cannot be expected to possess a detailed knowledge of various online services, query languages, and file contents. It does not mean, however, that effective information retrieval for him is not possible. On the contrary, by organizing a proper searching process and by extensive use of his knowledge in the search area, a subject expert can often gather information more effectively than can an intermediary.

Our Subject Expert Searching Technique allows the end-user to organize a search in such a fashion as to use the benefits of his knowledge of the subject rather than a detailed knowledge of the esoteric commands that are characteristic of a particular online service or a particular file.

MICROCOMPUTERS AS "SUPERINTERMEDIARIES"

Several microcomputer programs are intended to simplify the online searching procedure. They are specifically oriented for use with some of the most popular online services. These software packages are meant to be employed as intermediaries, making the searching procedure easier for the online searcher. Even though the idea is in principle laudable, its implementations are not at present powerful or user-friendly enough to be really helpful, nor do they provide the required degree of flexibility.

Sci-Mate, a "universal online searcher," is a menu-driven communication software package produced by the Philadelphia-based Institute for Scientific Information (ISI). In addition to automating connection/disconnection procedures and data capturing, it allows the user to employ a "universal" language in communicating with several online services. The five online services included (DIALOG, MEDLARS, BRS, ORBIT, and the ISI SEARCH NETWORK) were selected based on their popularity among the research community.

For some searchers, the universal language will make it easier to communicate with various online services that have different query languages. Others may find unacceptable certain limitations that this software may impose on the searcher.

The Santa Clara, California-based Menlo Corporation recently developed another microcomputer software package, *In-Search,* which also acts as an intermediary between the searcher and the online service. At present, this window-organized menu-driven software can connect the user only with the DIALOG, although negotiations are in progress with several other online services.

In-Search provides broad-term subject guides for different databases available on DIALOG. Thus, a searcher is presented with a list of files that deal directly with a certain subject area. This feature may be attractive to a new searcher. The user, however, should not rely exclusively on files that deal directly with the subject area. As our own experience shows, general subject files may have at least as much and often much more information on a given subject. The selection of files is a very important part of the subject expert's activity.

A convenient feature of In-Search is information on the contents and price structure of the individual files. Another convenient feature for the user is that he can formulate his search strategy statement before he connects online. When the online session starts, the microcomputer simply sends a prefabricated statement to the host computer.

It is not clear, however, whether the necessity to adapt the search strategy while online (described in more detail further in this book) may be effectively realized with this software.

> The user should be aware that as with any intermediary, a computerized software package is there only to assist him in his information gathering activities. However sophisticated it is, it cannot replace the user himself in building or adapting a search strategy statement or in deciding about the relevancy of a particular record to his problems.

CONCLUSIONS

Specialists and the general public are very much unaware of the potential of contemporary information retrieval systems. Even if they do know about the existence and the potential of such systems, there are certain barriers that prevent professionals and scientists from their active use.

This chapter describes the terms *precision* and *recall* which are often used in the evaluation of the results of a search. These concepts are related to the cost structure of an online search.

Commonly used searching techniques are aimed primarily at increased search precision even if it means a decrease in search recall. One of the primary reasons for such a situation is the fact that these techniques were primarily developed for the special intermediary and are generally unsuitable for use by the subject expert himself.

Online retrieval systems, query languages, file contents, retrieval techniques, training, and various reference manuals are also organized around the concept of increasing precision. This is because the intermediary often cannot properly distinguish between the relevant and irrelevant postings and has to rely on standard terminology (controlled vocabulary terms) attached by the producer to each record.

However, such an "intermediary-oriented" organization of online information activities does not have any objective basis. In fact, the most attractive feature of computerized information services for the subject expert is that online information activities reduce his reliance on the traditional library services. They also allow a great improvement in effectiveness and time response, and provide a significant reduction in cost of information gathering.

By using only controlled terms, a subject expert limits his ability to process information to the ability of the producer's indexers (which may be very low). This may formally increase the recall ratio to a significant degree, but also tends to narrow the subject expert's professional horizon by filtering out any potential for associative problem-solving based on the retrieved information.

Our Subject Expert Searching Technique allows the subject expert to match, under usual resource limitations, the immediate task of a particular project with his long-term objectives. The technique does not rely exclusively on index searching. Since a subject expert takes an active part in the searching process, he can easily distinguish between relevant and irrelevant postings.

Chapter 11

Building a Strategy

The development of an effective search strategy is one of the most important tasks for the subject expert in his information gathering activities.

A SEARCH STRATEGY AND ITS OBJECTIVES

The existing literature on information retrieval systems often defines a search strategy as a group of terms and computer commands, each of which specifies a certain class of unit records that can be retrieved from a file.

For example, a search for all unit records that are "assigned to the class" *cat* can be performed. The a priori existence of such a class is normally implied.

In our searching technique we call a collection of terms and commands a *search strategy statement* (search statement). Here the search strategy statement constitutes an important part, albeit only a part, of the overall search strategy.

> We define the *search strategy* as the science and art of using the subject knowledge of an expert and the potential of information retrieval systems. This is done in order to achieve both the immediate and long-term objectives of the subject expert and also to assure cost-effectiveness in his overall professional activity.

Our definition significantly differs from the conventional approach in several ways:

- The participation of the subject expert is seen as an essential element of a search. This, by the way, does not mean that a search is run exclusively by the subject expert himself. On the contrary, the technique allows the rationalization of the searching process to such an extent that most of the work that does not require an expert's participation could be done by support staff.
- The search strategy is not specifically oriented

to any online service or file but can be easily transformed for use on a particular online service.

- The cost-effectiveness of a search is seen as a part of the primary professional objectives of a subject expert. This allows the subject expert to balance the cost of the search against the professional value of the information retrieved.
- Assignment to a class (the classification process) for the retrieved unit records is primarily done by the subject expert himself. In addition to the index terms, the subject expert may use valuable information provided by authors (for example, words from titles and abstracts). This is in contrast to the conventional approach in which an intermediary has to limit himself to a classification developed and assigned by the indexers. Essentially, the subject expert creates his own classification scheme, which is especially important in cases of new knowledge, where existing classifications are not substantially developed. Several online modifications of a search strategy statement are usually necessary in order to transform the subject expert's objectives into a successful search strategy.
- When a search does not result in retrieval of any unit record, it is totally unsuccessful as far as an intermediary is concerned. However, from the subject expert's point of view the nonexistence of a certain class of unit records may indeed be quite informative. It may indicate, for example, that a certain area of knowledge is not sufficiently developed, and that the subject expert must deal with a far wider problem if he wishes to use existing knowledge. Or, it may be an indicator of the fact that the subject expert does not have knowledge of the working terminology in the area of the search. Also, new results in some areas may not be published for military, proprietary, or political reasons. Establishing proof of the existence of a certain class of unit records (or formulating a substitute in the case when such a class does not exist) is an integral part of any normal analytical process.
- A subject expert should never assume that the class of the unit records described by his search strategy statement necessarily exist. Neither should he presume that the results that he obtained with his search strategy are the only possible solutions for his problem. The most elegant and effective solutions are often taken from outside of a narrow circle of "core information," and may be unearthed only when the subject expert uses his power of associative logic. In any case, finding a new approach to a problem is to some degree a matter of luck and to a great degree the result of a large intellectual effort. The online interaction with the computer should at least help the subject expert to formulate clearly for himself the objectives of his investigation. The additional benefits of formulating the search strategy for the subsequent activity of the subject expert cannot be overestimated both for his immediate and long-term objectives.

The *Subject Expert Searching Technique* encompasses three kinds of searches:

- The subject search
- The name search
- The citation search

If necessary, all three kinds of searches can be combined within one search strategy statement.

We assume that a *subject search* is the most important kind of information activity for a subject expert in pursuing his professional objectives. Most of the following material relates primarily to the organization of such searches.

A *subject search* can be further divided into a *topical search* and a *comprehensive search.*

A topical search (demand search, problem-solving search, selective search) is narrow and loosely corresponds to the immediate task of the subject expert. It is primarily intended to solve a specific problem.

A comprehensive search (bibliographic search, retrospective search) is much wider, corresponds more to the long-term objectives of the subject expert, and may also be useful in compiling a "master bibliography" on the subject.

These are two extremes, although in practice

one cannot draw a definite boundary between them.

In this book we do not really examine the case of a quick reference inquiry, in which a user is trying to locate a document for which he already knows a title or an author. After all, according to our definition, such a search does not create information. Therefore, a topical search in many cases can easily be handled by an intermediary.

THE SEARCH STRATEGY FORM

In the Subject Expert Searching Technique a search strategy is organized with the help of a special *search strategy form* (see the Appendix). The information requested here is essential and therefore the form should be clearly and concisely filled out.

Date. Certain elements of a search (such as the availability of specific terms) depend on the date when the search was originally organized. Also, the results of the search depend on when the search was run. Therefore, a date is an important characteristic of a search and should be recorded.

Name. Searching is an art as much as it is a science and thus bears the individual characteristics of the person who created it. In the subject expert's practice, a search is often a part of a much wider professional project that may be conducted over a long time period and may involve a group of specialists. Therefore, it is important to include the name of the person who created the search so that its rationale and direction will be clear for any specialist who may be later involved in the same project. This allows for a better understanding of the direction and limitations of the search, and for its adaptation for other purposes.

Topic. This part should have two components, the name of the project to which the search belongs and the name of the search itself. It is desirable that the name of a search be clear, short, and captivating. At this stage of the search, it is unrealistic to expect that the search name will correspond totally to the search strategy statement. Such an attempt would impose an unnecessary limitation on the search strategy.

Online Services to be Searched. The choice of online services depends on many factors such as the kind of information sought, the searcher's knowledge of a particular online service, and time and money resources, The Subject Expert Search Technique allows the construction of a search strategy statement in such a way that it can easily be modified for use on a new online service.

An inexperienced user who does not know the information potential of different online services and files could discuss this problem with online service specialists. In most cases online services have their own free-of-charge hot lines (action desks, online service searching consultants) and may provide the user with useful information on the files. Based on this information, the user can make decisions concerning whether or not to use a specific online service and file; however, the user's own statistics on search results accumulated over time are the best guidance in this selection process.

It is advisable for a searcher to choose one online service as his *"principal resource" online service.* The choice of the principal online service depends on factors such as the following:

- The number of useful files in the online service
- The quality of the online service software, and the simplicity and flexibility of its query language
- The average price of file searching
- The accessibility and reliability of the online service, and the level of support services

Online information retrieval is a very competitive business. Online services with software that is more sophisticated and frequently updated usually provide better, more efficient, and cheaper service. Being financially successful, they continue to attract more and more files. The situation may be the reverse if the online service has outdated software. As a result, there may be slight variations in prices for searching the same file through different online services.

The difference in search cost may be further increased because of the variation in operational speed and service reliability of the different online services. In the end, the cost of the same search performed on the same file through different online services may vary by as much as 100 percent.

After it has been run through several files on the principal online service, the search can be modified in order to be run on other files through other online services.

Search Strategy Statement. The statement is organized with the help of a special form or table. The process of organizing the search strategy statement will be analyzed in more detail in the following chapters.

Online Service/File Tables. The tables should list all online services and files that might be accessed by the searcher. This list is important in the process of running a search, recording the number of unit records resulting from the search, and planning future searches.

THE SEARCH STRATEGY STATEMENT, CONCEPTS, AND TERMS

In our searching technique we define the *search strategy statement* as a specified collection of terms and logical operators arranged by a subject expert in order to retrieve certain kinds of information.

The complexity of a search strategy statement is directly related to the breadth of the search subject and to the degree that the terminology used is standardized. Thus, if the subject of a search is very narrow and the search terminology is so well-defined and established that each term represents only one concept, the search strategy statement may be very simple. Conversely, the ambiguity in terminology or the complexity of the search subject may result in an unavoidably complex search strategy statement.

In the search statement a set of terms constitute a concept that represents a common idea. A search statement in our technique would generally consist of one to three concepts.

A concept can be described by one word, such as *PREGNANCY* or by several words, such as *OCCUPATIONAL HEALTH AND SAFETY*. It is not the name of the concept that is all-important, but rather it is the single idea corresponding to this concept that is the focus of attention.

It is very seldom that only one term gives exhaustive coverage of a particular concept used in scientific or professional activities. More often, a concept is described by a number of terms. This is true for the following reasons:

- Different terms such as *pregnancy* or *pregnant* may have the same root. Various grammatical structures, singular and plural forms, and different spellings of the same terms can normally be retrieved by using truncation:
- New areas of knowledge may not have standardized terminology:
- Various scientific schools, especially those located in different countries, may use different terms:
- Multidisciplinary areas are often created as a result of the merging of several well established disciplines. Each of those disciplines tends to introduce terminology that is based on its own tradition.

Building a set of terms (term expansion) for a particular concept is one of the most important tasks of the subject expert in the information retrieval process. The careful completion of this task is of paramount importance in assuring the success of a search strategy. Such a task should not be entrusted to anybody else.

Developing a set of terms is time consuming and requires a detailed knowledge of the subject. Frequently it is an ongoing process. In order to produce an effective search, a given set of terms may have to be adapted to the requirements of a particular information retrieval system. Such a set may later be supplemented by a number of new terms.

In developing a set of terms based on a particular concept,the subject expert may use different sources, including the following:

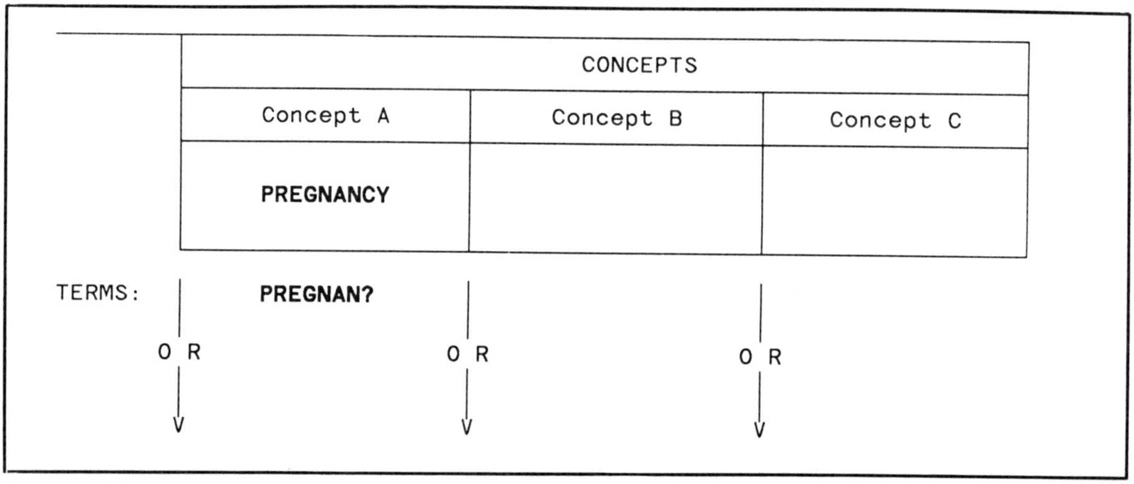

Fig. 11-1. The search strategy form with a truncated term that relates to the first concept.

- Personal knowledge
- General dictionaries
- Specialized subject dictionaries
- General thesauri
- Specialized subject thesauri
- Hierarchical thesauri of online files in printed or electronic form
- Special literature on the subject, such as manuals, handbooks, and literature reviews
- Results of previous searches

Let us examine the process of compiling a set of terms, using the example of the concept PREGNANCY.

It is clear that the first term included in our list should be PREGNAN? (A question mark here means truncation). Figure 11-1 shows how the search strategy form is filled out. This term covers both PREGNANCY and PREGNANT, as well as any possible variation of these two words (see Fig. 11-2). More terms related to the concept PREGNANCY can be retrieved through various dictionaries and thesauri.

Of course, not every term that is included in a thesaurus should be included in a search strategy statement. Only those terms whose meanings relate to the overall objectives of a particular search should be selected.

```
? e pregnan

Ref Items  Index-term
E1      1  PREGNADIOL
E2      1  PREGNADIONE
E3     77 *PREGNAN
E4   2123  PREGNANCIES
E5      1  PREGNANCNCY
E6      1  PREGNANCT
E7  11338  PREGNANCY
E8      4  PREGNANDIOL
E9      1  PREGNANDIONE
E10   123  PREGNANE
E11   103  PREGNANEDIOL
E12     3  PREGNANEDIOLS
                                -more-

? p

Ref Items  Index-term
E13    20  PREGNANEDIONE
E14     1  PREGNANEDIONES
E15    11  PREGNANES
E16     2  PREGNANETETROL
E17     1  PREGNANETRIAL
E18    41  PREGNANETRIOL
E19     7  PREGNANETRIOLONE
E20     1  PREGNANETRIOLS
E21     1  PREGNANGLIONIC
E22     1  PREGNANICES
E23    20  PREGNANOLONE
E24     1  PREGNANONE
                                -more-

? p

Ref Items  Index-term
E25  5954  PREGNANT
E26     1  PREGNANTMARE
E
```

Fig. 11-2. Variations of the term PREGNANCY. DIALOG online service. File 5:BIOSIS Previews.

Since the objectives of the search are set by the subject expert himself, the final list of terms always bears his individual stamp. There is no such thing as a universal search for a given concept.

Figure 11-3 shows different synonyms of the term PREGNANCY that you may find in a general thesaurus. Such a thesaurus may be a good source of commonly used words, but may not be too useful in the case of highly specialized scientific or professional terms. These latter terms may sometimes be found in a specialized subject thesaurus (see Fig. 11-4). Subject thesauri generally include more specialized terms. In addition, they are often organized in accordance with hierarchical principles. This makes it easier for an expert to organize a particular search statement. A subject thesaurus published as a standard on terminology may also include so-called "nonrecommended" terms. In order to be successful, a search strategy should also include nonrecommended terms widely used in the published literature.

Unfortunately, many areas of professional knowledge do not have published thesauri of currently used terms. As a result, a professional has to rely on specialized dictionaries and other literature that may be less convenient when a set of terms is compiled.

The use of a special medical dictionary in fin-

preference 372

preference, *n.* partiality, predilection, propensity (LIKING); choice, say (*colloq.*), option (VOICE).

PREGNANCY.—I. *Nouns.* **pregnancy,** fetation, gestation, gravity; conception, quickening, lightening, labor, term.
impregnation, fecundation, fertilization, insemination, artificial insemination.
birth control, contraception, planned parenthood.
abortion, feticide, aborticide, curettage, miscarriage, spontaneous abortion.
II. *Verbs.* **be pregnant,** gestate, conceive, quicken; miscarry, abort.
impregnate, inseminate, fecundate (*biol.*), fertilize (*biol.*).
III. *Adjectives.* **pregnant,** big, big with child, childing, *enceinte* (*F.*), expectant, expecting, full, gravid, great, great with child, heavy, heavy with child, laden, anticipating (*slang*).
See also BIRTH, CHILD, FERTILITY. *Antonyms*—See UNPRODUCTIVENESS.

pregnant, *adj.* big with child, *enceinte* (*F.*), expectant (PREGNANCY); meaty, pithy, pointed (MEANING); suggestive, redolent, remindful (SUGGESTION).
prehensile, *adj.* prehensive, prehensory, raptorial (TAKING).
prejudge, *v.* be prejudiced, forejudge, have

indoctrinate; sectar
jaundice, warp, twis
be prejudiced, preju
bias, be partial, fa
nate; show prejudic
distort.
III. *Adjectives.* **prej**
biased, squint-eyed,
unfair, jaundiced, d
tive; slanted, colore
partial, partisan, on
clined, favorable, i
zealotic.
narrow-minded, nar
al, provincial, petty
fined, hidebound,
Victorian, mid-Vict
tional, local, localis
See also INFLUENCE
TENDENCY, UNFAIR
IMPARTIALITY.

prejudicial, *adj.* injur
rimental (HARM).
preliminary, *adj.* in
preceding, prepar
PREPARATION).
prelude, *n.* introduct
amble, preface
ENCE); *Vorspiel* (
SIC).
premature, *adj.* unt

Fig. 11-3. Part of a page from *The New Roget's Thesaurus of the English Language in Dictionary Form, 1978 Edition,* with the synonyms to words *pregnancy and pregnant.* (Definition of *pregnancy* reprinted by permission of G.P. Putnam's Sons from *THE NEW ROGET'S THESAURUS IN DICTIONARY FORM* by Norman Lewis, copyright © 1978 by G.P. Putnam's Sons.)

Prednisoione

Preforms 1107

RT		Briquets
		Compacts
	—	Composite materials
		Green strength
	—	Molds
		Powder metallurgy
		Preforming

Pregnancy 0605

NT		Ectopic pregnancy
RT		Amniotic fluid
		Birth
		Placenta
	—	Pregnancy complications

Pregnancy complications 0605

NT	—	Abortion
		Chorioadenoma
		Choriocarcinoma
		Chorioepitrhelioma
		Dystocia
		Eclampsia
		Ectopic pregnancy
		Hyperemesis gravidarium
		Preclampsia
		Septic abortion
	—	Toxemias of pregnancy
RT	—	Edema
		Panhypopituitarism
	—	Phlebitis
	—	Pregnancy
		Thrombophlebitis
	—	Vaginitis

Pregnanediol 0601 0616

BT	Hormones
	Progestational hormones
	Sex hormones

Pregnenone 0601 0616

BT	Hormones
	Progestational hormones
	Sex hormones

Preheaters

USE	Heating equipment

Fig. 11-4. Part of a page from the *Thesaurus of Engineering and Scientific Terms, First Edition,* Engineers Joint Council, 1967, which includes the term PREGNANCY, several related terms *(RT),* and *narrower terms (NT).* (©1967, Engineers Joint Council; reprinted by permission, American Association of Engineering Societies.)

ding appropriate synonyms is shown in Fig. 11-5.

Certain computerized files maintain their hierarchical thesauri online. Some of them are regularly updated, and there may also be printed versions of them. An online thesaurus may be maintained as an integral part of an online file index (see Fig. 11-6) or may be organized as a separate vocabulary file (see Fig. 4-14).

The printed version of a hierarchical thesaurus is normally issued by a producer once a year (or even less frequently) and may range from several well published volumes (see Figs. 11-7 and 11-8) to a simple one-page list of principal subjects.

The hierarchal thesaurus of a particular file is generally intended for use in organizing a search in the same file. However, in our technique, such thesauri are used primarily to organize a universal search strategy statement to be used later in a number of online files and online services. Our final list of terms combined with the OR operator is shown in Fig. 11-9.

TRIMMING A LIST OF TERMS

Often terms that are taken from different sources, such as dictionaries, thesauri, and primary or secondary publications, are not concise, include redundant words, or have significant variations in their spelling. One of the major tasks to be performed by the subject expert is to simplify such a list of terms so that it expresses the original concept clearly and concisely.

In the following paragraphs we illustrate the process of trimming the list of terms for a concept based on a simple example, the subject of *fiber optics*.

First, known variations of this term were indiscriminately listed, as shown in Fig. 11-10.

Then, as a result of several cycles of trimming, the list of term variations was considerably reduced. For example, a proximity search could simultaneously describe several of the two-word terms shown in Fig. 11-10. In Fig. 11-11 the (w) logical operator substitutes for either a dash or a space between two words. The truncation sign (here, ?) consolidates terms with various endings.

Further examination of the terms on the list in Fig. 11-11 shows that it can be trimmed even more radically. Because the English language has only a limited number of other words starting with FIB, and their occurrence is unlikely in conjunction with the word OPTICS, we decided to reduce even further the length of the term FIBER/FIBRE, limiting

555 **presby-**

preganglionic (pre″gang-gle-on′ik) proximal to a ganglion.

pregenital (pre-jen′ĭ-tal) antedating the emergence of genital interests.

pregnancy (preg′nan-se) the condition of having a developing embryo or fetus in the body, after union of an ovum and spermatozoon. **abdominal p.**, ectopic pregnancy within the peritoneal cavity. **ampullar p.**, ectopic pregnancy in the ampulla of the uterine tube. **cervical p.**, ectopic pregnancy within the cervical canal. **combined p.**, simultaneous intrauterine and extrauterine pregnancies. **cornual p.**, pregnancy in a horn of the uterus. **ectopic p., extrauterine p.**, development of the fertilized ovum outside the cavity of the uterus. **false p.**, development of all the signs of pregnancy without the presence of an embryo. **interstitial p.**, pregnancy in the portion of the oviduct within the uterine wall. **intraligamentary p.**, ectopic pregnancy within the broad ligament. **multiple p.**, presence of more than one fetus in the uterus at the same time. **mural p.**, interstitial p. **ovarian p.**, pregnancy occurring in an ovary. **phantom p.**, false pregnancy due to psychogenic factors. **tubal p.**, ectopic pregnancy within a uterine tube. **tuboabdominal p.**, ectopic pregnancy occurring partly in the fimbriated end of the oviduct and partly in the abdominal cavity. **tubo-ovarian p.**, pregnancy at the fimbria of the uterine tube.

pregnane (preg′nān) a crystalline saturated steroid hydrocarbon, $C_{21}H_{36}$; *β-pregnane* is the form from which several hormones, including progesterone, are derived; *α-pregnane* is the form excreted in the urine.

pregnanediol (preg″nān′di-ol) a crystalline, biologically inactive dihydroxy derivative of pregnane, formed by reduction of progesterone and found especially in urine of pregnant women.

pregnanetriol (preg″nān-tri′ol) a metabolite of 17-hydroxyprogesterone; its excretion in the urine is greatly increased in certain disorders of the adrenal cortex.

pregnant (preg′nant) with child; gravid.

pregnene (preg′nēn) a compound which forms the chemical nucleus of progesterone.

pregneninolone (preg″nēn-in′o-lōn) ethister-

preleukemia (-lu-ke′me-ah) a stage of bone marrow dysfunction preceding the development of acute myelogenous leukemia. **preleuke′mic,** adj.

prelimbic (pre-lim′bik) in front of a limbus.

premalignant (pre″mah-lig′nant) precancerous.

premature (-mah-tūr′) 1. occurring before the proper time. 2. a premature infant.

prematurity (-tūr′ĭ-te) underdevelopment; the condition of a premature infant.

premaxilla (pre″mak-sil′ah) incisive bone.

premaxillary (pre-mak′sĭ-ler″e) 1. in front of the maxilla. 2. pertaining to the premaxilla (incisive bone).

premedication (pre″med-ĭ-ka′shun) preliminary medication, particularly internal medication to produce narcosis prior to general anesthesia.

premenarchal (-mĕ-nar′kal) occurring before establishment of menstruation.

premenstrual (pre-men′stroo-al) preceding menstruation.

premenstruum (-men′stroo-um) the period immediately before menstruation.

premolar (-mo′lar) in front of the molar teeth; see under *tooth.*

premonocyte (-mon′o-sīt) promonocyte.

premorbid (-mor′bid) occurring before development of disease.

premunition (pre″mu-nish′un) resistance to infection by the same or closely related pathogen established after an acute infection has become chronic, and lasting as long as the infecting organisms are in the body. **premu′nitive,** adj.

premyeloblast (pre-mi′ĕ-lo-blast″) precursor of a myeloblast.

premyelocyte (-sīt″) promyelocyte.

prenatal (pre-na′tal) preceding birth.

preneoplastic (pre″ne-o-plas′tik) before the formation of a tumor.

prenylamine (prĕ-nil′ah-men) a coronary vasodilator, $C_{24}H_{27}N$.

preoperative (pre-op′er-a″tiv) preceding an operation.

preoptic (-op′tik) in front of the optic chiasm.

preoral (-o′ral) in front of the mouth.

preparalytic (pre″par-ah-lit′ik) preceding pa-

Fig. 11-5. Part of a page from the *Dorland's Medical Dictionary* by W.A. Newman Dorland, 1980 Edition, which describes the term PREGNANCY. (Courtesy of Holt, Rinehart and Winston, Inc.)

```
? e pregnancy

Ref  Items   Index-term                      RT
E1       1   PREGNANCIS
E2       1   PREGNANCT
E3   31154  *PREGNANCY   DC=0038908           7
E4       1   PREGNANCY AFTER AGE 35
E5       1   PREGNANCY AFTER
               HYSTERECTOMY
E6       1   PREGNANCY AFTER SURGERY
E7       1   PREGNANCY AFTER TEST
E8      11   PREGNANCY ANEMIA
               DC=0120371                     2
E9           PREGNANCY ANOMALY                1
E10      2   PREGNANCY ASSOCIATED
                                          -more-

? e e3

Ref  Items   Index-term                      RT
R1   31154   PREGNANCY   DC=0038908           7
R2           CHILD BEARING                    1
R3     208   CHILDBEARING                     1
R4    4879   GESTATION                        1
R5      94   GRAVIDITY                        1
R6           INTRAUTERINE PREGNANCY           1
R7           PREGNANCY CONTROL                1
R8           UNINTENDED PREGNANCY             1
```

Fig. 11-6. Online display of a basic index. DIALOG online service. File 72:EMBASE.

The top part of the display has been retrieved online using the *expand (e)* command. The right column shows a number of *r*elated *t*erms to the words displayed. In the bottom portion of the display, a set of related terms to the term *e3 PREGNANCY* has been retrieved. These may be explored further through their related terms.

it to the first three letters to include both British and American spellings.

Such a short form of truncation should be used very carefully. It cannot always be recommended as a universal solution, as in some cases it could lead to the retrieval of too many undesirable postings.

Both variations of spelling inside the term FIBEROPTICS can be picked up with the internal truncation signs, ??, which in Fig. 11-12 substitute for any two characters.

The example of the trimming process shown above is very simple. Some real life examples may be considerably more complex. However, the subject expert is usually quite capable of evaluating beforehand whether a trimmed list of terms would result in the retrieval of concepts foreign to his subject. As will be shown later, if he were not careful enough in such a task, the results of the actual search would demonstrate that the search strategy was ambiguous by producing too many undesirable postings.

Through the process of simplifying his search strategy, the subject expert invariably gains a better understanding of the relationships among various concepts in his own area of knowledge. The impact of such intellectual activity on the subject expert's professional development cannot be overestimated.

In general, there is a tradeoff between the degree of simplicity in the terminology of the search strategy statement and the number of records, useful or not, that such a statement could retrieve.

It is quite obvious that the simpler and more common the terms that are used in the statement and the shorter they are truncated, the greater the number of records selected and the greater the number of undesirable ones.

On the other hand, the use of relatively simple terms may produce a winning strategy that would simultaneously be:

- Effective enough to retrieve all the term variations of the same concept, and
- Universal enough to be used with minimal modifications in numerous files and online services.

Only a subject expert himself can provide the balance between the requirements for simplicity and the necessity to reduce undesirable "noise." This is done through careful

selection of the terms that constitute his search strategy statement and by constant revision of the statement before and during the search.

Ideally, such revisions would allow the elimination of the terms that proved to be too wide in the context of the subject expert's quest. It should also permit the subject expert to reformulate the terms that he found vague and that, in addition to the required concept, also describe concepts that are of no interest to the searcher. Ambiguity in pro-

PREGNADIENETRIOLS
D4.808.745.432.769+
do not use /analogs
74
X TRIHYDROXYPREGNADIENES
XU DESONIDE
XU FLUCLORONIDE
XU FLUPREDNIDENE ACETATE

PREGNANCY
G8.520.769+
IM for articles on normal pregn, NIM as check tag; when IM, only /drug eff /rad eff; policy: Manual 18.4+, 28.29–28.34; in children or adolescents, see note under PREGNANCY IN ADOLESCENCE; pregn despite use of contraceptives is PREGNANCY + contraceptive term with no qualif; check tag FEMALE also; molar pregn = HYDATIDIFORM MOLE; note TEST-TUBE FERTILIZATION see FERTILIZATION IN VITRO
CATALOG: do not use /in inf or /in adolesc (= PREGNANCY IN ADOLESCENCE) or /in middle age (= MATERNAL AGE 35 AND OVER)
PRENATAL INFLUENCES was heading 1963–72
use PREGNANCY to search PRENATAL INFLUENCES 1966–72
see related
PRENATAL CARE
PSEUDOPREGNANCY
XU PREGNANCY, UNWANTED

PREGNANCY, ABDOMINAL
C13.703.733.536
check tags FEMALE & PREGNANCY

PREGNANCY, ADOLESCENT see PREGNANCY IN ADOLESCENCE
G8.520.769.420.770

PREGNANCY, ANIMAL
G8.520.769.618+
IM for articles on normal animal pregn but check also tag PREGNANCY; for NIM animal pregnancy do not index PREGNANCY, ANIMAL: merely check tag PREGNANCY; when IM, only /drug eff /rad eff; do not use /vet; check tags ANIMAL & FEMALE also; Manual 18.4.6
see related
ANIMALS, NEWBORN

PREGNANCY-ASSOCIATED ALPHA 2-GLOBULINS see PREGNANCY ZONE PROTEINS

PREGNANCY COMPLICAT
CARDIOVASCULAR
C13.703.634+ C14.58
coord IM with specific cardiovasc di
PREGNANCY; hemorrh during preg
HEMATOL; Manual 18.4.7; DF: PR
64

PREGNANCY COMPLICAT
C13.703.667 C15.37
for disord of formed elements or coag
excess or defic of substances in the blo
COMPL, not PREGN COMPL HEM
hematologic dis (IM); check tags FEMA
pregn goes under PREGNANCY COM
18.4.7; DF: PREGN COMPL HEMA
64

PREGNANCY COMPLICATI
C1.539.674+ C13.703.
coord IM with specific infectious dis (
PREGNANCY; Manual 18.4.7; DF: P
64

PREGNANCY, ECTOPIC
C13.703.733+
check tags FEMALE & PREGNANCY;
+ PREGNANCY, ECTOPIC or its sp

PREGNANCY, FIRST TRIMESTER see PR
G8.520.769.725.750

PREGNANCY IN ADOLESC
G8.520.769.420.770
pregn as a physiol, social, cultural, psyc
includes pregn in children under 13; che
PREGNANCY & ADOLESCENCE if
if under 13; do not confuse with PREG
(NIM) where ADOLESCENCE is picked
groups in the article CATALOG: d
& adolescence
79
X ADOLESCENT PREGNANCY
X PREGNANCY, ADOLESCENT
X PREGNANCY, TEENAGE

+ INDICATES THERE ARE INDENTED DESCRIPTORS IN MESH TREE STRUCTURES AT THIS NUMBER

Fig. 11-7. Part of a page from the U.S. National Library of Medicine *Medical Subject Headings—Annotated Alphabetic List*, 1982.

The index in the list refers a searcher to the corresponding part of the hierarchical thesaurus (see next figure). It also describes some related terms as well as terms not recommended for use.

G8 - PHYSIOLOGY-SEX, REPRODUCTION, UROGENITAL

REPRODUCTION, UROGENITAL PHYSIOLOGY (NON MESH)

REPRODUCTION, UROGENITAL PHYSIOLOGY (NON MESH)	G8			
REPRODUCTION	G8.520			
FERTILITY	G8.520.227			
FERTILIZATION	G8.520.277			
FERTILIZATION, DELAYED •	G8.520.277.300			
FERTILIZATION IN VITRO	G8.520.277.320	E5.820.490		
FERTILIZATION, POLYSPERMIC •	G8.520.277.350			
SPERM CAPACITATION	G8.520.277.760			
SPERM-OVUM INTERACTIONS •	G8.520.277.800			
FETAL ORGAN MATURITY	G8.520.290			
FETAL VIABILITY	G8.520.300	G7.553.370		
GESTATIONAL AGE	G8.520.340	G7.168.383	G7.553.417	
INSEMINATION	G8.520.392			
INSEMINATION, ARTIFICIAL	G8.520.392.492	E2.574	G5.414.133.	E5.820.520
OOGENESIS	G8.520.560			
OVIPOSITION	G8.520.581			
OVULATION	G8.520.631			
ANOVULATION	G8.520.631.50	C13.371.56.		
SUPEROVULATION •	G8.520.631.500	E5.820.150.		
OVUM TRANSPORT	G8.520.650	G4.335.283.		
PARTHENOGENESIS	G8.520.689			
PREGNANCY	G8.520.769			
BIRTH INTERVALS	G8.520.769.50	N2.421.143.		
CORPUS LUTEUM MAINTENANCE	G8.520.769.100			
CORPUS LUTEUM REGRESSION	G8.520.769.150			
LABOR	G8.520.769.326			
LABOR ONSET •	G8.520.769.326.200			
LABOR STAGE, FIRST •	G8.520.769.326.550			
LABOR STAGE, SECOND •	G8.520.769.326.570			
LABOR STAGE, THIRD •	G8.520.769.326.590			
UTERINE CONTRACTION	G8.520.769.326.700			
LABOR PRESENTATION	G8.520.769.362			
BREECH PRESENTATION •	G8.520.769.362.150			
MATERNAL AGE	G8.520.769.420	G7.168.990		
MATERNAL AGE 35 AND OVER •	G8.520.769.420.630			
PREGNANCY IN ADOLESCENCE	G8.520.769.420.770			
MATERNAL-FETAL EXCHANGE	G8.520.769.455			
NIDATION	G8.520.769.490			
NIDATION, DELAYED •	G8.520.769.490.660			
PARITY	G8.520.769.552			
PLACENTATION	G8.520.769.580			
POSTNIDATION PHASE	G8.520.769.600			
PREGNANCY, ANIMAL	G8.520.769.618			
LITTER SIZE	G8.520.769.618.400			
PREGNANCY MAINTENANCE	G8.520.769.640			
PREGNANCY, MULTIPLE	G8.520.769.654			
QUADRUPLETS	G8.520.769.654.469	M1.438.486		
QUINTUPLETS	G8.520.769.654.553	M1.438.587		
SUPERFETATION	G8.520.769.654.690			
TRIPLETS	G8.520.769.654.800	M1.438.768		
TWINS	G8.520.769.654.888	M1.438.873		
TWINS, DIZYGOTIC •	G8.520.769.654.888.920	M1.438.873.		
TWINS, MONOZYGOTIC •	G8.520.769.654.888.940	M1.438.873.		
PREGNANCY, PROLONGED	G8.520.769.689			
PREGNANCY TRIMESTERS (NON MESH)	G8.520.769.725			
PREGNANCY TRIMESTER, FIRST	G8.520.769.725.750			
PREGNANCY TRIMESTER, SECOND	G8.520.769.725.790			
PREGNANCY TRIMESTER, THIRD	G8.520.769.725.830			
PREGNANCY, UNWANTED •	G8.520.769.761			
PRENIDATION PHASE	G8.520.769.790			
PSEUDOPREGNANCY	G8.520.769.804	C13.371.580		
PUERPERIUM	G8.520.769.843			

• INDICATES MINOR DESCRIPTOR

391

Fig. 11-8. A page from the U.S. National Library of Medicine *Medical Subject Headings—Tree Structure*, 1982.

The term PREGNANCY is shown as a part of the general hierarchical tree for medical sciences.

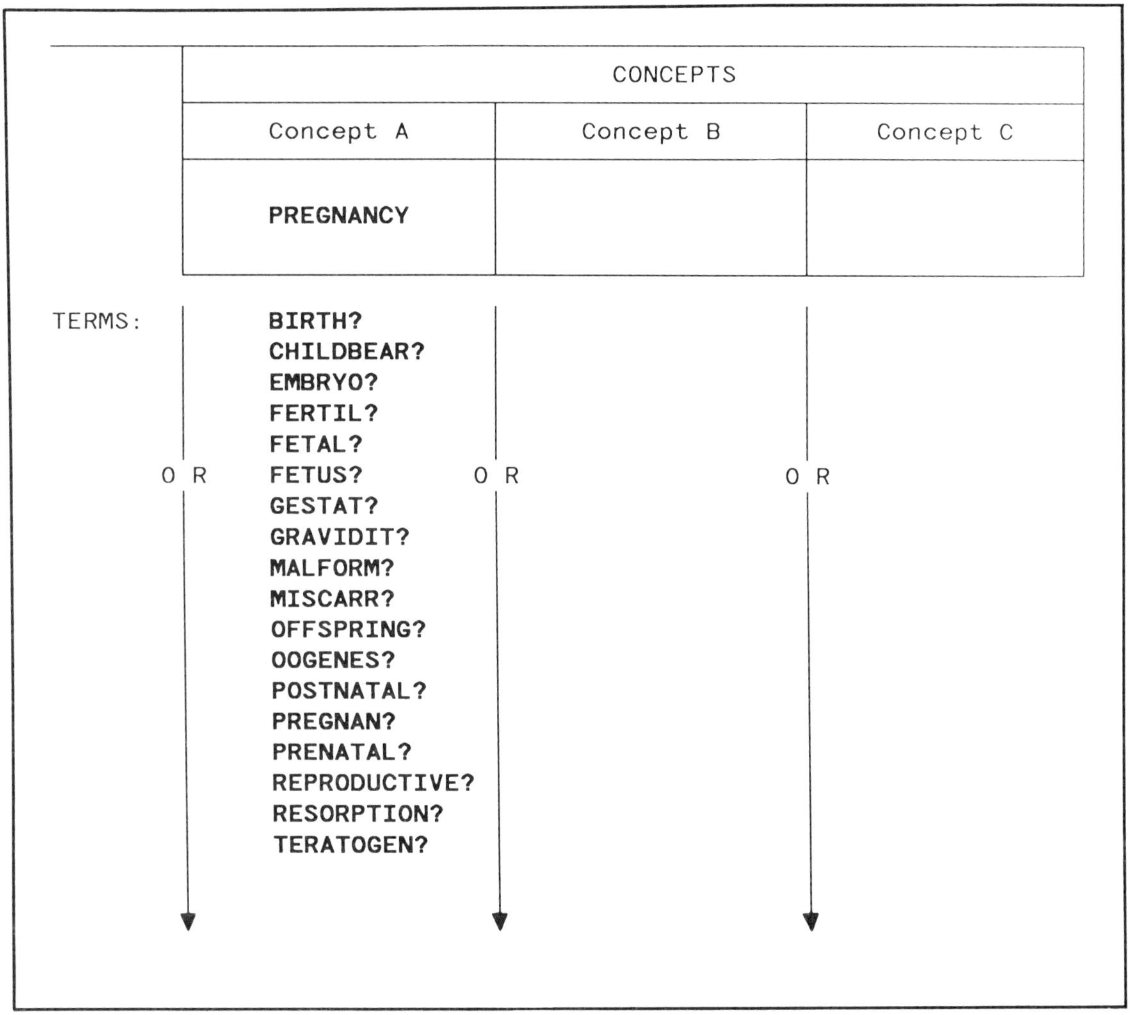

Fig. 11-9. The search form with truncated forms of all the terms identified as relating to the first concept.

fessional or scientific terminology makes terminological confusion between different fields of knowledge quite possible.

> With the help of our Subject Expert Searching Technique, it is possible for the subject expert to organize a search strategy statement that combines effectiveness and simplicity. Such a search would allow the user to obtain desirable results in a wide range of different databases and online services.

THE ONE-CONCEPT SEARCH

The *one-concept search* is not done very frequently in practice. This type of search is normally performed on a subject that is:

- Relatively new
- Well defined terminologically: there should be no words identical in spelling but different in meaning (homonyms) to confuse a searcher. If such spelling-twin terms do exist, they may be logically excluded with the NOT operator, providing their use is consistent, their application

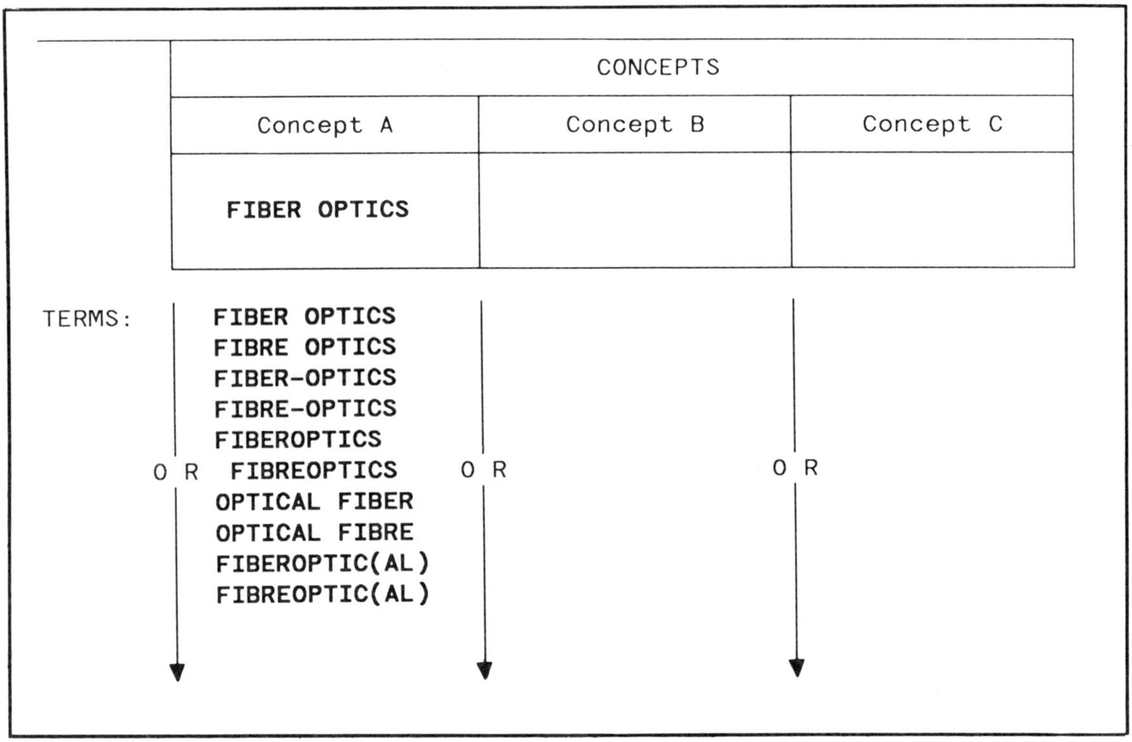

Fig. 11-10. An initial, untrimmed list of terms.

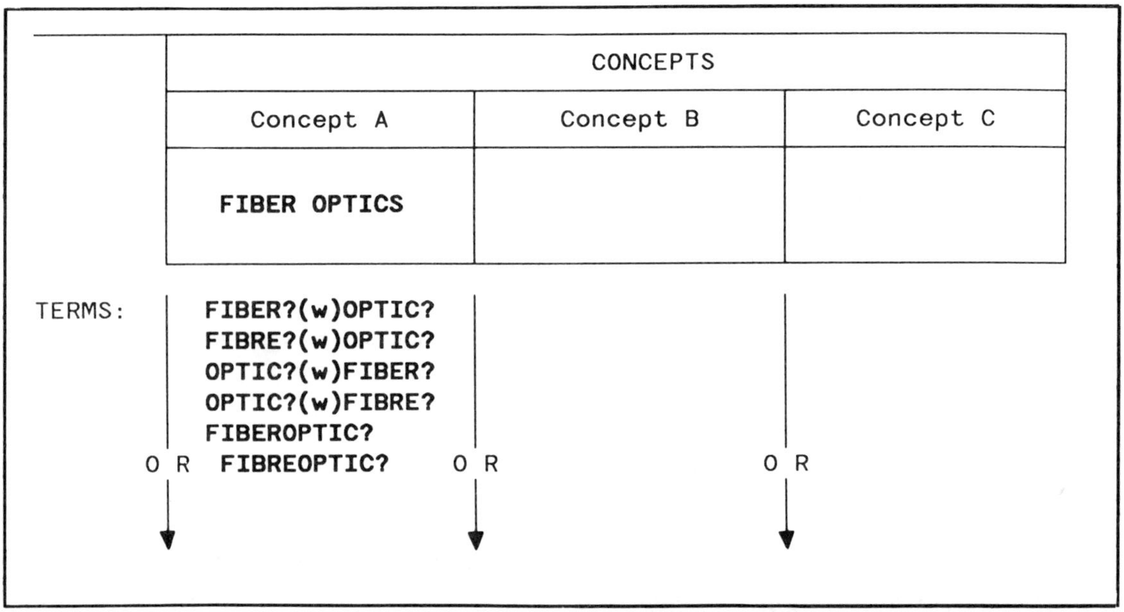

Fig. 11-11. The search form with a list of terms trimmed through the use of the proximity operator and truncation.

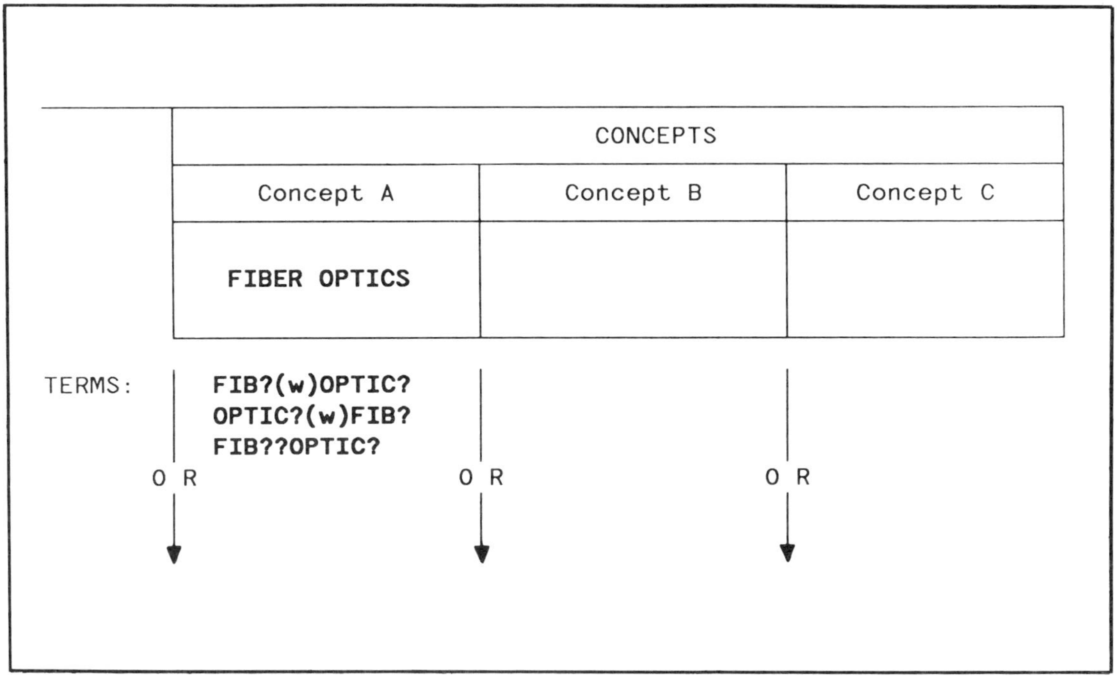

Fig. 11-12. The search form with the list of terms further trimmed through the use of truncation.

is limited, and they can be easily identified.

- Very small: the total number of publications for such a topic should not exceed 100. The subject expert is apt to make an error by presuming that there are not too many publications on a given subject.

The only time when one may exceed the threshold of 100 publications is when he or she is compiling a master bibliography. Even in this case, the total number of unit records retrieved online should not exceed 300-500.

In most cases, the subject expert will find that the one-concept search cannot be effectively managed because it produces too many postings.

Examples of a "very small" search are not very easy to come up with, although any subject expert could probably provide an example of the "moderately small" subject (up to 500 publications). An example of a search on a subject that we consider to be "very small," performed on the master index file of DIALOG online service, is shown in Fig. 11-13.

THE DEVELOPMENT OF A PRINCIPAL CLAUSE

The basic kind of search statement in our Subject Expert Searching Technique is the two/three-concept search. In the statement, two concepts constitute a *principal clause,* whereas the third concept may (or may not) be used as a *subordinate clause.*

As illustrated in Fig. 11-14, it is easy to see that the logic used when you are creating a search statement using our technique is similar to grammatical logic. (Grammatical units are the building blocks of language structure.) The first concept is loosely analogous to the subject of a sentence, the second to the predicate, and the third to the dependent (subordinate) clause, which complements the principal clause.

In order to use our searching technique, you should understand the process through which concepts are organized in a statement. When you are

```
? b411;sf pubaff,7,5

          2jul84 14:06:43 User12345
    $1.01  0.013 Hrs File72
    $0.10  Tymnet
    $1.11  Estimated Total Cost

File411:DIALINDEX(tm)
(Copr. DIALOG Inf.Ser.Inc.)

Unavailable files:184

File5:BIOSIS Previews 81-84/JuL BA7801;RRM2710
File7:SOCIAL SCISEARCH - 72-84/WK20
File47:Magazine Index -
File49:PAIS International - 76-84/Jul
File66:GPO Monthly Catalog - Jul 1976 to Jun 1984
File111:National Newspaper Index - 79-84/Jun
File167:World Affairs Report - 71-83/Sep
File211:NEWSEARCH
File244:LABORLAW - 61-84/Jun
File248:Middle East Abstracts and Index - 1980
File249:MIDEAST File - 1980-84/Jun
File260:UPI News - Apr 83 - Mar 84
File262:Canadian Business & Current Affairs 1982-8402

        File Items Description
        ---- ----- -----------

? s yeti or abominable

        (5)
                 1 YETI
                 0 ABOMINABLE
               1  YETI OR ABOMINABLE
        (7)
                 7 YETI
                 2 ABOMINABLE
               9  YETI OR ABOMINABLE
       (47)
                10 YETI
                35 ABOMINABLE
              43  YETI OR ABOMINABLE
       (49)
                 0 YETI
                 1 ABOMINABLE
               1  YETI OR ABOMINABLE
       (66)
                 0 YETI
                 0 ABOMINABLE
               0  YETI OR ABOMINABLE
      (111)
                 2 YETI
                 5 ABOMINABLE
               6  YETI OR ABOMINABLE
      (167)
                 0 YETI
                 2 ABOMINABLE
               2  YETI OR ABOMINABLE
      (211)
                 0 YETI
                 0 ABOMINABLE
               0  YETI OR ABOMINABLE
```

Fig. 11-13. An example of a one-concept two-term search in a MASTER INDEX file. DIALOG online service. File 411: Dialindex. (Continued on page 133.)

A master index file allows the user to determine the principal files that contain the sought-after unit records more quickly and less expensively. It is then necessary to search through each file individually in order to actually retrieve these unit records. The command *sf selects* a Set of Files in the master index file. *Pubaff* is a set of files composed by the online service (files 47, 49, 66, 111, 167, 211, 244, 248, 249, 260, 262) that includes material on *pub*lic *aff*airs.

```
(244)                                     (260)
              0 YETI                                     6 YETI
              0 ABOMINABLE                              24 ABOMINABLE
            0  YETI OR ABOMINABLE                     28  YETI OR ABOMINABLE
(248)                                     (262)
              0 YETI                                     0 YETI
              0 ABOMINABLE                               1 ABOMINABLE
            0  YETI OR ABOMINABLE                      1  YETI OR ABOMINABLE
(249)
              0 YETI
              0 ABOMINABLE
            0  YETI OR ABOMINABLE
```

Fig. 11-13. (Continued from page 132.)

writing a sentence, a knowledge of general grammatical principles does not assure that the sentence will be meaningful. Even though all sentences are constructed using a limited number of grammatical rules, the results produced by two different writers may differ significantly due to something indefinable that separates a good writer from a bad one. In order to produce a text of high quality, elements such as subject knowledge and talent must be present in addition to the rules of grammar.

As is the case with writing, a search may be good or bad. This depends on certain characteristics of the searcher, among which subject knowledge and experience play prominent roles.

In the search statement, it is the role of the AND operator to combine and limit several concepts. In order to be successful, the search statement should be built to satisfy the following criteria:

- It should produce a set of unit records that are meaningful and relevant to the problem posed by the end-user.
- The degree of limitation should be sufficient; that is, the number of postings in the set produced by ANDing several search concepts should be no more than half the number of postings that were retrieved by one of the concepts combined in this set when it was used alone.
- The number of postings retrieved by a search statement in each file should be *manageable* and correspond to the resources of the end-user. To be manageable, we recommend that the threshold number of postings retrieved in each file should be in the order of 40-60. If master bibliography is created, the number of postings retrieved from one file may reach as high as 80-100. In reality, the user should select for himself the maximum number of postings he believes is necessary or sufficient for his professional objectives. As in any other kind of activity,

CONCEPTS		
Concept A	Concept B	Concept C
Principal clause		**Subordinate clause**

Fig. 11-14. The logic used during the creation of a search statement.

the final results of the search should be evaluated taking into account the importance of the primary professional problem. What makes a good online search different from a good traditional bibliographic search is that an online search would normally retrieve many more useful postings.

We will demonstrate the development process for the two/three-concept statement with an example of a search request. The request is formulated as follows:

- What are the effects of *noise* on *pregnant women*, especially in the *occupational environment?*

It is clear to an expert on noise, especially to one who specializes in occupational health and safety issues, that this particular problem is well-defined and manageable. More precisely, one may expect that the world literature contains no more than one thousand publications on the effect of noise on pregnant women. Only a fraction of these publications would be devoted to the effect of noise in an occupational environment.

Therefore, the principal clause in our search statement is based on the concepts of NOISE and PREGNANCY, as shown in Fig. 11-15.

Note that not all of the words from the original request necessarily find their way to the search statement. This is neither possible nor even desirable. For example, the word *women* in our request is not informative in the sense that it is highly unlikely that anybody but a woman will become pregnant. Thus the word *women* is rarely mentioned in the original documents.

On the other hand, since the subject is relatively narrow, experimental data obtained on animals may also be of a certain interest to the end-user. The exclusive use of the concept of *female, human* would not allow us to explore this information.

In fact, the actual searching in our case unexpectedly resulted in a small number of publications discussing the effect of noise on male fertility. This result was found by the end-users to be not only appropriate, but informative because it added an interesting new angle to the original problem.

After developing a principal clause, we conducted an *online adaptation* of the first version.

In order to adapt the search strategy to the system, we normally run the search through a file that is one of the least expensive. This *first stage adaptation* allows the searcher to type a search statement manually, to make alterations in the case of misspellings or unusable terms, and to conduct further online adaptations without the fear of spending too much money in the process. Such a file may also be used for saving the first version of the search, which later can be executed automatically in other files. Examples of inexpensive files include File 1:ERIC in the DIALOG online service and File Orbit, a conditional file in the ORBIT online service that does not contain unit records.

We conducted the *second stage adaptation* of our search strategy by executing the first version of our temporarily saved search in another file. The file chosen at this point had to have the following characteristics:

- The file should be large and have a broad range of subjects relating to the problem explored. This should assure that a substantial number of useful postings will be retrieved from it;
- The file should be up-to-date so that relatively recent information can be expected from it.

In order to make our examples in this book more concise, we do not show here the first search in the cheapest file; rather we show searches in files that could immediately provide us with meaningful results. For example, the first version of our search on NOISE and PREGNANCY,shown in Fig. 11-16, was performed in File 5:BIOSIS Previews rather than in the inexpensive File 1:ERIC.

An analysis of the results of our search in File 5 shows that the search also includes an undesirable subconcept describing the use of ULTRASONIC DIAGNOSIS in pregnancy (see posting 1 at the end

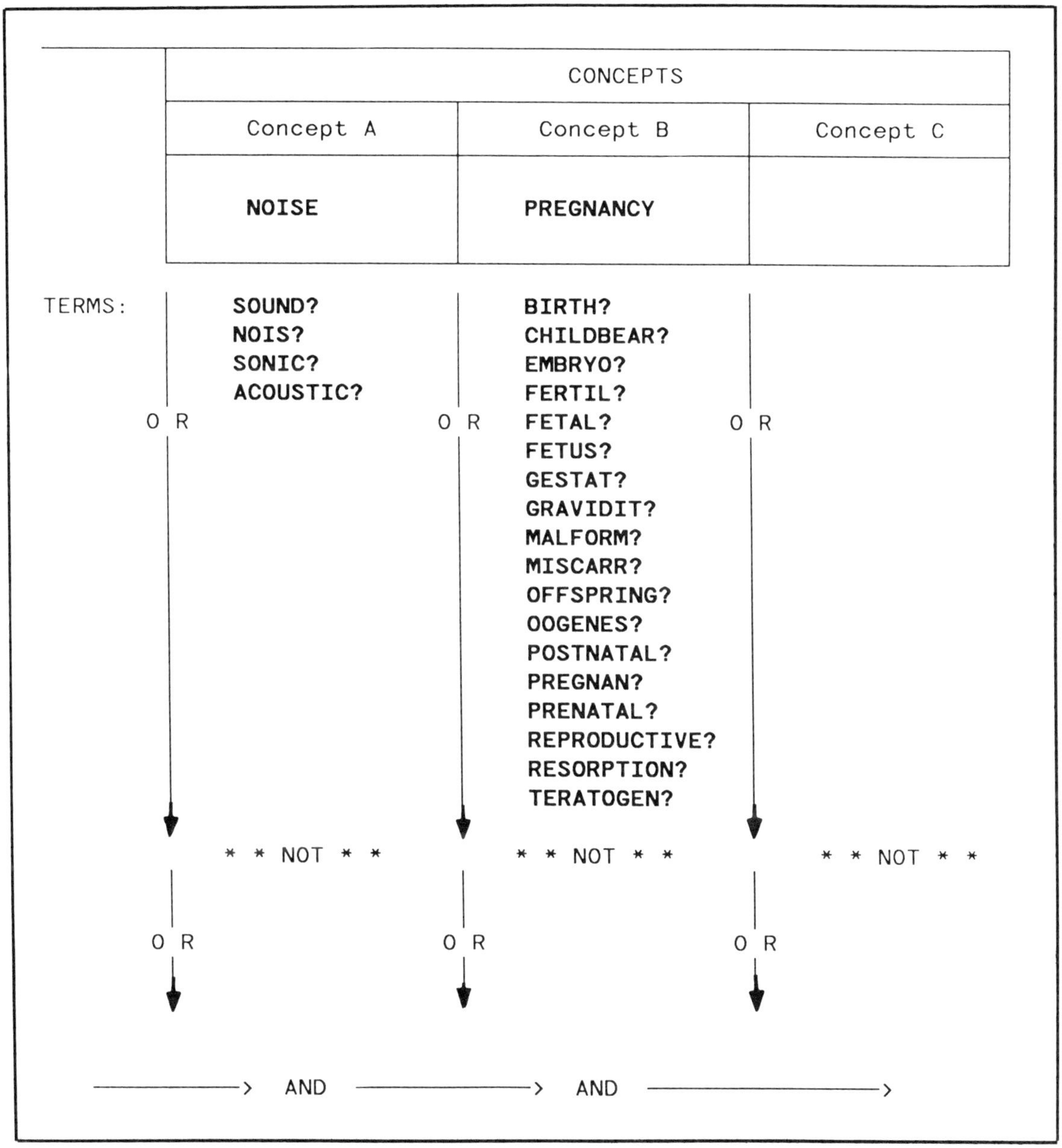

Fig. 11-15. The search form with the terms for a two-concept search.

of Fig. 11-16). This subconcept relates to both of the concepts NOISE and PREGNANCY but is not relevant to our particular concern.

Therefore, in developing the concept for NOISE in our search statement we had to exclude all unit records that describe any application of DIAGNOSTICS, with particular reference to ULTRASONIC SCANNING SYSTEMS. Such systems are widely used in everyday medical practice, and we would expect a large number of references in the specialized literature. The resulting search form is shown in Fig. 11-17.

```
? b5

          2jul84 14:08:13 User12345
    $0.91  0.016 Hrs File1  2 Descriptors
    $0.21  Tymnet
    $1.12  Estimated Total Cost

File5:BIOSIS Previews 81-84/JuL BA7801;RRM2710
(c.BIOSIS 1984)See File55,255
         Set Items Description
         --- ----- -----------
? s sound?
           1  3043 SOUND?
? s nois?
           2  2551 NOIS?
? s sonic?
           3  1318 SONIC?
? s acoustic?
           4  2105 ACOUSTIC?
? c 1-4/or
           5  8026  1-4/OR
? s birth?
           6  9102 BIRTH?
? s childbear?
           7   103 CHILDBEAR?
? s embrio?
           8     2 EMBRIO? <------------------  THE TERM WAS
? s embryo?                                     MISSPELLED
           9 20459 EMBRYO?                      BY THE SEARCHER
? s fertil?
          10 14354 FERTIL?
? s fetal?
          11 12929 FETAL?
? s fetus?
          12  6149 FETUS?
? s gestat?
          13  6297 GESTAT?
? s gravidit?
          14    91 GRAVIDIT?
? s malform?
          15  3147 MALFORM?
? s micarr?
          16     0 S MICARR? <----------------  THE TERM WAS
? s miscarr?                                    GARBLED IN
          17   125 MISCARR?                     TRANSMISSION
? s offspring?
          18  2490 OFFSPRING?
? s oogenes?
          19   538 OOGENES?
? s postnatal?
          20  2753 POSTNATAL?
```

Fig. 11-16. A first version of the two-concept search on NOISE and PREGNANCY. DIALOG online service. File 5:BIOSIS Previews. (Courtesy of BioSciences Information Service. © 1984 BioSciences Information Service.) (Continued on page 137.)

```
? s pregnant? ◄──────────────────────┐          A WIDER TERM
         21   5958 PREGNANT?            │          (SET 22)
? s pregnan? ◄──────────────────────┘          RETRIEVES MANY
         22 15727 PREGNAN?                         MORE CITATIONS
? s prenatal?                                      THAN SET 21
         23   1254 PRENATAL?
? s reproductive?
         24   7773 REPRODUCTIVE?
? s resorption?
         25   1616 RESORPTION?
? s teratogen?
         26   2031 TERATOGEN?
? c 6-26/or
         27 79200  7-27/OR
? c 5 and 27
         28    342  6 AND 28

? end/savetemp
Serial#T16E
         2jul84 14:17:20 User12345
  $10.03  0.152 Hrs File5 26 Descriptors
   $1.22  Tymnet
  $11.25  Estimated Total Cost

?t28/6/1-10
28/6/1
78005422
  SHORT-TERM AND LONG-TERM RISKS AFTER EXPOSURE TO DIAGNOSTIC ULTRASOUND IN
UTERO.

28/6/2
76052985
  THE  RISK OF INFERTILITY AND DELAYED CONCEPTION ASSOCIATED WITH EXPOSURES
IN THE DANISH WORKPLACE.

28/6/3
75068754
  AUDITORY BRAIN STEM RESPONSES IN HIGH RISK NEO NATES.
```

Fig. 11-16. (Continued from page 136.)

The results of using the second version of the search, based on two concepts NOISE and PREGNANCY with the excluded subconcept of ULTRASONIC DIAGNOSTICS, is shown in Fig. 11-18.

The reduction in the number of postings in the second version of our search to 311 (compared to the 342 postings in the first version) does not look too large. However, most of the 31 irrelevant postings would likely have found their way into the final results of our search. Thus, it is useful to eliminate them at this stage. Also, there would likely be more postings on ULTRASONIC DIAGNOSTICS in the medical files, which we will search later.

This new version of the search is still not finalized. Later in this chapter, we will show how to further increase the relevancy of these results.

ANALYZING THE RESULTS OF A TWO-CONCEPT SEARCH

At this stage, it is still unclear whether or not a second version of our search on NOISE and PREGNANCY would be manageable and successful. An analysis of postings retrieved with this two-concept strategy shows that many of them pro-

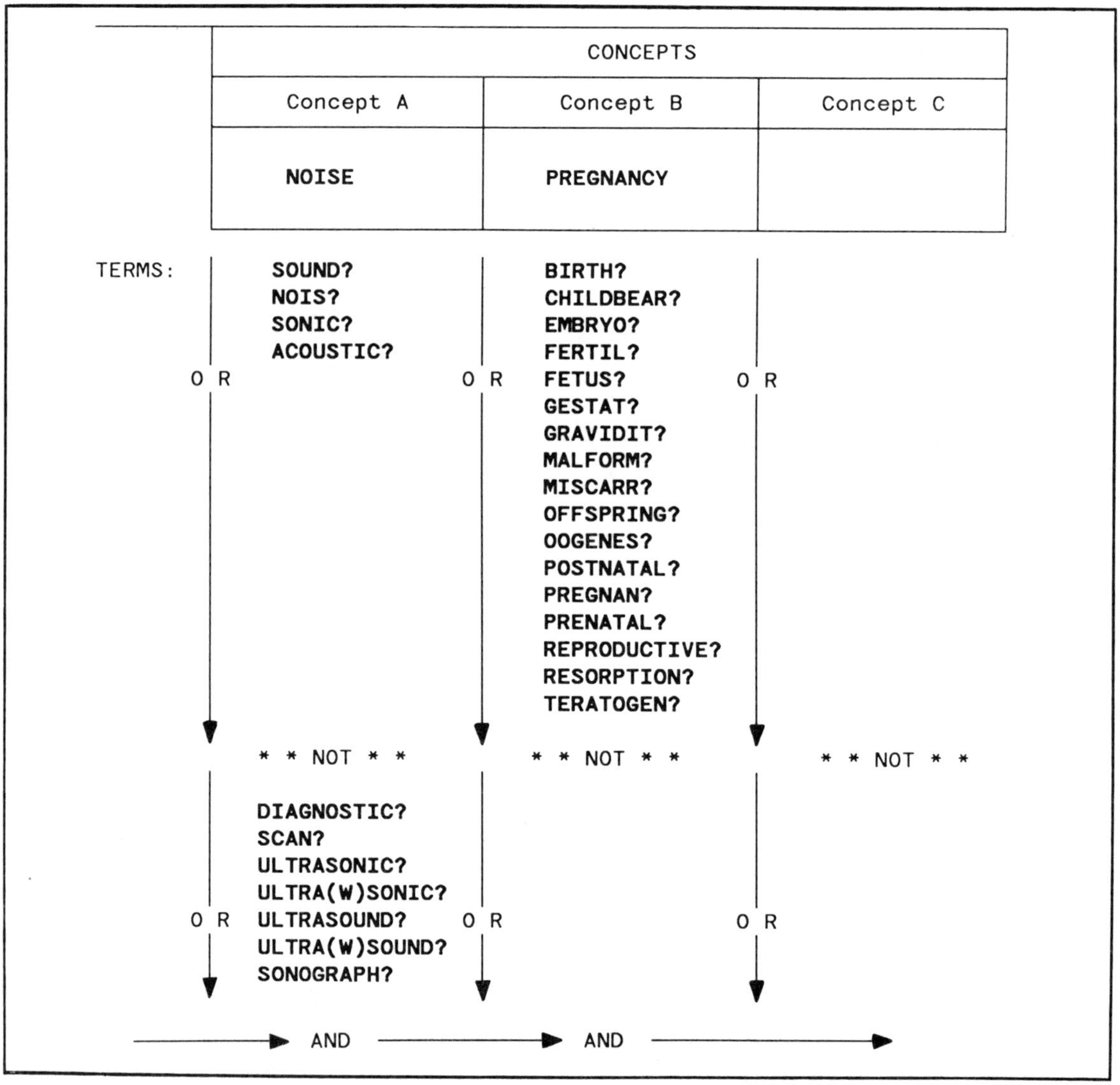

Fig. 11-17. Excluding an undesirable subconcept using the NOT operator. (See also Fig. 11-18.)

vide useful information. However, the degree of relevancy may vary significantly from unit record to unit record. More importantly, the number of postings retrieved with the two-concept strategy in File 5: BIOSIS Previews (311 postings) is far too large to be manageable in the sense described above.

In order to illustrate the last point better, we ran a saved two-concept search in several dozen DIALOG files in which we expected to find useful information. The number of postings retrieved in each of these files with our two-concept search strategy is shown in Fig. 11-19. The figure is based on our Search Strategy Form (see the Appendix).

In most of the files in which we ran our search, it was relatively easy to distinguish between the useful records and the records of no use to us just by the online printing of the titles of the unit records retrieved. A quick look at the titles allowed the subject experts to conclude that the two-concept search

```
b5;.exs t16e/1-5
            2jul84 16:42:57 User12345
     $0.45  0.010 Hrs File1*
     $0.18  Uninet
     $0.63  Estimated Total Cost

File5:BIOSIS Previews 81-84/JuL BA7801;RRM2710
(c.BIOSIS 1984)See File55,255
          Set Items Description
          --- ----- -----------
            1  3043 SOUND?
            2  2551 NOIS?
            3  1318 SONIC?
            4  2105 ACOUSTIC?
            5  8026  1-4/OR
? s diagnostic?
            6 18561 DIAGNOSTIC?
? s scan?
            7 15034 SCAN?
? s ultrasonic?
            8  2224 ULTRASONIC?
? s ultra(w)sonic?
            9     2 ULTRA(W)SONIC?
? s ultrasound?
           10  3375 ULTRASOUND?
? s ultra(w)sound?
           11     3 ULTRA(W)SOUND?
? s sonograph?
           12  1078 SONOGRAPH?
? c 6-12/or
           13 36833  6-12/OR
? .exs t16e/6-7
           14  9102 BIRTH?
           15   103 CHILDBEAR?
? .exs t16e/9-15
           16 20459 EMBRYO?
           17 14354 FERTIL?
           18 12929 FETAL?
           19  6149 FETUS?
           20  6297 GESTAT?
           21    91 GRAVIDIT?
           22  3147 MALFORM?
? .exs t16e/17-20
           23   125 MISCARR?
           24  2490 OFFSPRING?
           25   538 OOGENES?
           26  2753 POSTNATAL?
? .exs t16e/22-26
           27 15727 PREGNAN?
```

Fig. 11-18. The second version of the two-concept search on NOISE and PREGNANCY. DIALOG online service. File 5:BIOSIS Previews.

Execution of parts of a temporarily saved search allows the searcher to eliminate misspellings (see set 8 in Fig. 11-16), computer or communication line faults (set *16* in Fig. 11-16), or improperly truncated terms (set *21* in Fig. 11-16).

```
                    28   1254 PRENATAL?
                    29   7773 REPRODUCTIVE?
                    30   1616 RESORPTION?
                    31   2031 TERATOGEN?
? c 14-31/or
                    32 79200  14-31/OR
? c (5 not 13) and 32
                    33    311  (5 NOT 13) AND 32
? end/save
Serial#6Z6Z
                2jul84 16:49:05 User12345
     $6.86   0.104 Hrs File5 31 Descriptors
     $0.62   Uninet
     $7.48   Estimated Total Cost
```

Fig 11-18. (Continued from page 139.)

resulted in very useful information and to decide which of the records were relevant. A subsequent printing of selected records in full format, both online and offline, provided him with valuable material to analyze in more detail.

However, in 13 out of 39 files searched, we found the number of postings retrieved to be too large. A subject expert would experience significant difficulties in evaluating the results of a search with too many postings. It was, therefore, necessary to further limit the number of postings retrieved in those files. How a subject expert can perform such a task with relative ease is described later in this book.

Most of the files that we selected for this particular search are bibliographic. However, on many occasions we have been able to run a search initially developed for a bibliographic file through nonbibliographic databases as well. Depending on the subject, the use of a "universal" search strategy in nonbibliographic or even in nonreferral databases may be quite successful without any changes. However, it may require substantial modifications in some files.

> Often it is quite beneficial to start a complex investigation by conducting an online search in bibliographic databases and only then to proceed with searching in full text or source databases.

Even though our search is not yet finished, certain preliminary conclusions can be drawn based on the results presented in Fig. 11-19. Especially noticeable is the significant increase in the number of postings retrieved with our multiterm concept when compared with a search that was performed with only one term. In order to illustrate this point better, we ran a special search in File 411:DIALINDEX that shows that only a small fraction of the postings retrieved with our strategy was retrieved with a simple two-concept search that used only one truncated term per concept (see Fig. 11-20).

Note that large general subject databases may include more postings on a given narrow subject than certain smaller files that presumably specialize in this narrow subject. In our case, such large and general databases as 5,55,255: BIOSIS Previews; 72,73,172,173:EMBASE (Excerpta Medica); 152,153,154:Medline; 11:PSYCINFO; or 6:NTIS produced more records on the subject of noise and pregnancy than such databases as 40:Enviroline, 41:Pollution Abstracts, 68:Environmental Bibliography, or even 161:Occupational Safety & Health (NIOSH) that specialize in the area of environmental pollutants.

Not only is the number of postings retrieved in a large general file usually higher than the number retrieved from a specialized file, but also the information content of a specialized file is often inferior to that of a large file, even in the very area of a small file's specialization. A specialized file, however, may sometimes list certain kinds of useful information that are not included in a large general file (for example, government reports, regulations, or results of commissioned studies), and thus it is certainly worth searching.

Note that sometimes even the lack of records (or the very small number of records) retrieved in a particular file may be quite informative. For example, the lack of postings retrieved with our

Saved search # t16e   Saved search # ________
Saved search # 6z6z   Saved search # ________

DIALOG

	0	1	2	3	4	5	6	7	8	9
0						311/21	103/45	23	61	
10		226/26	32	54	0	17				
20	1									
30					15	103/35				
40	30	36						12		
50						247/24				
60									9	
70			321/71	48			252/22	16		
80								35		
90					26					
100		7								
110										
120										
130						0	0			
140	2									
150			138/11	374/76	445/99					
160		38				9	0			
170			249/45	666/54						
180							31			
190										
200										
210										
220										
230										
240					0					
250						117/5				
420							19			

Fig. 11-19. The number of postings retrieved by executing a second version of the two-concept search on NOISE and PREGNANCY. DIALOG online service.

The table is a matrix. The number of a file is uniquely specified by the row and column it is in. Thus, the file in the row labelled *10* and the column labelled *2* is file 12. The entry at the box represents the number of postings retrieved in the corresponding file. For example, *32 postings* were retrieved in File 12. (In the files where a three-concept search was performed later, the results are listed after a slash).

```
? b411;sf 5,8,40,41,55,72,73,152,153,154

            2jul84 14:19:16 User12345
     $1.04  0.016 Hrs File410
     $0.31  Tymnet
     $1.35  Estimated Total Cost

File411:DIALINDEX(tm)
(Copr. DIALOG Inf.Ser.Inc.)

File5:BIOSIS Previews 81-84/JuL BA7801;RRM2710
File8:COMPENDEX - 70-84/Jun
File40:ENVIROLINE - 70-84/Jun
File41:Pollution Abstracts - 70-84/May
File55:BIOSIS Previews - 1977 thru 1980
File72:EMBASE (Excerpta Medica) 80-84/Iss15
File73:EMBASE (Excerpta Medica) In process 84/Wk17
File152:MEDLINE - 66-72
File153:MEDLINE - 73-79
File154:MEDLINE - 80-84/Jul

        File Items Description
        ---- ----- -----------
? s nois? and pregnan?
         (5)
                2551 NOIS?
               15727 PREGNAN?
                  19  NOIS? AND PREGNAN?
         (8)
               32901 NOIS?
                 194 PREGNAN?
                   4  NOIS? AND PREGNAN?
        (40)
                2882 NOIS?
                 357 PREGNAN?
                   2  NOIS? AND PREGNAN?
        (41)
                5835 NOIS?
                 321 PREGNAN?
                   8  NOIS? AND PREGNAN?
        (55)
                2520 NOIS?
               13356 PREGNAN?
                   7  NOIS? AND PREGNAN?
        (72)
                3855 NOIS?
               32806 PREGNAN?
                  36  NOIS? AND PREGNAN?
        (73)
                 294 NOIS?
                2455 PREGNAN?
                   1  NOIS? AND PREGNAN?
```

Fig. 11-20. A simple two-concept search on NOISE and PREGNANCY in a Master Index file retrieved only a small fraction of the postings previously retrieved with a multiterm search (compare with Fig. 11-19). DIALOG online service. File 411:Dialindex.

```
                    (152)
                              2712 NOIS?
                             55170 PREGNAN?
                              20  NOIS? AND PREGNAN?
                    (153)
                              3531 NOIS?
                             76406 PREGNAN?
                              50  NOIS? AND PREGNAN?
                    (154)
                              3188 NOIS?
                             56906 PREGNAN?
                              42  NOIS? AND PREGNAN?

             ? b5

                         2jul84 14:21:30 User12345
                 $1.37   0.039 Hrs File411 20 Descriptors
                 $0.31   Tymnet
                 $1.68   Estimated Total Cost
```

search strategy in Files 135:Congressional Record, 136:Federal Register, 166:GPO Publications Reference, or 244:Laborlaw, which primarily reflect activities of the US government and congress, denotes an apparent lack of legislative activity in the area of our search. On the other hand, the single unit record retrieved with our strategy in File 20:Federal Index did reveal that a certain US congressman favors a bill to reduce aircraft noise at Washington National Airport, since ". . . new research links birth defects with jet zoom." Similarly important for the purpose of our investigation were at least two out of seven records retrieved in File 101:CIS (Congressional Information Service).

Another interesting observation based on the numbers presented in Fig. 11-19 concerns an obvious pattern; that is, the newer a file is, the more useful unit records were found on the subject of our search (of course, relative to the file size). This trend is quite typical of many other new areas of knowledge as well.

The distribution of postings retrieved with the two-concept search strategy in a number of files is shown in Fig. 11-21.

> The solid-line curve on this figure is typical of the distribution of results in a successful two-concept search.

THE DEVELOPMENT OF A SUBORDINATE CLAUSE

As illustrated in Fig.11-21, a user may expect that in several files the number of postings will exceed the limit that we consider to be manageable (40-60 postings), even if a search is well-constructed. In order to bring this number to a manageable level, we normally superimpose a third *subordinate concept* to be used only in those files where the number of postings exceed our chosen threshold level.

> For a subordinate concept we recommend the use of a saved search that covers a broad area of the subject expert's interest. Such a search can be permanently stored online and used only when needed. A subordinate clause search is normally used in order to increase the relevancy of the final results.

The area of specialization of the subject expert for whom the search was performed was OCCUPATIONAL HEALTH AND SAFETY. Working in this area, he and his colleagues frequently used as a subordinate clause a prefabricated auxiliary search that broadly describes this area. The search

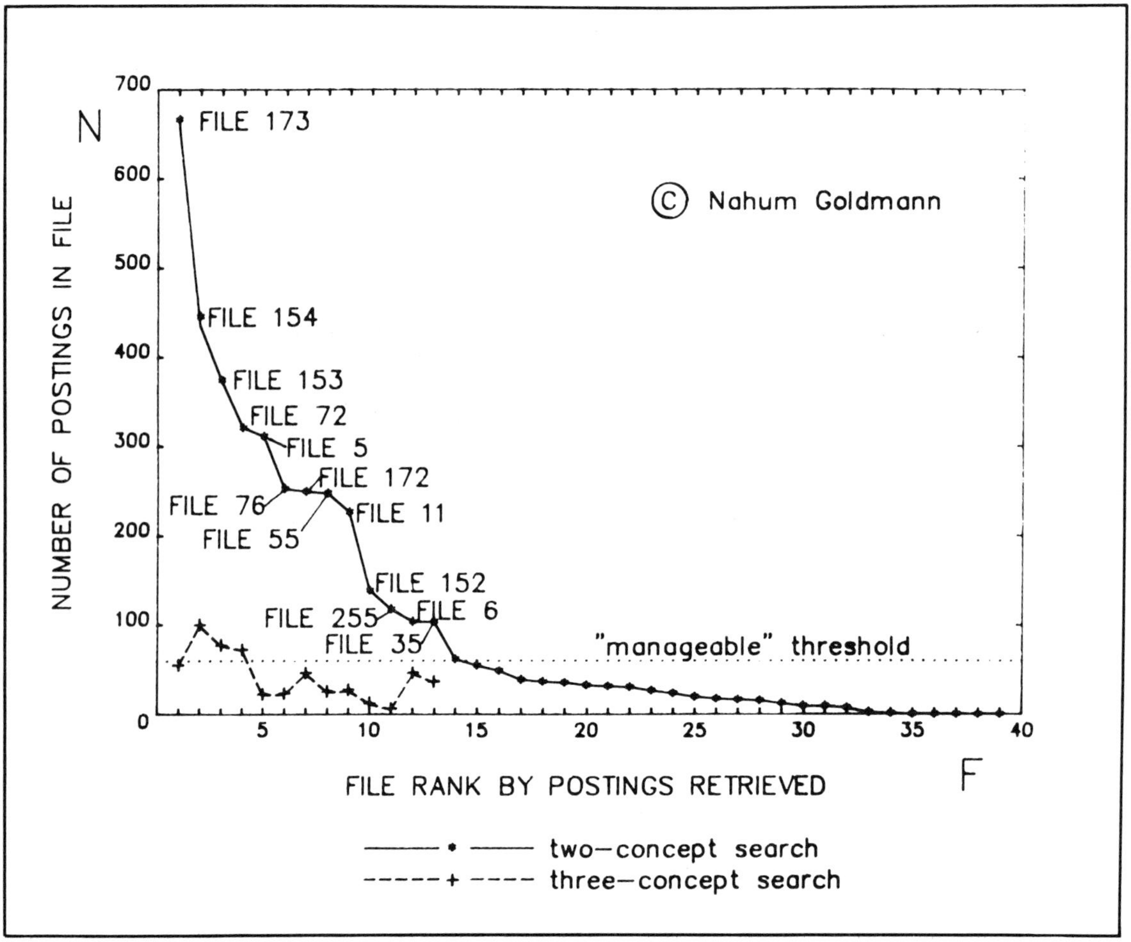

Fig. 11-21. The distribution of postings retrieved by executing a two/three-concept search on NOISE and PREGNANCY. DIALOG online service.

N is the number of postings in a file. F is the rank of a file which is assigned during the two-concept search in accordance with the number of postings retrieved from it. Thus, F = 1 is the file from which the largest number of postings have been retrieved, F = 2 is the file with the second largest number of postings, and so on.

was permanently stored online in DIALOG online service and used when needed (see Fig. 11-22).

You can see in Fig. 11-22 that the number of postings from File 5 was dramatically reduced when the principal clause (Fig. 11-18) was ANDed with the subordinate clause (from 311 to 21 postings). Many of these postings where found to be highly relevant to the subject under investigation.

Such a large reduction in the number of postings after using a subordinate clause does not happen very frequently. In practice, the degree of reduction with a subordinate clause would likely be three to five times. This is usually sufficient when bringing a two-concept search down to a manageable level.

In our example, we ANDed a principal clause with a subordinate third concept in only those 13 files where the number of postings for the two-concept search exceeded the 60-posting threshold. The results of the three-concept search are shown in the table (Fig. 11-19) and also in Fig. 11-21. The

```
? .exs 6g5y
            34  4961 OCCUPAT?
            35  5217 INDUSTR?
            36 17513 WORK?
            37 11188 EMPLOY?
            38  5862 SAFE?
            39   551 JOB?
            40  2580 HAZARD?
            41 13658 RISK?
            42  4887 ADVERSE?
            43    75 ANNOY?
            44 57676  34-43/OR

? c 33 and 44
            45    21  33 AND 44

? t45/6/1-3
45/6/1
76052985
  THE  RISK OF INFERTILITY AND DELAYED CONCEPTION ASSOCIATED WITH EXPOSURES
IN THE DANISH WORKPLACE.

45/6/2
74030591
  NEO  NATAL  BODY  WEIGHT  IN BABIES DELIVERED BY FACTORY WORKERS FROM THE
DEPARTMENT OF PROTECTED WORK.

45/6/3
71079414
  THE  RISK OF HEARING IMPAIRMENT IN CHILDREN FROM MOTHERS EXPOSED TO NOISE
DURING PREGNANCY
```

Fig. 11-22. Use of a third subordinate concept OCCUPATIONAL HEALTH AND SAFETY in a search on NOISE and PREGNANCY (see Fig. 11-18). DIALOG online service. File 5:BIOSIS Previews. (Courtesy of BioSciences Information Service. © 1984 BioSciences Information Service.)

end-users who conducted an analyses of the results of three-concept searches confirmed their usefulness.

> In practice, an end-user would execute a two-concept search in a set of selected files in order to get useful results. Every time a two-concept search results in a number of postings that exceeds your predetermined threshold, you can further limit the number of postings by using a third subordinate concept.

The subject expert should select for himself the posting threshold he believes is appropriate to his professional objectives. The chosen threshold depends on such factors as the desired completeness of the search results, the overall budget for information gathering (which includes direct online cost or the cost of professional labor necessary for preparation and running the search), and the expected cost-effectiveness of the information gathering activities.

In evaluating the last factor, the end-user should also take into consideration the overall reduction of project costs due to the use of results already obtained elsewhere. It pays not to repeat somebody else's costly mistakes.

Also relevant to the selection of the threshold

is the degree of novelty in the area of search. The newer the search subject and the less established its terminology, the higher the threshold required to retrieve useful information.

> **Evaluation by the end-user of the final results of an online search, be it a two- or a three-concept strategy, is absolutely necessary in order to select only these records that he will be using in his subsequent work. It is impractical now and in the future to expect that use of computer systems alone can assure the high relevancy of the results obtained. However, the end-user can gain quite a lot of new knowledge by examining data selected with the help of computer systems.**

In several files the final results exceeded our selected threshold of 60 postings even after the three-concept search was performed. The material obtained with our three-concept search, however, was judged by the end-user to be so highly relevant to the subject of the search that it was certainly worth the additional effort of scanning all the titles.

The alternative of further narrowing the prestored auxiliary concept was found to be less cost effective, taking into account the time that the subject expert would have to have spent in order to reformulate the third concept and to run a new search in the high-contents files. In addition, from the expert's point of view, it was highly desirable and worthwhile to scan all the records retrieved after using the third concept.

In only one case did our search not run smoothly. This occurred in File 173:EMBASE (Excerpta Medica), whose many large unit records resulted in an overflow of the computer disk memory when our search was processed. There were two principal reasons for this.

First, File 173 is almost three times larger than the more recent Files 172 or 72 of the same database (each of the last two files themselves contain more than 500,000 records). Second, EMBASE's records are well-indexed and typically include abstracts as well. Therefore, the number of useful records retrieved in this file was much higher than in similar sized files whose records are not as well described by abstracts and indexes.

A relatively minor modification of our original search strategy allowed us to conduct a search in File 173 and to obtain valuable results.

In practice, however, the likelihood of having to modify a properly designed search strategy in this way is low. Excerpta Medica is rather an exception amongst databases of its kind, having a reputation of being one of the best-maintained online databases on medicine and biology.

Some of the records retrieved with our search strategy were only indirectly related to the subject of the search as it was expressed initially. The end-user, however, stressed the importance of such supplemental results to their own work, as they provided information concerning new and unexpected aspects of the problem. It would be quite difficult to retrieve such records using conventional searching methods.

CONCLUSIONS

In this chapter we defined the search strategy as the science and art of using the subject knowledge of an expert and the potential of information retrieval systems. This is done in order to achieve both the immediate and long-term objectives of the subject expert and also to assure cost-effectiveness in his overall professional activity.

The Subject Expert Searching Technique includes three kinds of searches referred to as subject, name, and citation searches. Our technique is based on the assumption that a subject search is the most important kind of information activity for a subject expert in pursuing his professional objectives.

In our searching technique a search strategy is organized with the help of a special search strategy form. The information requested in the form is essential, and the form, found in the Appendix, should be clearly and concisely filled out.

The choice of online services on which a given search will be performed depends on many factors. In our technique, a search strategy statement is constructed in such a way that it can be easily modified for running on a new online service. It is, however, advisable for a searcher to choose one principal-resource online service. In this chapter, we formulated the criteria for selection of a principal online service.

We defined a search strategy statement as a specified collection of terms and logical operators arranged by a subject expert in order to convey a particular thought. Concepts in the search statement consist of sets of terms.

Building a set of terms for a particular concept is one of the most important tasks required of the subject expert during the information retrieval process. Such a task should not be entrusted to anybody else. We examined the use of different sources in the process of compiling a set of terms.

The basic kind of search statement in our Subject Expert Searching Technique is the two/three-concept search. In the statement, two concepts constitute a principal clause, whereas the third concept may (or may not) be used as a subordinate clause. AND operators combine and limit concepts in the search statement.

In order to be successful, the resulting combination of concepts should produce a set of unit records whose meaning is relevant to the original problem formulated by the end-user. The number of postings retrieved by a search statement in each file should be manageable. To be manageable, we recommend that the threshold number of postings retrieved in each file should be in the order of 40-60. In practice, the user should select for himself the posting threshold he believes is appropriate to his professional objectives.

The chosen threshold depends on such factors as the desired completeness of the search results, the overall budget for information inquiry (which includes direct online cost or the cost of professional labor that is necessary for the preparation and running of (a search), and the expected cost effectiveness of the information gathering activities.

We demonstrated the development of a two/three-concept statement using a particular search request as an example. After developing a principal clause, we conducted its online adaptation. Then, we discussed various techniques, such as temporarily saving searches, that are useful during the adaptation process. In order to bring the number of postings to a manageable level, we added a third subordinate concept to be used only in those files where the number of postings exceeded our threshold level.

The end-user's evaluation of the final results of an online search, whether it uses two or three concepts, is absolutely necessary in order to select only these records that will be used in his subsequent work. It is impractical now and in the future to expect that the use of computer systems alone can assure high relevancy of the results obtained. The end-user, however, can gain quite a lot of new knowledge by examining data selected with the help of computer systems.

For a subordinate concept, we recommend the use of a saved search that covers a broad area of the subject expert's interest. Such a search can be permanently stored online and used only when needed.

An analysis of the material retrieved online confirmed that the three-concept search produced very useful information.

Chapter 12

Running A Search

A search strategy statement developed before a searching session starts inevitably undergoes certain changes during the search itself.

TWO OR THREE CONCEPTS?

We did not use a full three-concept search in all the files investigated in the previous chapter (see Figs. 11-19 and 11-21) for the following reasons:

- To execute a third concept in a search requires on the average 50 percent more time than a two-concept search. This operation does not make much sense when a two-concept search has already resulted in a relatively small number of postings.
- However well a third concept has been defined, thereby increasing the relevancy of the final results, it is never ideal and may eliminate some useful unit records. If the number of postings retrieved with a two-concept search is relatively small, it is easier and more efficient to search manually. The subject expert is, after all, a better judge of the relevancy of the material retrieved than a computer is.
- In small files specializing in a particular subject, a search focusing on the subject of a file could be useless. For example, a search on the concept of POLLUTION in File 41:Pollution Abstracts would be unproductive, as most of the unit records in this file deal with pollution. It is also unlikely that the unit records in File 41 would include the index term POLLUTION.

Therefore, it is more efficient to use a two-concept search statement to search in all selected files and then to AND the results of such a search with a subordinate clause concept. Such an ANDing takes place only in files where the number of postings retrieved with the principal clause exceeds the chosen manageable threshold.

In practice, only about one-third of all selected files would require the use of a third subordinate concept.

Our auxiliary search statement shown in Fig. 11-22 effectively retrieved such commonly used terms as OCCUPATIONAL HEALTH AND SAFETY, INDUSTRIAL HYGIENE, and ADVERSE EFFECTS. In order to evaluate its efficiency, we executed this search in File 72:EMBASE (Excerpta Medica). The choice of File 72 was based on its large number of unit records and its very well-developed classification scheme. The high quality of EMBASE's indexing and abstracting services and its consistency in application of the thesaurus terms are, unfortunately, the exception rather than the rule amongst various databases currently available online.

The auxiliary search, after being ANDed with the principal clause, further limited the results to 71 unit records (see Fig. 12-1, set number 45). ANDing the same two-concept search with the portion of File 72 that is exclusively devoted to the subject of our auxiliary search (subfile 35:Occupational Health, set number 46) resulted in only 18 postings (see set number 47).

It is very important to note that all of the postings from subfile 35 were also retrieved with the auxiliary search strategy. This is despite the fact that the search was initially organized in a database with a different subject.

Thus, a "universal" search strategy that is suitable for most of the bibliographic files could retrieve all the records that are described with special controlled vocabulary. It is not really necessary to build as many searches as there are databases to search—a very time consuming, costly, and ineffective operation.

We examined in detail the citations retrieved. The unit records retrieved using subfile 35 all dealt directly with the occupational environment. The additional 53 unit records retrieved using the subordinate clause (see set number 48) varied in their relevancy. Many unit records in this additional set were judged by the end-user to be very useful in his subsequent work.

The usefulness of the "universal" auxiliary search strategy is even more apparent in files with less consistently developed and applied controlled vocabulary than EMBASE.

SELECTING FILES

The files in our sample were chosen to be representative of all banks of data that might include information on the subject of interest to us; this information should present the investigated problem from different angles.

Thus, such files as 5,55,255:BIOSIS Previews; 152,153,154:Medline; 72,73,172,173:Excerpta Medica; 11:Psychinfo; 140: Psycalert; and 76:Life Sciences Collection present this information from the point of view of biomedical sciences. In these files, an expert would expect to find information primarily devoted to the effects of different environmental conditions on human reproduction.

Files 8:Compendex; 12,13:Inspec; 14:Ismec; 165:Engineering Meetings may provide information that emphasizes noise effects in the industrial environment, whereas File 15:ABI/Inform is often a good source of information on occupational health problems in the office environment.

File 7:Social Scisearch is devoted to social, behavioral, and related sciences. Files 40:Enviroline, 41:Pollution Abstracts, 68:Environmental Bibliography, and 161:Occupational Safety and Health (NIOSH) are selected since they are devoted to information on pollutants, especially in the occupational environment.

On the other hand, in such files as 34,87,94,186:Scisearch one can find information in all areas of scientific and technical knowledge. The same can be said of files like 6:NTIS, 35:Comprehensive Dissertation Abstracts, 426:MARC (Library of Congress catalogs), and 77:Conference Papers Index, except that they also

```
? b72;.exs 6z6z

          23mar85 17:41:21 User13482
    $0.91 0.029 Hrs File75 31 Descriptors
    $0.21 Tymnet
    $1.12 Estimated Total Cost

File72:EMBASE (EXCERPTA MEDICA) 82-85/Iss08
Copr. ESP BV/EM 1985
        Set Items Description
        --- ----- -----------
          1  2767 SOUND?
          2  2431 NOIS?
          3   566 SONIC?
          4  1921 ACOUSTIC?
          5  6452  1-4/OR
          6121441 DIAGNOSTIC?
          7  9927 SCAN?
          8  2308 ULTRASONIC?
          9     3 ULTRA(W)SONIC?
         10  7066 ULTRASOUND?
         11    20 ULTRA(W)SOUND?
         12  1540 SONOGRAPH?
         13129146  6-12/OR
         14  7414 BIRTH?
         15   144 CHILDBEAR?
         16  4446 FERTIL?
         17 27228 EMBRYO?
         18 12161 FETAL?
         19 18339 FETUS?
         20  5823 GESTAT?
         21    88 GRAVIDIT?
         22 13983 MALFORM?
         23    80 MISCARR?
         24  1407 OFFSPRING?
         25   476 OOGENES?
         26  4220 POSTNATAL?
         27 22359 PREGNAN?
         28  3254 PRENATAL?
         29 41944 REPRODUCTIVE?
         30   974 RESORPTION?
         31  8214 TERATOGEN?
         32103760  14-31/OR
         33   321  (5 NOT 13) AND 32

? .exs 6g5y

         34 19586 OCCUPAT?
         35 40567 INDUSTR?
         36 21758 WORK?
         37  9634 EMPLOY?
         38  8288 SAFE?
         39   974 JOB?
         40  3765 HAZARD?
```

Fig. 12-1. An example of a three-concept search executed in one file. DIALOG online service. File 72;EMBASE.

```
                41 16852 RISK?
                42 33095 ADVERSE?
                43    91 ANNOY?
                44110954  34-43/OR

? c 33 and 44

                45    71  33 AND 44

? s sf=035

                46 16504 SF=035  OCCUPATIONAL HEALTH

? c 33 and 46

                47    18  33 AND 46

? c 45 not 47

                48    53  45 NOT 47
```

Fig. 12-1. (Continued from page 150.)

represent such bibliographic materials as reports, dissertations, conference presentations, and research proposals. File 47:Magazine Index is an important source of information from several hundred popular U.S. and Canadian magazines.

Information from the last two files, as well as from File 165:Engineering Meetings, is often more up-to-date than that from other files because of the nature of data in them, and thus they may be of special interest to the end-user. Results found in book files, such as File 426:MARC, may be especially important, since few databases include descriptions of nonperiodic publications. Existing book files, unfortunately, are not well indexed and do not include abstracts in the unit records.

Finally, as noted previously, searching in the U.S. Government Files 20:PTS Federal Index, 101:CIS (Congressional Information Service), 135:Congressional Record Abstracts, 136:Federal Register Abstracts, 166:GPO Publications Reference File, and 244:Laborlaw produced modest results, which suggest at least some interest in this subject on the part of the U.S. Congress and Government. At the same time, it also proved the lack of serious legislative activity in the United States in this area.

Of course, searches done in a number of files result in a certain degree of duplication with several unit records describing the same publication. However, the degree of duplication is not as large as one may expect. Descriptions of three to five articles may be found in most of the bibliographic files and a dozen more are covered in two, and sometimes three different files. Those duplicates should be recognized as core information. The majority of the records (up to 80 percent) did not have any duplicates at all. Most of the files from our sample contributed at least several unit records to the final set.

Even postings from different files that describe the same article may significantly vary in their information content. Some may not list all the authors or provide crucial information concerning the organizational source or the article's language; others do not include the abstracts. Sometimes, it requires several unit records to assemble the necessary information. This may be especially important when the original publication is not easily obtainable or is published in a foreign language.

The average cost of executing the saved two/three-concept search in one file listed on the printouts, as shown in Fig. 12-1 was US$3.61 (the cost of printing the records is not included here). The time taken to run a saved search through a file was always less than 3 minutes. Although this cost is not excessive for such an intensive search, it can be further reduced. Savings due to a high volume of searching or use of nonbusiness hours can cut this figure by as much as half.

The records can be printed out inexpensively in the offline mode (US$10-30 per 100 unit records). As a consequence, the price of online searching may be significantly lower than that of manual searching and may provide much more effective results.

Before starting a search, the end-user should consult the latest list of accessible files and mark on the search strategy form all the files to be searched. A manageable saved search can later be executed in all those files by a delegated searcher in order to save the subject expert's time.

MAKING A SEARCH MANAGEABLE

For an online searcher, it is desirable that a two-concept search be *manageable*. In more precise terms, the distribution of postings should be similar to the solid curve in Fig. 11-21. The number of postings should exceed your conditional threshold level in only a few files.

What if this condition is not met? In this case, a common recommendation of conventional searching techniques is to limit further the final concept by ANDing it with additional concepts. This limiting procedure is usually repeated until the final number of postings is small enough.

However, superimposing numerous additional concepts is an artificial solution that may create even more problems than it solves. Additional concepts cannot be suddenly pulled out of the air because they should be an integral part of an already developed overall strategy in which concepts have been related and interconnected. This strategy is the result of intensive intellectual activity on the part of a subject expert. It should first and foremost correspond to the expert's objectives and assure the success of his professional task. In addition, the development of another set of terms and the running of these through a number of files requires extra time and resources.

In the multiconcept search statement, there is a great difference between the first concept and any subsequent concepts that are combined with the AND logic. The very first concept introduces a certain subject into the search statement. An additional concept is used primarily in order to exclude undesirable subjects from the set of unit records formed by the first concept.

Thus, the additional concept reduces the number of unit records produced by the first concept. Of course, this does not mean that the second concept in the principal clause is subordinate to the first concept; they are coequal. The superimposing of the second concept makes the end-user's work easier as the total number of unit records that he has to analyze is dramatically reduced.

Due to the ambiguity of language structure and special terminology, each subsequent reduction by an additional concept may exclude certain unit records that are potentially useful for the subject expert. As additional concepts are introduced, it is more likely that some useful information will be omitted from the final set of unit records. When conventional searching techniques are used, this problem is further exaggerated because of their reliance upon index term searching.

On the other hand, properly developing a concept in your searching technique also means locating as many terms as possible that describe this concept. This is a time consuming task. Often, an improperly chosen concept has a high degree of correlation with a concept already used in the search statement. This could lead to a situation where the additional concept does not significantly reduce the number of postings and thus is useless. The time, money and other resources used in developing a concept would be lost.

Our experience shows that a properly

organized two/three-concept search should be sufficient to retrieve useful information in most practical situations. When more than three concepts are combined with the AND logic, it may be conceptually confusing and unnecessarily restrictive. This is the primary reason for the introduction of the two/three-concept search statement as the basic kind of search statement in our technique.

Instead of superimposing additional concepts, the subject expert has other options in formulating more precise search statements. We consider those options more powerful and better suited to the objectives of a search. If the subject expert is not satisfied with the existing search strategy, he may:

1. Eliminate *noise.*
2. Reformulate each of the two principal concepts so that the resulting search statement will cover a much narrower subject.
3. Combine two or more concepts into one, using the proximity searching feature.

ELIMINATION OF "NOISE"

Elimination of "noise," that is of an undesirable subconcept, is effective only if this subconcept is:

- Easily defined
- Consistently present in the unit records retrieved in several files with the first version of the search strategy
- Constitutes a significant share of the search results

In order to clarify the final search statement and make future modifications easier, we usually exclude a noisy subconcept from one of the concepts of the principle clause immediately. This operation is done with the help of the NOT operator.

The procedure of noise elimination was illustrated in the previous chapter, particularly in Fig. 11-18.

If any of the above criteria for the existence of a noisy subconcept is not met, it is beneficial to select one of the alternative routes for making a search manageable.

REFORMULATING A SEARCH

Several examples shown before illustrate the process of creating a search strategy. The final version of the search on NOISE and PREGNANCY (Fig. 12-1) was successful in accordance with our criteria. This is particularly true because it produced a manageable number of postings. Our analysis showed that a significant proportion of these postings were relevant to the original problem.

The success of this particular search was to a large extent based on the proper formulation of the problem being investigated. Unfortunately, in many cases we are not as lucky when formulating a search strategy. However, the skill of developing a search strategy is something that can be mastered over a relatively short period, provided the searcher knows the subject area well.

Suppose that a two-concept search is not successful; that is, when executed in one or several important files, it retrieves too many postings even when a third subordinate concept is used. Moreover, most of the unit records retrieved with such a search do not really relate to the problem under investigation. It also appears that the useless records are not a well-defined subset easily excluded from the search statement with the NOT operator.

In this case, the subject expert can reformulate his search using narrower concepts in building his search strategy.

The fundamental solution is to narrow down one or two concepts in the principal clause. Such a reformulation of the concepts can be very effective and should be used as much as practically possible.

Suppose that a search is performed on the existing and proposed REGULATIONS on NOISE EXPOSURE, especially in the INDUSTRIAL ENVIRONMENT.

The first version of the search strategy is shown in Fig. 12-2. The results of the first version of this search are shown in Fig. 12-3.

The analysis of the search results showed that it was not manageable since it retrieved too many irrelevant postings.

Instead of trying to AND the existing search results with more and more additional concepts, the subject expert can reformulate the search by choosing narrower concepts in the principal clause. Suppose that instead of dealing with the whole wide area of noise regulations, we choose to concentrate only on REGULATIONS specifically devoted to IMPULSE NOISE.

The second version of our search strategy would include the concepts and terms shown in Fig. 12-4.

We then create a second version of our search in an online service by introducing a new concept, IMPULSE, and ANDing this new concept with two old concepts, NOISE and REGULATIONS, from

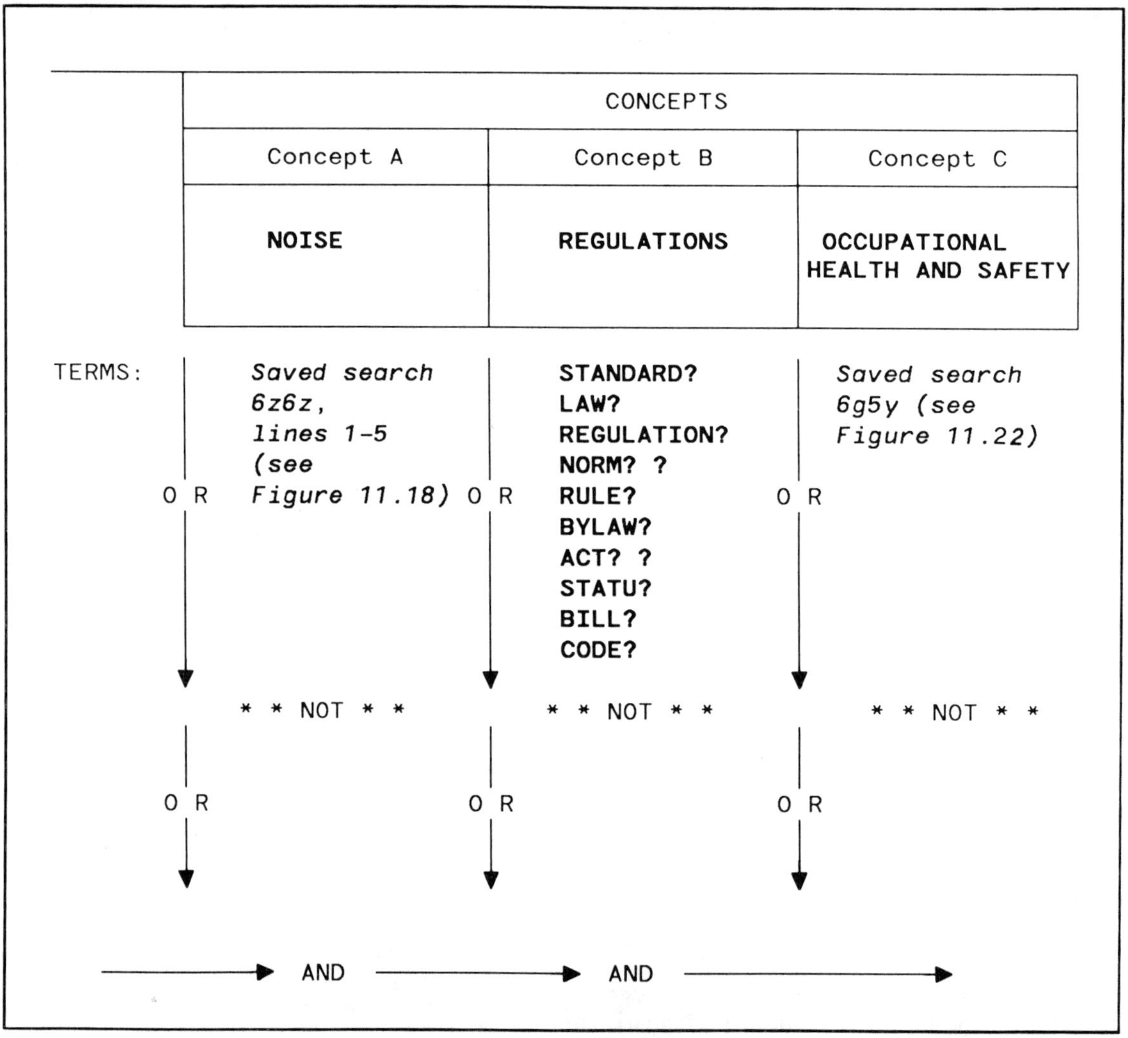

Fig. 12-2. The search form with the first version of a three-concept search strategy.

```
File153:MEDLINE - 73-79
         Set Items Description
         --- ----- -----------
? .exs 6z6z/1-5
           1  3692 SOUND?
           2  3531 NOIS?
           3  1312 SONIC?
           4  6212 ACOUSTIC?
           5 12976  1-4/OR
? s standard?
           6 38497 STANDARD?
? s law?
           7  3028 LAW?
? s regulation?
           8 16692 REGULATION?
? s norm? ?
           9  1346 NORM? ?
? s rule?
          10  3129 RULE?
? s bylaw?
          11   100 BYLAW?
? s by(w)law?
          12     0 BY(W)LAW?
? s act? ?
          13  9199 ACT? ?
? s statu?
          14 15494 STATU?
? s bill?
          15   975 BILL?
? s code?
          16  3931 CODE?
? c 6-16/or
          17 88683  6-16/OR
? c 5 and 17
          18   829  5 AND 17
? .exs 6g5y
          19 20963 OCCUPAT?
          20  9385 INDUSTR?
          21 28874 WORK?
          22 12781 EMPLOY?
          23  7786 SAFE?
          24  1412 JOB?
          25  3688 HAZARD?
          26 17152 RISK?
          27 95874 ADVERSE?
          28    86 ANNOY?
          29170765  19-28/OR
? c 18 and 29
          30   215  18 AND 29
```

Fig. 12-3. The first version of a search on Noise Regulators. DIALOG online service. File 153:Medline.

The block consisting of lines 1-5 is taken from our previous search on *noise* and *pregnancy* (see Fig. 12-1, and 12-2).

the previous search version.

The results of the second version (Fig. 12-5) show that our new search strategy is more manageable than the first version. It is now easier to put together a final version of our search by selecting only those parts of a temporarily saved search statement that are actually needed. The final version will be shorter than the version shown in Fig. 12-5 since it does not include saved search 6g5y on OCCUPATIONAL HEALTH AND SAFETY and several auxiliary logical statements. This "cleaned up" final version of the search on IMPULSE NOISE REGULATIONS can then be rapidly executed in all selected files.

The subject expert should remember, though, that the selection process for a narrower primary concept is not always easy. Certain conceptually narrow terms may be mentioned more often in the literature than broader terms (see Fig. 12-6). The user should be aware of such a possibility and be ready to modify his search strategy accordingly.

COMBINING TWO CONCEPTS INTO ONE WITH A PROXIMITY SEARCH

In Chapter 9 we illustrated the use of a proximity operator in the retrieval of standard terms consisting of two or more separate words. The proximity search can also be used for combining two or more concepts into one narrower and more precise concept.

Suppose that we have to perform a search on CONTROL of IMPULSE NOISE, particularly in the INDUSTRIAL ENVIRONMENT. The first version of our search statement is shown in Fig. 12-7.

The first version of our search, performed in File 13:Inspec, was not manageable as the search retrieved too many postings (see Fig. 12-8).

In order to make the search manageable, we can combine two principle clause concepts into one with the help of the proximity operator, as shown in Fig. 12-9.

The results of a search performed with the second version of the search strategy are shown in Fig. 12-10.

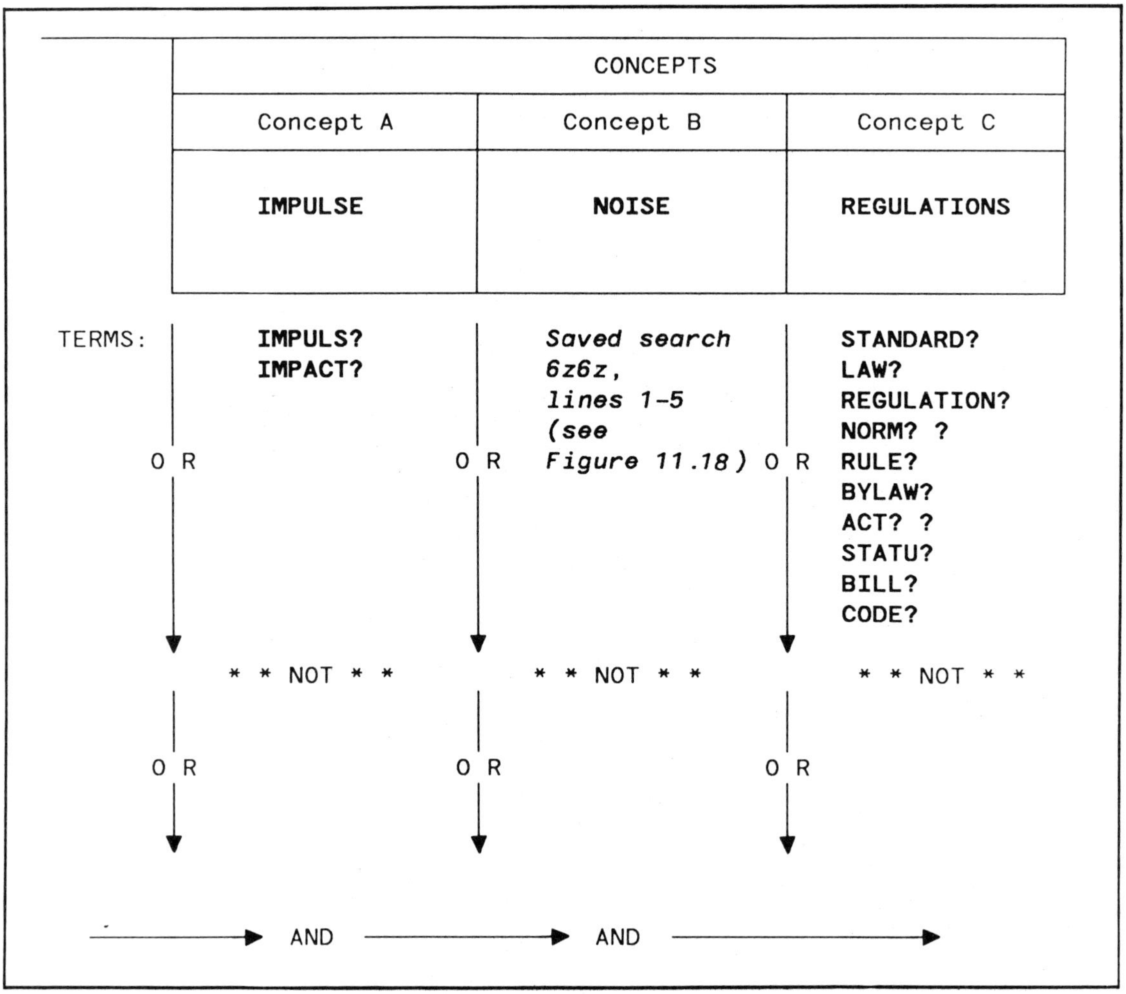

Fig. 12-4. The search form with the second version of the search strategy.

```
? s impuls?
          31   2628 IMPULS?
? s impact?
          32   3742 IMPACT?
? c 31 or 32
          33   6354   31 OR 33
? c 33 and 18
          35     19   34 AND 18
```

Fig. 12-5. The second version of the search on IMPULSE NOISE REGULATIONS is a continuation of the search shown in Fig. 12-3. DIALOG online service. File 153:Medline.

The use of the proximity operator in combining two concepts into one may increase the precision of a search; however, the disadvantage of such term combinations is the increased number of terms to key in. Also, the subject expert should remember that such combinations are effective only when the terminology of the investigated problem is well-established. Being well-established means that the two words have become a stable word combination and are frequently used together in the special literature and in practical situations. Until a word combination reaches such a point, a proximity search would be ineffective.

```
SS 1 /C?
USER:
scandinavia

PROG:
SS 1 PSTG (827)

SS 2 /C?
USER:
denmark

PROG:
SS 2 PSTG (1094)

SS 3 /C?
USER:
finland

PROG:
SS 3 PSTG (1922)

SS 4 /C?
USER:
norway

PROG:
SS 4 PSTG (3541)

SS 5 /C?
USER:
sweden

PROG:
SS 5 PSTG (3428)
```

Fig. 12-6. The broader term (*Scandinavia*) retrieved fewer unit records than some of the narrower terms (such as *Denmark* or *Sweden*). ORBIT online service. File Georeff.

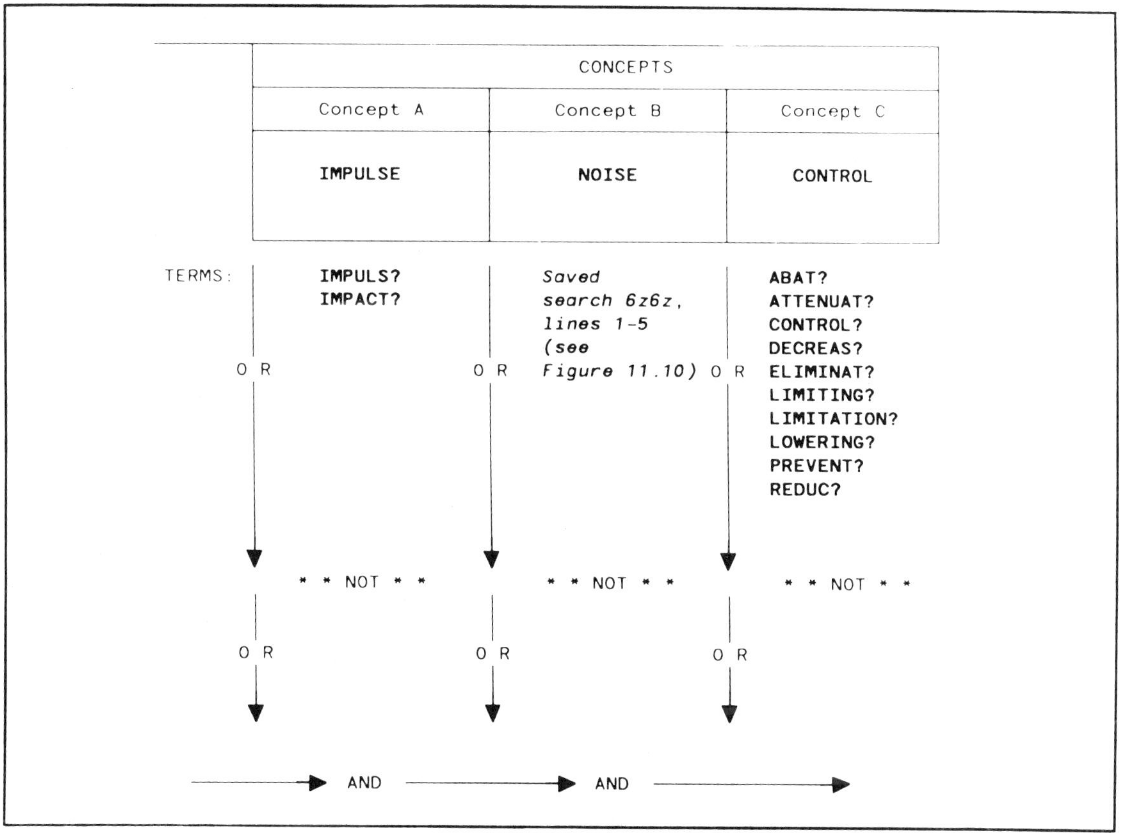

Fig. 12-7. The search form with a version of a search that does not use the proximity operator.

Some inexperienced searchers may misuse the proximity search feature and sometimes connect three or even more words using proximity operators. An increase of precision here is almost always done at the expense of reduced information value. This is because such a search does not allow for the retrieval of newly established word combinations that may have a high information value from the end-user's point of view.

CONCLUSIONS

In our technique, we use a two-concept search statement to search in all selected files. We AND the results of such a search with a subordinate clause concept only in files where the number of postings retrieved with the principal clause exceeds the chosen manageable threshold.

Several examples in Chapters 11 and 12 illustrate the use of a two-three concept search. The files in these examples were chosen to be representative of all banks of data that might include information on the subject of interest to us; the variety of files used presents the investigated problem from different angles.

The average cost of executing a saved two/three-concept search in one file in our case was US$3.61. The time taken to run a saved search through a file was always less than 3 minutes. Although this cost is not excessive for such an intensive search, it can be further reduced through the use of nonbusiness hours and large volume searching. The records can be printed inexpensively in the offline mode (US$10-30 per 100 unit

Fig. 12-8. The first version of a search on CONTROL of IMPULSE NOISE. DIALOG online service. File 13:INSPEC.

We use two terms LIMITING? and LIMITATION? rather than a truncation after the first t in order to eliminate confusion with the frequently used term LIMIT (meaning *threshold).*

```
File13:INSPEC - 77-84/ISS14
(Copr. IEE)
See File 12(1969 Thru 1976)
           Set Items Description
           --- ----- -----------
             1  6707 IMPULS?
             2 21813 IMPACT?
             3 28264  1 OR 2
             4 12918 SOUND/
             5 16027 SOUND?
             6 30283 NOIS?
             7   766 SONIC?
             8 26530 ACOUSTIC?
             9 61661  4-8/OR
            10  1233 ABAT?
            11 10772 ATTENUAT?
            12140002 CONTROL?
            13 36604 DECREAS?
            14 14599 ELIMINAT?
            15  9085 LIMITING?
            16 11021 LIMITATION?
            17  1914 LOWERING?
            18  7670 PREVENT?
            19 74612 REDUC?
            20274209  10-19/OR
            21   558  3 AND 9 AND 20
```

records). As a consequence, the price of online searching may be much lower than that of manual searching and provide more effective results.

Before beginning a search, the end-user should consult the latest list of accessible files and mark on the search strategy form all the files to be searched. A manageable saved search can later be executed in all those files by a delegated searcher in order to save the subject expert's time.

Our experience shows that a properly organized two/three-concept search should be sufficient to retrieve useful information in most practical situations. When more than three concepts are combined with the AND logic, the search can be confusing and unnecessarily restrictive.

Instead of superimposing additional concepts, the subject expert has other options in formulating more precise search statements. We consider those

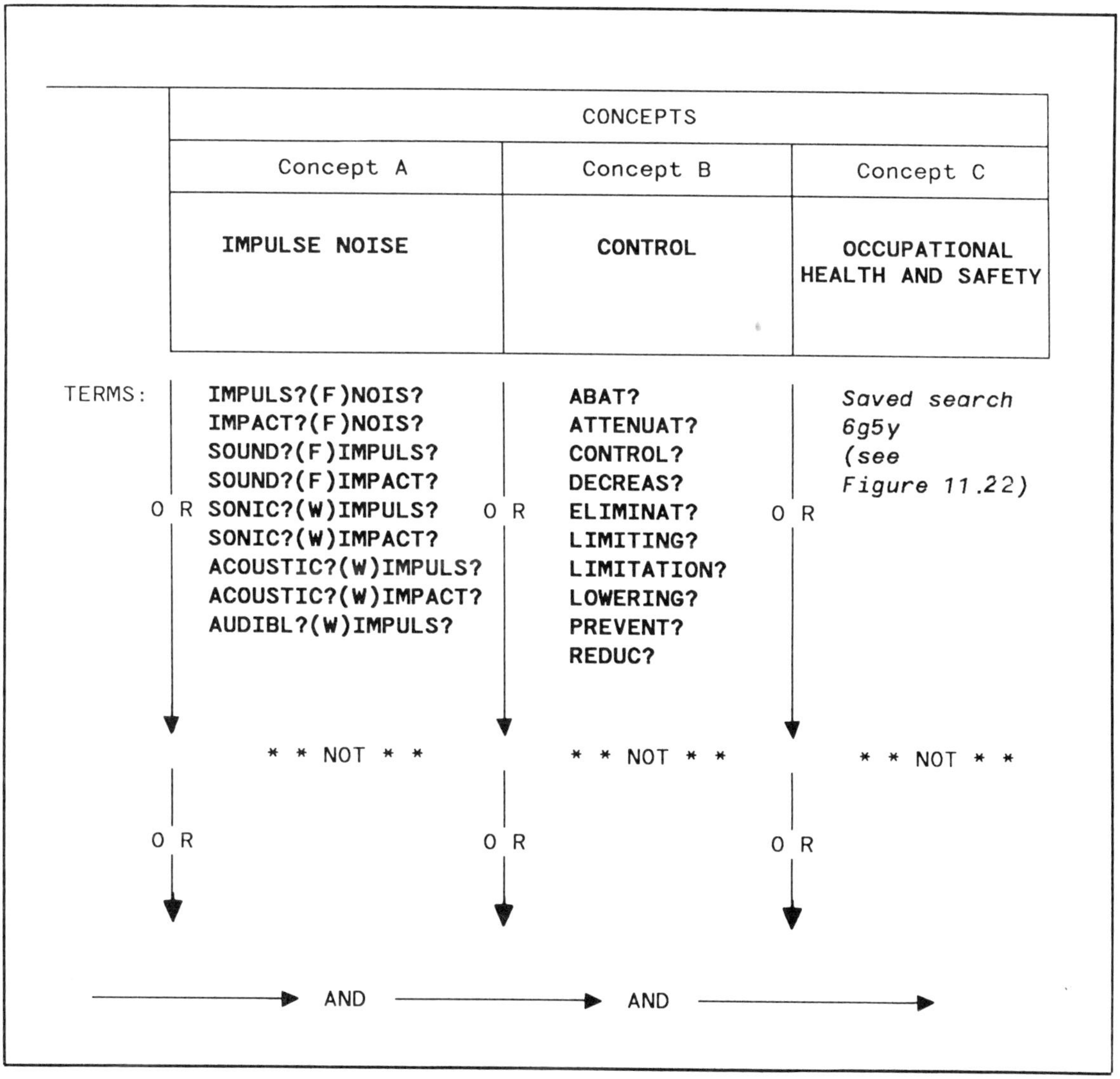

Fig. 12-9. A new version of a search from Fig. 12-7 and 12-8 in which the proximity operator has been used to combine two concepts into one.

```
File13:INSPEC - 77-84/ISS14
(Copr. IEE)
See File 12(1969 Thru 1976)
        Set Items Description
        --- ----- -----------
          1   686 IMPULS?(F)NOIS?
          2   372 IMPACT?(F)NOIS?
          3   221 SOUND?(F)IMPULS?
          4   137 SOUND?(F)IMPACT?
          5     2 SONIC?(W)IMPULS?
          6     0 SONIC?(W)IMPACT?
          7    31 ACOUSTIC?(W)IMPULS?
          8     4 ACOUSTIC?(W)IMPACT?
          9     0 AUDIBL?(W)IMPULS?
         10  1283  1-9/OR
         11  1233 ABAT?
         12 10772 ATTENUAT?
         13140002 CONTROL?
         14 36604 DECREAS?
         15 14599 ELIMINAT?
         16  9085 LIMITING?
         17 11021 LIMITATION?
         18  1914 LOWERING?
         19  7670 PREVENT?
         20 74612 REDUC?
         21274209  12-21/OR
         22  1743 OCCUPAT?
         23 40020 INDUSTR?
         24 75270 WORK?
         25 34322 EMPLOY?
         26 19748 SAFE?
         27  3437 JOB?
         28  3619 HAZARD?
         29  4134 RISK?
         30  1434 ADVERSE?
         31   236 ANNOY?
         32164907  23-32/OR
         33    80  10 AND 21 AND 32
```

Fig. 12-10. The second version of a search on CONTROL of IMPULSE NOISE, especially in the INDUSTRIAL environment. DIALOG online service. File 13:INSPEC.

Several two-word terms in the first concept are combined with the F operator. This operator retrieves two terms that appear in either order (both combinations of IMPULSE NOISE and NOISE IMPULSES will be retrieved using the F operator). Note also that a new term AUDIBLE IMPULSES was found during the previous searches and was included in our search strategy statement, although without any success in this particular file.

options more powerful and better suited to the objectives of a search. If the subject expert is not satisfied with the existing search strategy, he may: 1) eliminate "noise;" 2) reformulate each of the two principal concepts so that the resulting search statement cover a much narrower subject; or 3) combine two or more concepts into one, using proximity searching features.

Chapter 13

Other Approaches

In addition to the subject search, several other approaches can be quite effective in online information gathering.

THE NAME SEARCH

A name search may be conducted for the following reasons:

- It is necessary to reconstruct the methodology and history of achievements of an author, a group of authors, or a scientific school, whose publications were found with a subject search;
- The monitoring of the work of a scientist or a professional prominent in the investigated field is important since his publications are always original and represent state-of-the-art achievements;
- A narrow area of research is not well-developed terminologically and the formulation of a subject search presents certain difficulties. In this case, publications of several key specialists may encompass most of the achievements in this area.

Thus, an author's name may be a valuable identifying characteristic of his particular area of expertise. Since the author may work for an extended period in the same area, his publications could reflect the development of such an area over a period of time. The author's affiliation (organizational source, corporate source) often gives an additional inside look at such factors as the scientific school to which he belongs, the establishment (private, military, or government) that is financing his works, and his general scientific credentials.

> In the information gathering process, it is beneficial to specify a small number of authors contributing the most interesting publications in the area of interest and to monitor their work on a permanent basis.

At first glance it would appear that searching with the name of an author would not cause many difficulties. Most of the reference and source files include an author index that lists the names of

```
File 04: COMPENDEX:1969-84,06
SET ITEMS DESCRIPTION (+=OR;*=AND;-=NOT)
--- ----- ------------------------------
? e au=von gierke

       EXPAND AU=VON GIERKE
REF  INDEX-TERM              TYPE ITEMS RT
E1   AU=VON GERMERSCHEIM,
       KURT------------------       1
E2   AU=VON GERMERSHEIM, KURT       2
E3   AU=VON GERMERSHEIM,
       KURT EDLER------------       1
E4   AU=VON GERSDORFF, B.----       1
E5   AU=VON GESTZKOW,
       WOLFGANG--------------       1
E6  -AU=VON GIERKE-----------
E7   AU=VON GIERKE HE--------       4
E8   AU=VON GIERKE, G.-------       1
E9   AU=VON GIERKE, H. E.----       3
E10  AU=VON GIERKE, HENNING
       E.--------------------       2
E11  AU=VON GIERKE,H. E.-----       1
E12  AU=VON GLADISS, FRITZ---       1
E13  AU=VON GLAHN, PETER-----       1
E14  AU=VON GLAHN, U.--------       3
E15  AU=VON GLAHN, UWE H.----       1
                                     -MORE-
```

Fig. 13-1. Examples of online displays of several parts of the Author Index. ESA online service. File 04:COMPENDEX.

Generally, the name of an author sought online can be found in several places in an author index. If all the variations are not listed in a search, many unit records may not be retrieved. Note that the exact position of punctuation marks and spaces has a crucial role in retrieval of the particular form of a name.

```
586902   DATABASE: NNI File 111
  Kadafi flap: the conflict comes in public relations. (Muammar Qadhafi)
  Geyelin, Philip
  Los Angeles Times   v102   Section II  p7  Feb 25  1983
  col 5   017 col in.
  illustration; cartoon
  EDITION: Fri
  GEOGRAPHIC CODE: NNUS; FFLY   SIC CODE: 9721
  NAMED PEOPLE: Quadhafi, Muammar-foreign relations
  DESCRIPTORS: military policy-political aspects; United States-relations
with Libya; Libya-relations with the United States; detrrence
(strategy)-political aspects; international relations-political aspects


    Last name variations found in File 211:NEWSEARCH:
         el-Qaddafi
         Kadafi
         Kaddafi
         Qaddafi
         Qadhafi
         Quaddafi
         Quadhafi
         Qudhafi
    First name variations found in File 211:NEWSEARCH:
         Muamar
         Muammar
         Muammer
```

Fig. 13-2. The spelling of some difficult names from a non-Latin alphabet may vary even in the same record. DIALOG online service. File 111:National Newspaper Index. (Courtesy of Information Access Company. ©Information Access Company.)

published authors in alphabetical order. An automatic cross-file retrieval of author names, however, is not very simple even in files maintained in the same online service. This is true for the following reasons:

- Significant variations exist in the presentation of an author's name in different files. Sometimes, name variations even in the same file make its retrieval very difficult. For example, some files present only the initials of the author, others his full first name; yet others may present numerous combinations of such name elements as the last name, the first name, the initials, prefixes, punc-

```
File65:SSIE Current Research - 78-82/Feb
(Copr. SSIE Inc.)
         Set Items Description
         --- ----- -----------
? s in=francis n
           1     2 IN=FRANCIS N

? t1/3/1
1/3/1
0324611    SSIE NO.: GQN 75561
  TRENDS IN UNIVERSITY, INDUSTRIAL, AND GOVERNMENT
PARTICIPATION IN BASIC AND APPLIED PHYSICS RESEARCH
  INVESTIGATORS: Francis N
  PERFORMING ORG: Computer Horizons Inc.,1050 Kings Hwy.
N.,Cherry Hill,New Jersey,08034,United States of America
  SPONSORING ORG: U.S.  Dept.  of Defense,Navy,Office of
Naval Research,800 N. Quincy St.,Arlington,Virginia,
22217,United States of America
  CONTRACT/GRANT NO.: DN075561; N00014-80-C-0731
  7/80 TO CONT     FY: 81    FUNDS: $12,578

? s in=narin f
           2     7 IN=NARIN F

? t2/3/1
2/3/1
0398563    SSIE NO.: FX   802
  CROSS NATIONAL BIBLIOMETRIC COMPARISONS
  INVESTIGATORS: Narin F
  PERFORMING ORG: Computer Horizons Inc.,1050 Kings Hwy.
N.,Cherry Hill,New Jersey,08034,United States of America
  SPONSORING ORG: U.S. National Science Foundation,
Directorate for Scientific Technological & Internat.
Affairs,Div.  of  Science  Resources Studies,1800 G St.
N.W.,Washington,District of Columbia,20550,United States
of America
  CONTRACT/GRANT NO.: SRS81-04942
  8/81 TO 1/83   FY: 81   FUNDS: $71,092
```

Fig. 13-3. An example where the first and last names of a person (FRANCIS NARIN) are mistakenly interchanged in set number 1. DIALOG online service. File 65:SSIE Current Research 78-82/Feb.

This file is a source of information on past U.S. research contracts. The mistake occurred despite the fact that the investigator is well-known in information science circles. Note that instead of a usual AU = (author index), the file includes an IN = (investigator index), which makes a cross-file name search impossible to run in this file.

tuation marks and spaces, degrees, personal and seniority titles, and so on (see Fig. 13-1);

- Names are misspelled and interchanged much more often than even text words are, especially if they have been translated from languages with non-Latin alphabets (see Figs. 13-2 and 13-3);
- Certain names such as Smith or Johnson are so common that their proper retrieval is not an easy task (see Fig. 13-4).

Due to numerous misspellings and differences in the presentation of names, it is often necessary to display the appropriate parts of an Author Index before performing a detailed name search. This allows the searcher to find all existing name variations. Such a search, of course, is slow and time consuming but necessary to assure the retrieval of relevant information.

Sometimes a personal name becomes known as a part of a company name, as a brand name for a certain product, or as a name describing a scientific, medical, or technological process. When retrieving such a name, it may be necessary to truncate it in order to find all spelling variations (see Fig. 13-5).

If an author has a common last name, or if he has a large number of publications on several different topics, it is easier and faster to select only those works that are of interest to the searcher. This can be done by ANDing the results of a name search with a one-concept subject search (see Fig. 13-6).

THE CITATION SEARCH

The citation search is one of the most powerful of the information retrieval methods made possible by the introduction of computerized information retrieval systems. The power of the citation search is due to the fact that the searcher indirectly uses the judgment of the published scientists. The latter are usually the experts in the area of their publications and have a tendency to cite only the most useful papers on the subject. Thus, the relevancy of the cited material is far superior to the relevancy of index terms assigned to the article by the producer's indexers.

As a practical bibliographic tool, citation searching started in 1964 when E.Garfield introduced a new kind of secondary publication - the *Science Citation Index*. Later, the Philadelphia-based Institute for Scientific Information (ISI) also developed an electronic version of the Science Citation

```
File8:COMPENDEX - 70-85/Jan
Copr. Engineering Information Inc.)
        Set Items Description
        --- ----- -----------
? ss au=smith ? or au=smith, ?
          1  1435 AU=SMITH ?
         S AU=SMITH, ?
         >2,000 terms; respecify
         C 1 OR 2
         Invalid set value
```

Fig. 13-4. An example of an unsuccessful search on a common name. DIALOG online service. File 8:Compendex.

This relatively simple search took considerable online time to perform. It is, of course, virtually impossible to list all the first name variations in such a case.

```
? s parkinson(1w)disease?
           1     34 PARKINSON(1W)DISEASE?

? s parkinson?(1w)disease?
           2    644 PARKINSON?(1W)DISEASE?
```

Fig. 13-5. An example of the use of name truncation. DIALOG online service. File 255:BIOSIS Previews.

Even though the term *Parkinson's disease* has a standard spelling in most of the medical dictionaries, many publications also list it in such forms as *Parkinson disease* or *Parkinsons disease*. The latter form may be retrieved only by using truncation (see set number *2*).

```
File8:COMPENDEX - 70-84/Jun
Copr. Engineering Information Inc.)
          Set Items Description
          --- ----- -----------
? s au=johnson, d. l.
             1    39 AU=JOHNSON, D. L.
? s au=johnson dl
             2     7 AU=JOHNSON DL
? s au=johnson d
             3    11 AU=JOHNSON D
? s au=johnson, d.
             4    36 AU=JOHNSON, D.
? s au=johnson, daniel l.
             5     5 AU=JOHNSON, DANIEL L.
? c 1-5/or
             6    98  1-5/OR
? s nois? or acoustic? or sound? or sonic? or audibl? or hearing? or ear?
                 32901 NOIS?
                 23742 ACOUSTIC?
                 15226 SOUND?
                  1522 SONIC?
                   402 AUDIBL?
                  1099 HEARING?
                 43719 EAR?
             7101601  NOIS? OR ACOUSTIC? OR SOUND? OR SONIC? OR AUDIBL? OR
HEARING? OR EAR?

? c 6 and 7
             8    16  6 AND 7

? t8/6/1-10

8/6/1
 1360149
  EFFECTS  OF  GUNFIRE  ON  HEARING  LEVEL  FOR SELECTED INDIVIDUALS OF THE
INTER-INDUSTRY NOISE STUDY.

8/6/2
 1290693
  LONGITUDINAL STUDY OF HEARING IN CHILDREN -  2.   CROSS-SECTIONAL STUDIES
OF NOISE EXPOSURE AS MEASURED BY DOSIMETRY.
```

Fig. 13-6. An example of a combined name-subject search. DIALOG online service. File 8:Compendex. (Courtesy of Engineering Information, Inc. No part of this work may be reproduced or transmitted in any form or by any means, electronic or mechanical, including photocopying or by any information storage and retrieval system, without permission in writing from Engineering Information, Inc.)

Index. ISI online files, such as Scisearch or Social Scisearch, have been marketed through different online services.

In the DIALOG online service, for example, Files 34, 186, 94:Scisearch (in the natural sciences area) and File 7:Social Scisearch (in the social sciences area) allow the user to perform citation searches as well as use the more conventional retrieval techniques. With the help of a special *cited reference* command (CR =), the searcher can iden-

```
File34:SCISEARCH - 84/Wk20
(Copr. ISI Inc.)
See Files 87, 94 & 186
         Set Items Description
         --- ----- -----------
? e cr=johnson dl
Ref Items  Index-term
E1      1  CR=JOHNSON DK, 1982,
             V221, P399
E2      2  CR=JOHNSON DK, 1982,
             V67, P159
E3     17 *CR=JOHNSON DL
E4      1  CR=JOHNSON DL, V11, P137
E5      1  CR=JOHNSON DL, V36, P275
E6      1  CR=JOHNSON DL, 1957,
             V3, P411
E7      7  CR=JOHNSON DL, 1963,
             V46, P541
                                   -more-

? p
Ref Items  Index-term
E8      4  CR=JOHNSON DL, 1963,
             V46, P545
E9      2  CR=JOHNSON DL, 1963,
             V7, P1359
E10     1  CR=JOHNSON DL, 1964,
             V12, P1173
E11     3  CR=JOHNSON DL, 1966,
             V75, P84
E12     1  CR=JOHNSON DL, 1967,
             P393
E13     6  CR=JOHNSON DL, 1967,
             V158, P376
                                   -more-

? s e12
           1     1 CR=JOHNSON DL, 1967, P393

? t1/3
2/3/1
0044675  OATS ORDER#: KY602  20 REFS
  CHARACTERIZATION OF SINTERED MGO COMPACTS WITH FLUORINE  (ENGLISH)
  IKEGAMI T; KOBAYASHI M; MORIYOSHI Y; SHIRASAKI SI
  NATL  INST  RES  INORGAN  MAT/NIIHARI/IBARAKI  305/JAPAN/;  TOKYO  INST
TECHNOL,MEGURO KU/TOKYO 152//JAPAN/
  JOURNAL OF THE AMERICAN CERAMIC SOCIETY , V63, N11-1, P640-643, 1980
```

Fig. 13-7. An example of a citation search. DIALOG online service. File 34:Scisearch. (Copied with the permission of the Institute for Scientific Information, © 1985.)

The first command displays a part of the *C*ited *R*eference Index. A description of the papers which cite a particular publication may be retrieved with the *select (s)* command.

```
? s cr=johnson d, ? or cr=johnson dl, ?
                 542 CR=JOHNSON D, ?
                 463 CR=JOHNSON DL, ?
           1    996   CR=JOHNSON D, ? OR CR=JOHNSON DL, ?

? s nois? or acoustic? or sound? or sonic? or audibl? or hearing? or ear?
                3959 NOIS?
                4163 ACOUSTIC?
                2495 SOUND?
                 207 SONIC?
                  23 AUDIBL?
                1007 HEARING?
               17950 EAR?
           2 29163   NOIS? OR ACOUSTIC? OR SOUND? OR SONIC? OR AUDIBL? OR
HEARING? OR EAR?

? c 1 and 2
           3    34   1 AND 2

? t3/3/1-2

3/3/1
2055579  OATS ORDER#: SQ207  21 REFS
  EFFECTS ON COCHLEAR MICROPHONICS IN GUINEA-PIGS INDUCED BY PROLONGED
EXPOSURE TO LOW-FREQUENCY SOUND  (ENGLISH)
  MAEHARA N; SADAMOTO T; YAMAMURA K
  ASAHIKAWA MED COLL,DEPT HYG/ASAHIKAWA 07811//JAPAN/;   SAPPORO MED
COLL,DEPT PUBL HLTH/SAPPORO/HOKKAIDO 060/JAPAN/
  EUROPEAN JOURNAL OF APPLIED PHYSIOLOGY AND OCCUPATIONAL PHYSIOLOGY , V52,
N3, P305-309, 1984

3/3/2
0677642  OATS ORDER#: NB436  14 REFS
  LONGITUDINAL-STUDY OF HEARING IN CHILDREN .2.  CROSS-SECTIONAL STUDIES OF
NOISE EXPOSURE AS MEASURED BY DOSIMETRY  (ENGLISH)
  SIERVOGEL RM; ROCHE AF; JOHNSON DL; FAIRMAN T
  WRIGHT STATE UNIV,SCH MED,DEPT PEDIAT/YELLOW SPRINGS//OH/45387;
USAF,AEROSP MED RES LAB,BIOACOUST BRANCH/WRIGHT PATTERSON AFB//OH/45433;
WRIGHT STATE UNIV,SCH MED,FELS RES INST/YELLOW SPRINGS//OH/45387
  JOURNAL OF THE ACOUSTICAL SOCIETY OF AMERICA , V71, N2, P372-377, 1982
```

Fig. 13-8. An example of a citation search. DIALOG online service. File 34:Scisearch. (Copied with the permission of the Institute for Scientific Information, © 1985.)

The first command retrieves all the unit records that cite a given author. Note that only a certain way of presenting the name, initials, punctuation signs, spaces, and questions marks required by this file will successfully retrieve the necessary data. In order to select only the unit records on a particular subject, we ANDed the results of a citation search with the results of the subject search.

tify the papers that cite an earlier paper of special interest. This establishes a subject relationship between the papers doing the citing and being cited (see Figs. 13-7 and 13-8).

The citation search may be used for purposes such as the following:

- Information gathering on a subject that is not

```
File186:SCISEARCH - 74-77
(Copr. ISI Inc.)
See also Files 34 and 94
          Set Items Description
          --- ----- -----------
? e cr=redmond ck, 1969

Ref Items   Index-term
E1      3   CR=REDMOND CE, 1959,
              V23, P61
E2      1   CR=REDMOND CE, 1975
E3         *CR=REDMOND CK, 1969
E4      5   CR=REDMOND CK, 1969,
              V11, P513
E5     12   CR=REDMOND CK, 1972,
              V14, P621
E6      1   CR=REDMOND CK, 1972,
              V16, P621
E7      1   CR=REDMOND CK, 1974
                                       -more-

? s e4
            1      5 CR=REDMOND CK, 1969, V11, P513

? t1/3/1
1/3/1
1190796  OATS ORDER#: BV117  14 REFS
  CANCER MORTALITY IN STEEL-INDUSTRY  (EN)
  RADFORD EP
  JOHNS   HOPKINS   UNIV,SCH   HYG   &   PUBL   HLTH,DEPT   ENVIRONM
MED/BALTIMORE//MD/21205
  ANNALS OF THE NEW YORK ACADEMY OF SCIENCES, V271, MAY28, P228-238, 1976


? b94;e cr=radford ep, 1976

            10jul84 18:13:30 User12345
    $6.60   0.040 Hrs File186 1 Descriptor
    $0.32   Tymnet
    $6.92   Estimated Total Cost
```

Fig. 13-9. An example of a citation search on a subject that is terminologically not well-defined. DIALOG online service. Files 94,186:Scisearch. (Copied with the permission of the Institute for Scientific Information, © 1985.) (Continued on page 169.)

The objective of this search was to find publications on OCCUPATIONAL HEALTH PROBLEMS related to COAL TAR PITCH VOLATILES. Unfortunately, this problem is related closely to such problems as environmental contamination, combustion emissions, and health effects in such industries as steel production, petrochemicals, and coal gas. It was very difficult to pinpoint the relevant articles from the numerous publications that dealt with a large number of poorly defined compounds in these industries. It was helpful to us that we had on hand one publication on this subject by Redmond C.K, Smith E.M, Lloyd J.W, and Rush H.W. "Long-term mortality study of steelworkers," *Journal of Occupational Medicine,* 1969, v. 11, pp. 513-521. A citation search performed in ISI files allowed us to find several articles that cited this publication (for example, a 1976 publication by Radford). Several subsequent author and citation search cycles added a number of useful publications on this subject. This was done by finding a useful publication, identifying its authors, and using their names for further author and citation searches. In due coarse, all citations found irrelevant were eliminated from subsequent search cycles. One of the "second cycle" citation searches in File 94:Scisearch (which is more up-to-date), retrieved a work by Woods where the problem of risk assessment with implications for occupational standard setting was explored. This allowed us to investigate the theoretical basis of the original problem in more depth. The establishment of such an important link to the subject of our search, especially because it is indirect, was possible only with the help of citation analysis.

```
File94:SCISEARCH - 78-80
(Copr. ISI Inc.)
See also Files 34 and 186
          Set Items Description
          --- ----- -----------
Ref Items   Index-term
E1      1   CR=RADFORD EP, 1972,
              V143, P247
E2      1   CR=RADFORD EP, 1974
E3         *CR=RADFORD EP, 1976
E4      1   CR=RADFORD EP, 1976, P26
E5      2   CR=RADFORD EP, 1976,
              V18, P310
E6      2   CR=RADFORD EP, 1976,
              V271, P228
E7      1   CR=RADFORD EP, 1977,
              P567
                                   -more-

? s e6
            1     2 CR=RADFORD EP, 1976, V271, P228

? t1/5/1
1/5/1
0745565  ARTICLE  OATS ORDER#: GR619  29 REFS
  EPIDEMIOLOGIC CONSIDERATIONS IN THE DESIGN OF TOXICOLOGIC STUDIES -
APPROACH TO RISK ASSESSMENT IN HUMANS  (ENGLISH)
  WOODS JS
  NIEHS,ENVIRONM TOXICOL LAB/RES TRIANGLE PK//NC/27709
  FEDERATION PROCEEDINGS , V38, N5, P1891-1896, 1979
```

Fig. 13-9. (Continued from page 168.)

well defined terminologically but for which the user has an existing reference (see Fig. 13-9).

- Evaluating the contribution of a particular scientist in his area of expertise. This, roughly speaking, may be done by subtracting the number of self-citations of a given author from the total number of citations to his works (see Fig. 13-10).
- Tracing the history of a scientific school or a particular thought (see Fig. 13-11).

```
File7:SOCIAL SCISEARCH - 72-84/WK22
(Copr. ISI Inc.)
          Set Items Description
          --- ----- -----------

? s cr=indow t, ?
            1   140 CR=INDOW T, ?

? s au=indow t?
            2    14 AU=INDOW T?

? c 1 not 2
            3   129  1 NOT 2
```

Fig. 13-10. An example of a simple citation analysis performed on a given author. DIALOG online service. File 7:SOCIAL SCISEARCH. (Copied with the permission of the Institute for Scientific Information, © 1985.)

Several self-citations included in set number *2* are logically subtracted from the total number of citations to his works (set number *1*). It is easy to find that 11 out of *140* citations to this author are self-citations.

ADAPTING A SEARCH TO A DIFFERENT ONLINE SERVICE

The transfer of a search from one online service to another is generally not an easy task. This is because different online services vary in the notation they use, and the meaning and the execution order priority of their logical operators.

One of the most important characteristics of an

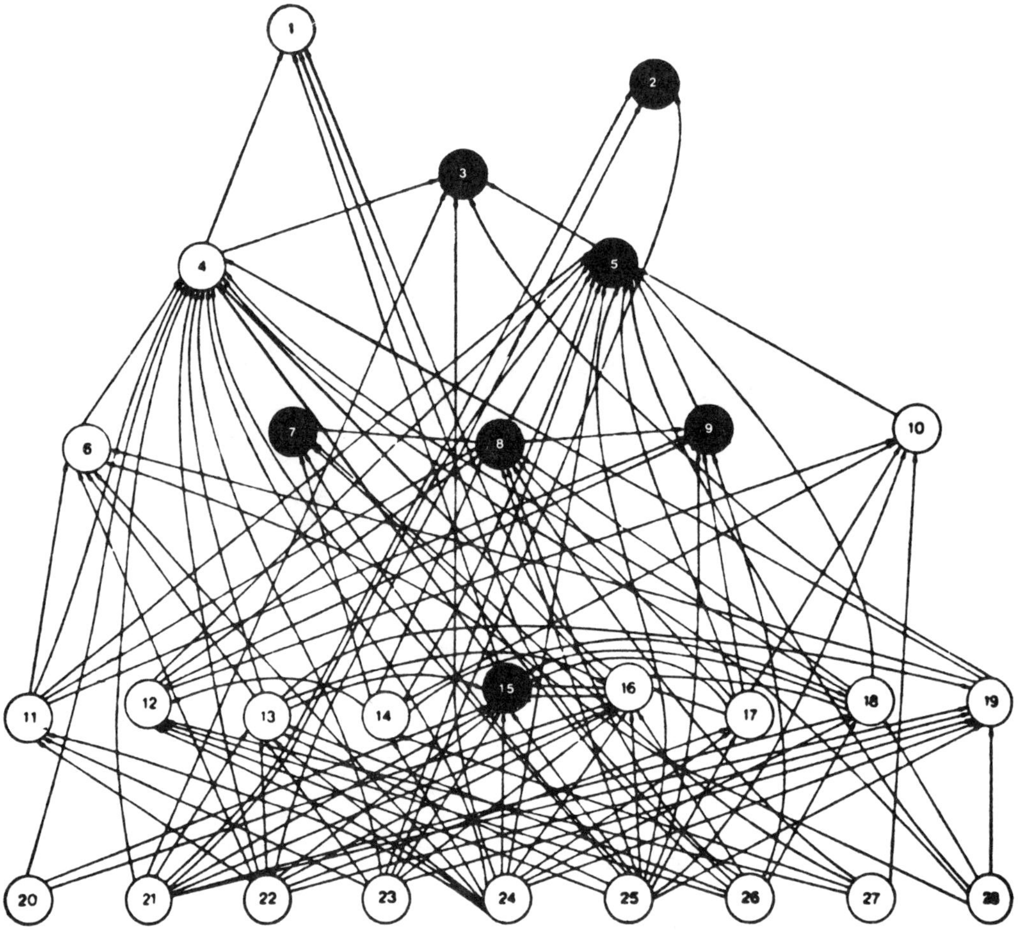

1, Sheehan 1958; 2, Bray 1960; 3, Nirenberg 1961; 4, Marcker 1964; 5, Nirenberg 1964; 6, Marcker 1965; 7, Brenner 1965; 8, Khorana 1965; 9, Nirenberg 1965; 10, Khorana 1965; 11, Marcker 1966; 12, Khorana 1966; 13, Marcker 1966; 14, Khorana 1966; 15, Adams 1966; 16, Webster 1966; 17, Nirenberg 1966; 18, Ochoa 1966; 19, Nakamoto 1966; 20, Berberich 1967; 21, Lucas-Leonard 1967; 22, Caskey 1967; 23, Ochoa 1967; 24, Khorana 1967; 25, Nirenberg 1967; 26, Ochoa 1967; 27, Khorana 1967; 28, Ochoa 1967.

Fig. 13-11. A historiograph of the major advances in genetics between 1958 and 1967, based on a citation analysis of a review of the 1967 literature. (Reproduced with permission from *Eugene Garfield, Citation Indexing,* ISI Press, 1983, ©Eugene Garfield.)

Each circle represents a paper cited five or more times by the papers listed in the bibliography of the review. The papers represented by solid black circles were cited 15 times or more in *1967 Science Citation Index.*

online service is the quality of its software. To a large degree it assures the success of a search. If the software is obsolete, the search may take too much online time, as well as too much of the expert's time. In some cases, the computer may not be able to handle the search at all.

The transfer of a search from one file or online service to another is especially difficult when a search statement relies exclusively on index terms or very complex logical statements. This is the usual practice in conventional searching techniques that have been developed primarily for use by intermediaries. Such a search is normally tailored to a particular file, and to adapt it for another file or another online service requires significant effort.

Adapting a search for another online service is not a mechanical task and requires a certain level of flexibility and compromise. The adaptation of a successful search strategy statement for another online service only makes sense when the expert expects to obtain original data from a particular file not included in his principal online service.

Presumably one of the most important criteria on which the searcher selects his principal online service is its high quality software. Therefore, he should expect to experience certain difficulties in the process of adapting a search strategy for a less-developed online service. The quality and flexibility of the query language of a second online service may be lower than that of the principal online service, and the same search may take much longer. The user may also be required to make his search strategy simpler, as the second online service may not be able to support a search as large as the one done on the principal online service. In addition, a search that takes longer may cost more. This last factor may be further aggravated by the fact that less popular online services tend to charge higher online prices.

Therefore, the user should examine all files beforehand and decide whether or not a particular file not included in his principal online service has sufficient merit for him to perform a search in it. To make the effort worthwhile, the file must be able to provide important information not obtainable from his principal online service.

An example of a search adapted from DIALOG online service and executed in ORBIT online service is shown in Fig. 13-12. Analyzing this search, you may note certain similarities as well as differences between it and the one shown for the DIALOG online service in Chapter 12.

Transfer of a search from one online service to another can be made easier for the occasional user with the help of a special glossary that compares similar commands on different online services. An example of such a glossary is shown in Fig. 13-13.

Recently, some companies have started to advertise microcomputer software that provides automatic translation of several of the most popular query languages into a "universal" query language. Searching with the universal query language may be easier for the occasional searcher conducting a search in an unfamiliar online service.

The use of even the most sophisticated computerized intermediary, however, cannot assure a successful search. A lot depends on the quality of the search statements. Computerized intermediaries are not very effective in dealing with complex search statements, mnemonics, and esoteric commands. They may also introduce certain restrictions that further limit the capabilities of the online information retrieval process.

SELECTIVE DISSEMINATION OF INFORMATION

The *Selective Dissemination of Information* (SDI) capability is a very useful feature in maintaining current awareness in the subject of interest. The SDI allows the user to have a search automatically run every time a file is updated (usually monthly, biweekly, or weekly).

Organizing an SDI search makes sense after the user has performed a

```
USER:
impact: or all impuls:

PROG:
MM (IMPACT:) (8)
    1      1551     IMPACT/BI
    2        18     IMPACTED/BI
    3        20     IMPACTING/BI
    4        13     IMPACTION/BI
    5         1     IMPACTLESS/BI
    6         9     IMPACTOR/BI
    7         3     IMPACTORS/BI
    8       216     IMPACTS/BI
SPECIFY NUMBERS, ALL, OR NONE

USER:
all

PROG:
SS 1 PSTG (1920)

SS 2 /C?
USER:
all sound: or all nois: or all sonic: or all acoustic: or
all audibl:

PROG:
SS 2 PSTG (1503)


SS 3 /C?
USER:
1 and 2

PROG:
SS 3 PSTG (45)

SS 4 /C?
USER:
prt ti 1

PROG:

-1-
TI  - Noise and Acoustical Vibration of Hammer Mills
```

Fig. 13-12. An example of a search on IMPULSE NOISE. ORBIT online service. File Paper (Paperchem). (Courtesy of The Institute of Paper Chemistry.)

successful search and compiled a bibliography. The bibliography can later be updated with the material received through the SDI.

If an SDI feature exists on an online service, it is usually easy to convert a savesearch to an SDI search. An example of the organization of an SDI in DIALOG online service is shown in Fig. 13-14.

ONLINE ORDERING SERVICES

Online ordering of documents is the next logical step in the online information retrieval process after the necessary citations to the original documents have been found online.

Most online services allow the user to order primary documents directly online. This is usually

- 16 - Goldmann's Glossary

SUBJECT	DIALOG	ORBIT	MEDLARS
	6. <u>Logical Operators</u>		
A or B	OR	OR	OR
A and B	AND	AND	AND
A but not B	NOT	NOT	NOT
Combining terms from previous statements	Examples: C 1 AND 2 NOT 3 SS S2 AND CAT (when using previous set #2 and a new term CAT)	Example: 2 AND CAT (when using previous set #2 and a new term CAT)	Example: 2 AND CAT (when using previous set #2 and a new term CAT)
Parentheses	() Used to specify order of the execution	Up to 10 levels of priorities inside one another can be used with the brackets. E.g.: ((A OR (B OR C)) AND D)	N/A
Priority of execution	() Parentheses; NOT; AND; OR	()Parentheses; AND and NOT have equal priority; OR	AND NOT; AND; OR E.g.: A OR B AND C = = A OR (B AND C)
	7. <u>Commands</u>		
File selection	B0 Allows to change over from one database to another, e.g.: B5 (File Biosis Previews).	FILE NAME Allows to change over from one database to another, e.g.: FILE LISA	FILE NAME Allows to change over from one database to another, e.g.: FILE TDB

Fig. 13-13. An excerpt from the description of the logical operators in different online services. *Goldmann's Glossary of Online Services and Databases*. Sixth edition. 1985.

```
File132:Standard & Poors Daily News, 79-84
(Copr. Standard & Poors Corp.1984)
         Set Items Description
         --- ----- -----------
? s northern(w)telecom?
           1   246 NORTHERN(W)TELECOM?

? pr1/5/1-10
Printed1/5/1-10  Estimated cost: $1.50 (To cancel, enter PR-)

? end/sdi

Serial#NQ5D
           10jul84 18:15:02 User12345
    $0.51  0.006 Hrs File132 2 Descriptors
    $0.05  Tymnet
    $0.56  Estimated Total Cost

? t1/5/1
1/5/1
503581
  NORTHERN TELECOM LTD.   840702
  Initial  Quarterly  Dividends  on  $2.1875 Class A Preferred Series 1 and
$2.22 Class A Preferred Series 2
   Initial quarterlies of $0.546875 and $0.2623 declared  on  $2.1875  Cum.
Redeem. Retract. Cl. A Pfd. Ser. 1 and $2.22 Cum. Redeem.  Retract.  Cl.  A
Pfd. and Ser.  2,  respectively,  both payable July 25 to holders of record
July 10, 1984.
   (Standard & Poor's NEWS)
```

Fig. 13-14. An SDI search set up in DIALOG online service. File 132:Standard & Poor's News. (Courtesy of Standard & Poor's Corporation.)

This is a source file containing textual and numeric business information, including financial reports on more than 10,000 publicly held corporations. This SDI search allows the subject expert to monitor the activity of a particular company (*Northern Telecom*). When selecting the number of potential postings for an SDI search with a print command, we presumed that any updating on the subject of interest will not produce more than *10* postings in this file.

done by sending a message through an online service to one of many document suppliers, which are listed by the online service.

The great variety of document suppliers currently existing in North America and Western Europe assures that most of the requests can be filled in a reasonable time period and at a reasonable cost. Some suppliers specialize in a particular area of knowledge or deliver documents to the end-user from a particular country or

```
1715576  OATS ORDER#: SA272  0 REFS
  PHYSIOLOGICAL MODELS AND GEOMETRY OF VISUAL SPACE  (EN)
  INDOW T
  UNIV CALIF IRVINE,SCH SOCIAL SCI/IRVINE//CA/92717
  BEHAVIORAL AND BRAIN SCIENCES , V6, N4, P667-668, 1983
```

Fig. 13-15. Online Order Number (OATS ORDER#: SA272) assigned by the producer (Institute for Scientific Information) in addition to the DIALOG Accession Number. DIALOG online service. File 7:Social Scisearch. (Copied with the permission of the Institute for Scientific Information, © 1985.)

geographic zone; others provide any document listed or even those not retrieved through an online service. Suppliers range from world-class libraries to online file producers to one-man establishments.

Certain producers also act as suppliers, as they keep in stock all documents listed in their file. Sometimes the original documents are stored and distributed in the form of standard microfiches. One of the major functions of computerized files for such producers-suppliers is to make document delivery easier. Therefore, the unit records in those files frequently include a unique order number, which is assigned by a producer in addition to the accession number assigned by the online service (see Fig. 13-15). Supply of the original documents by the file producers may greatly enhance the document accessibility for the end-user.

Large online services such as DIALOG or ORBIT attach descriptions of suppliers associated with them to their manuals. This is usually done on separate sheets referred to as "yellowsheets". An example of a yellowsheet included with the DIALOG manual is shown in Fig. 13-16.

Some systems allow the searcher to convert a unit record into an online ordering message. This process is fast and relatively foolproof. In others, the order is made by keying in necessary data, and the online service actually acts as a telecommunication medium.

An example of an online ordering procedure is shown in Fig. 13-17.

A comparison of fees charged by different document suppliers (based on their own advertisements) shows that the cost for a copy of a typical 10-20 page journal article is about $6.50 to $12. Higher costs may be charged for documents that are difficult to trace or whose citations are inaccurate or incomplete.

Response time for different suppliers may vary, although normal response time is about two to seven days. Some suppliers also provide rush service. This may cut service time to 24 hours or even less.

Generally, an end-user should shop around in order to find a supplier that suits his particular needs and resources.

Online information retrieval in combination with online ordering is a very powerful tool for bringing information to the end-user. When properly organized, this approach is much more effective than traditional information gathering methods, and at the same time, may be much less expensive. Unlike the traditional library, online information retrieval and document ordering do not require the end-user to be physically located in a recognized information center. This may have fundamental implications for the level of work of many subject experts and institutions, not only in developed areas but also in developing countries.

CONCLUSIONS

Several features of online information retrieval systems can supplement the subject search that is most frequently used in professional and scientific work.

The name search and the citation search can be powerful tools in the subject expert's practice. This chapter examines various reasons for performing such searches. The merits and the difficulties that a subject expert may anticipate in the organization of such searches are illustrated.

Adapting a search to another online service is not a mechanical task and requires a certain level of flexibility and compromise. The user should determine beforehand whether a particular file not included in his principal online service has sufficient merits for him to perform a search in it.

Transfer of a search from one online service to another may be made easier for the occasional user through the help of a special glossary that compares similar commands on different online services. An example of such a glossary is presented.

The selective dissemination of information (SDI) capability is a very useful feature in maintaining current awareness in the subject of interest. The SDI allows the user to have a search automatically run every time a file is updated.

IFIPATS

DIALOG* DIALORDER™ SERVICE

IFI/PLENUM DATA COMPANY

IFIPATS

SCOPE OF SERVICE

IFI/Plenum Data Company provides copies of U.S. and non-U.S. patents. Patents found in the CLAIMS™ Files 23, 24, 25, 125, 223, 224, and 225 may also be obtained from IFI.

OPTIONS AVAILABLE

Patent copies are sent via first class mail in the U.S. and via airmail to countries outside the U.S. Copies may also be sent by Federal Express to U.S. cities at an additional charge.

Orders are retrieved Monday through Friday and copies sent within 5 working days.

CHARGES AND TERMS

IFI charges $4.00 per patent plus a photocopy charge of $.30 per page for U.S. patents and $.75 per page for non-U.S. patents. Rush service available at $10.00 per patent (copies sent within 48 hours).

CONTACT

Once an order has been retrieved by IFI Plenum, and a date and time appear in the .LIST TRANSMITTED column, all questions about the order should be referred to:

IFI/Plenum Data Company
302 Swann Avenue
Alexandria, Virginia 22301

Telephone: 703/683-1085

*Trademark Reg. U.S. Pat. & Trademark Office.

(January 1983) IFIPATS-1

Fig. 13-16. An example of a yellowsheet for a document supplier. DIALOG online service. (Courtesy of IFI/Plenum Data Company.)

```
File150:Legal Resource Index - 80-84 Jun
          Set Items Description
          --- ----- -----------

? s trademark? and canad?
                405 TRADEMARK?
               2662 CANAD?
            1     8  TRADEMARK? AND CANAD?

? t1/3/1-8

1/3/1
1931850   DATABASE: LRI File 150
  Canadian Trademark Law: a bridge between United States and foreign law.
  McMahon, Thomas J.
  Chitty's L.J.   30  1-14  Jan  1982

1/3/2
1876943   DATABASE: LRI File 150
  Notes from Canada. (trademark applications filed by nonresidents)
  Fogo, James G.
  Trademark Rep.   71  173-179  March-April  1981

1/3/3
0876533
  Notes from Canada. (Johnny Carson trademark case)
  Bereskin, Daniel R.
  Trademark Rep.   70  165-168  March-April  1980

? k1/1-2
          KEEP 1/1-2

? .order candoc   please send airmail

2 items Ordered
Order# 4295

Item 1
  1931850   DATABASE: LRI File 150
    Canadian  Trademark  Law:   a bridge between United States and foreign

Item 2
  1876943   DATABASE: LRI File 150
    Notes from Canada. (trademark applications filed by nonresidents)

? logoff
           13jul84 17:58:03 User12345
    $2.88  0.032 Hrs File150 3 Descriptors
    $0.26  Tymnet
    $3.14  Estimated Total Cost
```

Fig. 13-17. An example of ordering while searching online. DIALOG online service. File 150:Legal Resource Index. (Courtesy of Information Access Company. ©Information Access Company.)

A special command (*k*) keeps only those unit records that the user intends to order. Documents in this example are ordered through *Candoc* (Micromedia Ltd, Toronto, Ontario, Canada). The ordering command includes an optional instruction to the supplier to send the required materials by airmail.

Online ordering is the next logical step in the online information retrieval process. Most online services allow the user to order primary documents directly online. This is usually done by sending a message through an online service to one of many document suppliers that are listed by the online service.

Online information retrieval in combination with online ordering is a very powerful tool for bringing information to the end-user. When properly organized, this approach is much more effective than traditional information gathering methods, and at the same time it may be much less expensive. Unlike the traditional library, online information retrieval and document ordering does not require the end-user to be physically located in a recognized information center. This may have fundamental implications for the level of work of many subject experts and institutions, not only in developed areas but also in developing countries.

Chapter 14

Do's and Don'ts

In this chapter the principal elements of our Subject Expert Searching Technique are presented in a step-by-step fashion. The chapter concludes with a set of rules that the user or online services may take into account in planning and running a search.

STEP-BY-STEP

The major concepts upon which our *Subject Expert Searching Technique* is founded are presented in step-by-step fashion below. Samples of all forms to be filled in are found in the Appendix in this book.

Step 1: Organizing a Strategy

1a) Formulate the request.

Formulate the request for a search in the form of a written question. The question should consist of one or two sentences and should be concise and clear to you. Underline the most important words in the request. If a resulting search looks too broad to you, reformulate the request so that it will deal with several smaller problems. From these, several smaller searches can be developed.

1b) Fill out the first page of the search strategy form from the Appendix.

Put the date, your name, and the topic of the search, as well as online services that are accessible and merit searching.

1c) Formulate a principal clause.

Select two principal concepts that together describe the main problem. Compare these two concepts with the words underlined in your request in order to find out whether you omitted any important information. If yes, reformulate the principal clause. Check whether the principal clause concepts overlap (if they do, they will not limit each other effectively).

1d) Select files in your principal online service that you are planning to search.

Look through the list of files, and analyze whether or not a particular file may have information that is of use to you. Do not prejudge your choice—sometimes a file that did not have a high priority on your list may provide information from an unusual angle. Mark the files that you have selected in the table found in the Appendix for your principal online service.

1e) Compile sets of terms for the principal clause concepts.

Use all general and special thesauri and dictionaries that are accessible to you. Look through the manuals, handbooks and other literature in order to refresh your memory of the subject and find terminology commonly used. Review the list of files that you have selected and find which of these files has online or printed thesauri. Order printed thesauri from the producers. Retrieve online all the related terms in files that have online thesauri. Write all the terms down in the column under the corresponding concept. Analyze one more time whether or not a particular term relates to the subject of your search; if it does not—delete it from your list.

1f) Truncate terms included in the first version of your search.

Truncation should be sufficient to retrieve all variations of the term that may exist. The truncated part of a word should not be too short as this may lead to the retrieval of many unrelated terms and thus make the retrieval process too slow or even impossible.

Step 2: Inputting the First Version

2a) Select the least expensive file in your principal online service.

Use this file to formulate and to save a search.

2b) Type in terms for the principal clause concepts in this file.

Combine terms in a clause with the OR operator. Organize a two-concept search statement with the help of the AND operator. Save the resulting search temporarily. Don't be confused at this stage with misspellings, or insufficient or excessive numbers of postings. This file was chosen primarily for typing your search inexpensively. The quality of the results in this file is unrelated to the quality of your search strategy.

2c) Review a printout of the first version of your search.

Note all misspellings and omissions. Record all ideas for a more rational online organization of your search statement.

Step 3: Initial Online Adaptation

3a) Execute a temporarily saved first version of your search in a second file that will assure a substantial number of useful postings and is representative of a group of files covering the broad subject area of interest.

Execute only the correct lines of a temporarily saved search. Correct all misspelled and omitted lines.

3b) Print out at least 10 titles of the unit records retrieved with your strategy and briefly review them.

If you are not satisfied with the search results, find what caused the search statement to retrieve useless records. If this search strategy was not formulated properly, you may do the following:

- Revise the sets of terms in the principal clause, modifying them in such a fashion that they will not retrieve useless data.
- Go back to step 1 and try to reformulate the search request.
- Analyze whether or not a useless search result is caused by an undesirable subconcept that is easily defined and consistently present in the unit records, and constitutes a significant share of the search results. If this is so, try to exclude such a subconcept immediately from one of the principal clause concepts using the NOT operator.

Step 4: Organization of a Final Search Version

4a) If you are generally satisfied with the quality of results retrieved by the second version of your search, save this version permanently online.

4b) If the number of unit records retrieved in this file is in excess of your chosen manageable threshold (for example, 40-60 postings), **use a third subordinate concept.**

Increase the relevancy of the final results, for example, by using the auxiliary search that broadly describes your area of interest. If you have not organized such an auxiliary search previously, do it now.

Step 5: Running a Final Version through Selected Files

This is the most time-consuming stage of your search and it may be conducted by support staff providing you already have a successful search strategy. The knowledge of several simple online commands is sufficient for running such a search through different files.

5a) Execute the final two-concept version of your search in each of the files selected.

If the number of unit records retrieved in a file exceeds your chosen manageable threshold, superimpose an auxiliary search describing the subordinate concept.

5b) Print the unit records retrieved by your search offline.

Choose the print format that is needed for your subsequent work.

5c) Alternatively, print online the titles of the unit records retrieved. After their analysis, print online in a desirable format only those unit records that you would like to work with.

5d) Note the number of useful postings retrieved with this strategy on your search strategy form.

This statistic may be useful in your subsequent searching activity.

Step 6: Adapting a Search to a Different Online Service

6a) Analyze the merits of running a search in files that are not included in your principal online service.

6b) Adapt the search strategy if you decide to run a search in another online service.

Step 7: Upon Completion of a Subject Search

7a) Compile a bibliography from the unit records retrieved by your search.

If there is more than one record describing the same original document, select that record that is most informative. If needed, combine the information contained in different records to better describe an original document. If the bibliography is going to be published, receive necessary permissions from the database producers.

7b) Order the originals of the documents.

This may be fully or partially done online.

7c) Organize name and citation searches for the most important authors found with your subject search.

7d) Organize an SDI search by using previously developed subject, name and citation searches.

7e) Update your master-strategy with the terms found during your information gathering activity.

GOLDMANN'S GOLDEN RULES OF SUCCESSFUL INFORMATION RETRIEVAL

First Rule:

DO NOT RELY ON AN INTERMEDIARY!

Second Rule:

DO NOT RELY ON AN INTERMEDIARY, BECAUSE HE DOES NOT KNOW WHAT YOU ARE TALKING ABOUT!

Third Rule:

DO NOT RELY ON AN INTERMEDIARY, BECAUSE HE DOES NOT KNOW WHAT HE IS TALKING ABOUT!

Fourth Rule:

If an intermediary retrieved a unit record for you, think about the hundred that he missed in the process.

Fifth Rule

Do not act as an intermediary:
TRUNCAT?

Sixth Rule:

One gets only the information that one deserves.

Seventh Rule:

The only person who know precisely what he is looking for, is the one who does not know the subject.

Eight Rule:

The only real reason for ever visiting a library is a blonde* assistant librarian.

Ninth Rule:

The least expensive search is one that has never been performed; BUT YOU CAN AFFORD IT? . . .

Tenth Rule:

You never know what they might put online.

Eleventh Rule:

If the searching software is bad, forget about using an online service unless YOU REALLY HAVE TO.

Twelfth Rule:

The usefulness of an online service is inversely related to the length of its connecting procedure.

Thirteenth Rule

No one book has all the answers, no one file provides all the information.

Fourteenth Rule:

Don't be afraid of damaging a host computer - it is rather difficult, If you did manage to damage it, don't worry: it is so expensive they cannot recover their losses from you in any case.

Fifteenth Rule:

Anyone who organizes a search statement with less than two concepts is primitive. Anyone who organizes a search statement with more than three concepts is confused.

*It may be male or female - don't be sexist . . .

Appendix

The Search Strategy Form

SEARCH STRATEGY FORM

Date 1985/________ Name________________

Topic

Online services to be searched: Dialog |__| Medlars |__|

Orbit |__| BRS |__| Others: ________

CONCEPTS		
Concept A	Concept B	Concept C

TERMS:

O R	O R	O R
V	V	V
* * NOT * *	* * NOT * *	* * NOT * *

Temporarily saved search ________________________

Permanently saved search ________________________

ORBIT

Numbers in brackets correspond to Dialog files

ACCOUNTANTS	APILIT	APIPAT	ASI (102)
BANKER	BIOTECHNOLOGY	BIO74 (5)	BIO80 (5)
CASSI	CAS6771 (308)	CAS7276 (309)	CAS77 (320)
CA82 (311)	CHEMDEX (31)	CHEMDEX2 (30)	CHEMDEX3
CIN (19)	CIS (101)	COLD	COMPENDEX (8)
CRECORD	DBI	EBIB	EIMET
ENERGYLINE (69)	ENVIROLINE (40)	EPIA	ERIC (1)
FEDREG	FOREST	FSTA (51)	GEOREF
GRANTS (85)	INFORM	INSPEC (12,13)	LABORDOC
LC/LINE	LISA (61)	MANAGEMENT (75)	MDF/I
METADEX	MONITOR	NDEX	NTIS (6)
NUC/CODES	P/E NEWS	PAPERCHEM	PIE
POWER	PSYCHABS (11)	SAE	SPORT
TROPAG	USCLASS	USGCA	USPA
USPB	USP70	WATERLIT	

MEDLARS

Numbers in brackets correspond to Dialog files

MED (154)	B79 (153)	B77 (153)	SDI
B75 (153)	B72 (152)	B69 (152)	B66 (152)
AV	BIOETHICS	CANCER	CANCERPROJ
CAT	CHEM	CLINPROT	HEALTH (151)
HIST	MESH	NAF	NEW MESH
OLD MESH	POP	RTECS	
SER	TDB	TOX	TOX74

Others: (specify)

Saved search #__________ Saved search #__________
Saved search #__________ Saved search #__________
Saved search #__________ Saved search #__________
Saved search #__________ Saved search #__________

DIALOG

**Also available on Orbit*
&Also available on Medlars

	0	1	2	3	4	5	6	7	8	9
0										
10		*		*						*
20										
30	*	*								
40	*									
50		*								
60		*								*
70						*				
80										*
90										
100										
110	*	*								
120										
130										
140										
150		&	&	&	&					
160										
170										
180										
190										
200										
210										
220										
230										
240										
250										
300									*	*
310	*									
320	*									
330										
410										
420										
470										
500										
510										

Index